Professional Attributes and Practice

Drawing on the success of the first, second and third editions of *Professional Values and Practice for Teachers and Student Teachers*, this fully updated, comprehensive and accessible fourth edition provides practical advice to help student teachers and teachers prepare for their professional life.

This new edition contains completely new chapters in response to the changing Standards and an updated chapter by the editor, Mike Cole, entitled 'Education and equality – conceptual and practical considerations'. This introductory chapter will enable readers to situate the topics discussed in the rest of the book, which deal with each of the Professional Attributes related to the 2007 Standards for the award of Qualified Teacher Status (QTS).

Professional Attributes and Practice is essential reading for student teachers, newly-qualified and practising teachers, teaching assistants, teacher educators, all others working in educational settings, and everyone interested in education.

Professor Mike Cole is Research Professor in Education and Equality and Head of Research at Bishop Grosseteste University College Lincoln, UK.

Professional Attributes and Practice

Meeting the QTS Standards

Fourth Edition

Edited by Mike Cole

Routledge
Taylor & Francis Group

LONDON AND NEW YORK

First Published 1999 by David Fulton Publishers
Second edition 2002
Third edition 2005

This edition published 2008 by Routledge
2 Park Square, Milton Park, Abingdon, Oxon, OX14 4RN

Simultaneously published in the USA and Canada
by Routledge
270 Madison Ave, New York, NY 10016

Routledge is an imprint of the Taylor & Francis Group, an informa business

© 1999, 2002, 2005, 2008 Mike Cole editorial matter and selection;
individual chapters the contributors

Typeset by RefineCatch Limited, Bungay, Suffolk
Printed and bound in Great Britain by Antony Rowe Ltd, Chippenham, Wiltshire

British Library Cataloguing in Publication Data
A catalogue record for this book is available from the British Library

Library of Congress Cataloging in Publication Data
A catalog record for this book has been requested

ISBN 10: 0-415-44725-9
ISBN 13: 978-0-415-44725-6

Contents

Acknowledgement

I would like to thank Tracey Riseborough for her help in formulating the contents of this book, a completely revised edition.

About the authors

Camilla Baker was educated as a primary school teacher in east London after completing her Education Masters at the University of Pennsylvania, USA. She taught in a large, urban primary school with a large percentage of bilingual learners, before moving to rural Wiltshire to be a peripatetic advisory EMAS teacher. Her ICT-based project with Nepalese Gurkha children has been cited by both NUT and DfES as good practice for isolated minority ethnic students in mainly white schools. She currently works in Hackney as a Primary EAL/EMAS consultant supporting language development and underachieving groups.

Dr Maud Blair was a lecturer at the Open University from 1991–2002. She was based in the Faculty of Education and Language Studies. Her main areas of teaching and research related to issues of race, ethnicity and gender. In 2001 she was seconded as an advisor on ethnicity to the Department for Education and Skills. She joined the DfES on a permanent basis and works in the School's directorate on issues of ethnicity and education. She is co-author of the DfES report, *Making the Difference: teaching and learning in successful multi-ethnic schools* published in 1998. She has written and published widely on issues of gender and ethnicity.

Professor Mike Cole is Research Professor in Education and Equality, and Head of Research at Bishop Grosseteste University College Lincoln. He is the author of *Marxism and Educational Theory: origins and issues* (Routledge 2008) and the editor of *Education, Equality and Human Rights: issues of gender, 'race', sexuality, disability and social class*, 2nd edition (Routledge 2006).

Valerie Coultas taught in London comprehensive schools for 25 years before becoming a Senior Lecturer in the School of Education at Kingston University. She has recently published a book, *Constructive Talk in Challenging Classrooms* (Routledge 2007), that gives teachers advice on how to use talk to promote positive relationships in urban schools. She is also a member of the editorial board of the *Socialist Education Journal*.

Malini Mistry is an experienced early years teacher and has had senior management experience before joining the University of Bedfordshire as a senior lecturer in early years.

Jeff Nixon began his teaching career in a boys' secondary modern school in 1972. He then worked in the Community Studies department of a 13–18 community college in West Yorkshire, where he became Head of Department and then Head of House. Since 1983 he has worked for the National Union of Teachers at the Union's Haywards

Heath Regional Office, initially as a District Officer and now as a Regional Officer. The views expressed in his chapter are his own, rather than those of the NUT.

Carol Smith taught for many years in mainstream primary schools, and was a SENCo for ten years, before becoming a Senior Lecturer in Education Studies at Bishop Grosseteste University College Lincoln. She is also an Associate Lecturer in Inclusion with the Open University. Her main areas of interest are inclusion, special needs and specific learning difficulties.

Dr Krishan Sood has over 30 years of teaching, leadership and management experience gained from working in schools, advisory work and in the higher education sector. He is currently an assistant head at an inner city, multicultural school in the Midlands, UK.

Dr Ian Woodfield has been a Head of Social Studies, Head of History and Head of the Faculty of Humanities in a large comprehensive school on the south coast of England. He has served for many years as a Senior Examiner and worked on the introduction of the GCSE examination system. He gained a Masters Degree in Education from the University of Sussex and has recently completed a doctoral thesis at the University of Brighton. The views expressed in the chapters to which he contributed are his own.

Dr Richard Woolley is a Senior Lecturer in Primary Education and Fellow in Learning and Teaching at Bishop Grosseteste University College Lincoln. He taught in five primary schools in North Yorkshire, Derbyshire and Nottinghamshire as well as working as Director of Studies and Social Studies Tutor at Cliff College. He has had curriculum responsibility for a broad range of subjects across the primary school curriculum, as well as time as a deputy head teacher and special needs coordinator. His current interests include professional issues in education, children's spiritual development and education for global citizenship.

Preface

Those awarded QTS [Qualified Teacher Status] must understand and uphold the professional code of the General Teaching Council [GTC] for England.

(Training and Development Agency (TDA) 2006: 8)

To gain qualified teacher status, a teacher needs to demonstrate ten attributes, as laid out in Training and Development Agency for Schools (TDA) (2007) (see Table overleaf). The chapters of this book deal with each of these attributes, each chapter considering one of them.

The five aims of the Government's *Every Child Matters* (DfES, 2004a, b, 2005), referred to throughout this book are for children to:

- be healthy;

- stay safe;

- enjoy and achieve;

- make a positive contribution;

- achieve economic well-being.

While these are certainly laudable ones, they might be seen as rhetorical in the light of the actual material and psychological situation of Britain's young people after a decade of the Blair Government. In a recent UNICEF report of 21 industrialised countries issued on St. Valentine's Day (UNICEF 2007), the UK came joint-last with the USA for 'child well-being'. The report revealed that younger children had the highest rates of ill health, complaining that they were in only 'fair or poor' condition, ranking the UK bottom of the 21 countries. Child poverty is double what it was in 1997, and the report singled out the UK for high rates of infant mortality and low birth weight. Children of all ages reported being dissatisfied with life and unhappy in family relationships. The UK has the highest proportion of young people in families where no one has a job, while homelessness among children is at an all-time high. The UK came second to bottom to the US in terms of the rates of children in households with incomes 50 per cent less than average. Only in education standards did the UK make it out of the bottom ten. However, at the same time, less than half of UK teenagers said they had 'kind and helpful' friends, the worst score of all the countries surveyed (Prince 2007: 15). This possibly reflects the excessive competition apparent in schools. Al Aynsley Green, the children's commissioner for England acknowledged that the UN has produced an accurate report and commented: 'There is a crisis at the heart of our society and we must not continue to ignore the impact of our attitudes towards children and young people and the effect this has on their wellbeing' (cited in Boseley 2007: 1).

The contributors to this book recognise the economic and political constraints that are placed on the well-being of children in a global capitalist economy that puts profit before need. Nevertheless, they are acutely aware that education can be a force

Professional Standards for Teachers in England from September 2007

The framework of standards . . . is arranged in three interrelated sections covering:

   a   Professional attributes

   b   Professional knowledge and understanding

   c   Professional skills . . .

The recommendation for the award of qualified teacher status and registration with the GTCE is made by an accredited Initial Teacher Training (ITT) provider following an assessment which shows that all of the QTS standards have been met . . .

All the standards are underpinned by the five key outcomes for children and young people identified in Every Child Matters and the six areas of the Common Core of skills and knowledge for the children's workforce. The work of practising teachers should be informed by an awareness, appropriate to their level of experience and responsibility, of legislation concerning the development and well-being of children and young people expressed in the Children Act 2004, the Disability Discrimination Acts 1995 and 2005 and relevant associated guidance, the special educational needs provisions in the Education Act 1996 and the associated Special Educational Needs: Code of Practice (DfES 2001), the Race Relations Act 1976 as amended by the Race Relations (Amendment) Act 2000, and the guidance Safeguarding Children in Education (DfES 0027 2004).

Note on the terminology used in the standards

- The term 'learners' is used instead of 'children and young people' when learning per se is the main focus of the standard. It refers to all children and young people including those with particular needs, for example, those with special educational needs, looked after children, those for whom English is an additional language, those who are not reaching their potential or those who are gifted and talented.

- The term 'colleagues' is used for all those professionals with whom a teacher might work. It encompasses teaching colleagues, the wider workforce within an educational establishment, and also those from outside with whom teachers may be expected to have professional working relationships, for example early years and health professionals and colleagues working in children's services . . .

- The term 'workplace' refers to the range of educational establishments, contexts and settings (both in and outside the classroom) where teaching takes place . . .

- Where the phrase 'parents and carers' is used, it is understood that the term 'parents' includes both mothers and fathers.

- The term 'well-being' refers to the rights of children and young people (as set out and consulted upon in the Every Child Matters Green Paper and subsequently set out in the Children Act 2004), in relation to:

     - physical and mental health and emotional well-being

- protection from harm and neglect

- education, training and recreation

- the contribution made by them to society

- social and economic well-being.

- The term 'personalised learning' means maintaining a focus on individual progress, in order to maximise all learners' capacity to learn, achieve and participate. This means supporting and challenging each learner to achieve national standards and gain the skills they need to thrive and succeed throughout their lives. 'Personalised learning' is not about individual lesson plans or individualisation (where learners are taught separately or largely through a one-to-one approach).

Qualified Teacher Status . . .
Professional Attributes

Those recommended for the award of QTS should:

Relationships with children and young people

Q1 Have high expectations of children and young people including a commitment to ensuring that they can achieve their full educational potential and to establishing fair, respectful, trusting, supportive and constructive relationships with them.

Q2 Demonstrate the positive values, attitudes and behaviour they expect from children and young people.

Frameworks

Q3 (a) Be aware of the professional duties of teachers and the statutory framework within which they work.

(b) Be aware of the policies and practices of the workplace and share in collective responsibility for their implementation.

Communicating and working with others

Q4 Communicate effectively with children, young people, colleagues, parents and carers.

Q5 Recognise and respect the contribution that colleagues, parents and carers can make to the development and well-being of children and young people, and to raising their levels of attainment.

Q6 Have a commitment to collaboration and co-operative working.

Personal professional development

Q7 (a) Reflect on and improve their practice, and take responsibility for identifying and meeting their developing professional needs.

(b) Identify priorities for their early professional development in the context of induction.

Q8 Have a creative and constructively critical approach towards innovation, being prepared to adapt their practice where benefits and improvements are identified.

Q9 Act upon advice and feedback and be open to coaching and mentoring.

2 Professional knowledge and understanding

Those recommended for the award of QTS should:

Teaching and learning

Q10 Have a knowledge and understanding of a range of teaching, learning and behaviour management strategies and know how to use and adapt them, including how to personalise learning and provide opportunities for all learners to achieve their potential.

FIGURE P.1

---

for change in the 21st century. With this in mind, the book addresses specifically how student teachers and teachers can meet the standards specified by the TDA. In so doing, each author adopts a broad and critical perspective.

If student teachers and teachers are to begin to challenge the material deprivation and despair faced by masses of our children and young people; if they are to make a positive contribution with respect to health, safety, happiness, achievement, and economic and general well-being; if they are to empower pupils to make positive contributions to humankind, they need first to be aware of some conceptual and practical issues with respect to equality and equal opportunity issues. In the introductory chapter, therefore, I examine the key equality concepts of 'race' and racism; gender; disability; sexuality and social class. I argue that we are not born 'ist/phobic',[1] that 'ism/phobia' is a product of the society or societies in which we live. I suggest six steps that might be taken to check, unlearn, counteract and get beyond 'isms/phobia'. I conclude that while we can make important changes in societies as they are, in order to fully eradicate oppression in all its forms, we need to change society.

Camilla Baker and Maud Blair, in Chapter 1, address themselves to Q2:

> Have high expectations of children and young people including a commitment to ensuring that they can achieve their full educational potential and to establishing fair, respectful, trusting, supportive and constructive relationships with them.

This chapter provides a context for the new teacher to understand developments of 'race', diversity, and underachievement in education. A brief review of recent history is undertaken to inform new teachers of the politics and aims behind the new Standards. This chapter takes the key principles of recent policy and research on minority ethnic achievement as its starting point, in particular the statement that while children of certain groups persistently remain at the bottom end of achievement tables, there is no inherent reason for them to be there. This statement locates the barriers in the context of the pupil, and challenges professionals and schools to consider the 'unwitting' aspects of institutional racism, as institutions are being required to do in light of the Stephen Lawrence enquiry and the Race Relations Amendment Act 2000.

The link between high expectations and high achievement is well known and this link is reviewed, followed by an expanded discourse on how reflection inwards to assumptions held can provide a framework for considering how teachers create their expectations.

While the Government documents have taken a general language of universality, the authors argue that the positive movement away from 'culture' or 'colour blind' policies should not be lost in the new semantics. At the same time, they are aware of non-colour-coded xeno-racism. Linguistic, social, cultural and religious diversity are explored from the perspective of the daily reality of a teacher. Taking the Government's 'social renewal' as the context for public service reform, the emphasis in these new Standards is on developing productive relationships, which are essential for achievement to be improved. Practical strategies and reflective approaches are suggested as steps to support a new teacher begin the career-long process of reflective self-evaluation and improvement.

In Chapter 2, Carol Smith considers Q2:

Demonstrate the positive values, attitudes and behaviour they expect from children and young people.

She argues that the term, 'positive values', is open to interpretation. An individual's values are shaped by their past experiences and their ideals. This chapter identifies and discusses some key values that are common to all and how these values impact on a teacher's practice. Teachers draw on their values and beliefs to become reflective practitioners. This goes beyond the student teacher's reflection on the effectiveness of the delivery of individual lessons to a consideration of how legislation, central policies and initiatives should be interpreted and put into practice. The way in which they interact with pupils,[2] parents/carers and colleagues is underpinned by their values. With a continuing move towards inclusive schools and the implementation of the *Every Child Matters* agenda, teachers will need to develop inclusive approaches in which there are high expectations for all. This is a complex task and success can only be achieved by listening to pupils, valuing their opinions and reflecting on how these should inform their practice.

Jeff Nixon, in the third chapter of the book, takes on Q3:

(a) Be aware of the professional duties of teachers and the statutory framework within which they work.

(b) Be aware of the policies and practices of the workplace and share in collective responsibility for their implementation.

Nixon considers a very wide range of issues relating to the teacher's duty of care, and conditions of service. In doing so, he takes his readers through some important documents, such as the 'Blue Book' and the 'Burgundy Book'. Nixon also deals with grievance and disciplinary procedures, with local agreements, and with the changing face of conditions of service. He addresses such fundamental issues as the welfare of the child, and appropriate physical contact and restraint. Nixon concludes his chapter with a consideration of some important legislation concerned with equality and equal opportunity, to do with 'race', disability, age, sexuality, gender, and part-time workers' rights.

The subject of Richard Woolley's first chapter, Chapter 4, is Q4:

Communicate effectively with children, young people, colleagues, parents and carers.

Since teachers relate to a broad spectrum of people within their work, and the range of stakeholders in a school is diverse and each has different interests, outlooks, backgrounds and concerns, effective communication, Woolley argues, requires that teachers are aware of the individual needs and attitudes of different stakeholders and take these into account when fostering relationships. The chapter explores communication with three broad groupings: children and young people; colleagues; and parents and carers. Whilst this list is by no means exhaustive, it encompasses a very wide spectrum of people with an interest in the running of a school and in its educational provision at a range of levels. Woolley focuses on what is communicated, how this happens and the ways in which teachers need to be aware of the messages, both explicit and implicit, passed on by their communication. This chapter is particularly concerned with implicit communication: how messages are conveyed through values and attitudes on a macro level. There is a constant focus on standards that are measured by the achievement of attainment targets and results in national tests. Schools have been driven by the curriculum, rather than driving forward a curriculum that is relevant to the needs and context of the learners. For Woolley, the key question here is what this communicates to children, young people and those who care for them. The chapter explores how teachers can communicate the message that learning and individual progress are valuable in their own right, to create classroom environments where the individuality of each child is valued.

The second chapter by Woolley, Chapter 5, addresses Q5:

Recognise and respect the contribution that colleagues, parents and carers can make to the development and well-being of children and young people, and to raising their levels of attainment.

This chapter explores key relationships with parents and carers, teaching assistants and other colleagues and considers how teachers can use these to develop productive and supportive ways of nurturing the development of learners. It explores the place of informal and formal methods of reporting on children's progress, and explores the benefits and limitations of developing opportunities for out of school learning in the home. Woolley also considers how a teacher's philosophy of education impacts on her/his approach to children's well-being and attainment, and how individual values and attitudes can affect a teacher's perceptions, and how the messages that teachers present may be understood and interpreted by children and young people. Fundamental to this is the provision of safe and supportive learning environments where all people are valued and where there is a clear vision for the role of education. In schools, Woolley argues, we need to ensure that the importance of well-being is not overshadowed by a standards-driven agenda. The chapter also explores what is meant by well-being and where the focus should be in considering the development and attainment of children and young people. Student teachers and teachers, it is suggested, should reflect on the nature of progress and how it is measured and valued in schools. Woolley contends that some progress is difficult to measure, and that personal growth and the development of attitudes and values are not given sufficient priority in an education system that is driven by market forces. He encourages teachers to consider the development and well-being of the whole child and to see academic progress as one facet within a much broader picture.

Chapter 6, by Malini Mistry and Krishan Sood looks at Q6:

Have a commitment to collaboration and co-operative working.

As Mistry and Sood point out, the education world is changing fast. There are now government expectations to work in new ways, the new terminology being partnerships and collaborations. With the implementation of *Every Child Matters* and the Workforce Reform acts, schools are required to work collaboratively with many different agencies such as social services, the health service and many others to support the learning of children and young people. How this partnership works out in practical terms in schools across the primary and secondary sector is analysed in this chapter. The authors conclude that there are no ready-made solutions, but suggest creative ways to engage with partners to provide the highest quality education for all.

Chapter 7, by Valerie Coultas, deals with Q7:

(a) Reflect on and improve their practice, and take responsibility for identifying and meeting their developing professional needs
(b) Identify priorities for their early professional development in the context of induction.

Coultas suggests that an effective teacher is someone who sees herself or himself as a learner. Teachers who evaluate and change their own practice to benefit their pupils are rewarding colleagues to work with. Teachers should use peer observations, team planning and team teaching to reflect on their practice and refine and develop their teaching repertoires. Schools can encourage teachers to reflect on their teaching and promote collaborative ways of working through creating structures, such as strong teams, that draw on teachers' expertise and give teachers the intellectual space to become creative professionals. Coultas argues that teachers need this space to develop and innovate in all schools, but particularly in challenging settings where the most flexible approaches are required. The imposition of quantitative targets, through performance management, and the new divisive pay scales being introduced into schools are not the best methods, she argues, for promoting genuine reflection, creativity, intellectual initiative and collaboration since they serve to undermine collegiality.

Chapter 8, the first of three chapters by Ian Woodfield, is concerned with Q8:

> Have a creative and constructively critical approach towards innovation, being prepared to adapt their practice where benefits and improvements are identified.

The chapter seeks to develop an argument that neo-liberal, public sector educational reforms as championed by New Labour can be interpreted as superficial and transient as they lack any sense of a deep and lasting commitment to social democracy, let alone socialism, and fail to make a realistic attempt to address the fundamental concerns of social justice. However, for the engaged professional this does not mean that these policies should be ignored in the futile hope that they will simply disappear. It is argued that the development of a 'bunker mentality' is ultimately a surrender of professional responsibility. The lack of a unifying social movement creates both problems *and* opportunities and it is for a new generation of teachers to engage with these as they struggle to meet the needs of their students in the collegiate culture of a new professional learning community. It is further argued that if we are truly to meet our future educational needs as a society, we need a creative and dynamic workforce of engaged and socially aware professional educators.

Woodfield also sounds a note of caution for those who champion the technocratic interpretation of teaching as a series of skill sets that can be learned by paraprofessionals, to be delivered in a context-free, cost-effective social vacuum. There are lessons to be learned, he argues, from the mistakes of the past and from other areas of social life. A managerialist culture that neither empowers nor engages creative professionals, Woodfield concludes, is a culture ultimately lacking in any real understanding of the fundamental challenges that face our unequal society.

In Chapter 9, Woodfield addresses Q9:

> Act upon advice and feedback and be open to coaching and mentoring.

The chapter seeks to alert new teachers to the powerful *rhetoric* of change – a rhetoric that can present 'streaming' as if it were a new and fresh approach, that can use the language of 'appropriate pathways' to conceal mechanisms for selection and the labelling of a generation of students as educational failures. Woodfield suggests that it is only by drawing on the experiences of a past generation of teachers that these ideas can be fully exposed to critical review and that it is essential for new teachers to become engaged in an on-going professional conversation with experienced teaching colleagues about the nature of teaching and learning. The problem lies in the adoption of strategies that are marketed as new but are in reality the failed attempts of previous generations repackaged for a new generation of teachers often kept ignorant of their own professional culture. It is made clear that this is not to say that talented young teachers should not seek to innovate and change. A successful mentoring relationship will do much to 'bridge the cultural gap' between generations of teachers and should help to build a more secure sense of professional identity. Woodfield further argues that the loss of vocation and its replacement with 'playing the game', with teachers acting out the new assigned social identity in inspection situations, is *not* a firm foundation upon which to build a committed and successful teaching force for the 21st century. What *is* needed is the construction of a secure mechanism for the seamless transmission of professional values from one generation to the next – the adoption of successful models for mentoring and coaching that nurture a new generation of teachers seeking to avoid rather than repeat the errors of the past, a generation committed to the highest professional standards, founded on the best available classroom practice, but also secure in a sense of professional identity.

The last chapter of the book, also by Woodfield, addresses Q10:

> Have a knowledge and understanding of a range of teaching, learning and behaviour management strategies and know how to use and adapt them, including how to personalise learning and provide opportunities for all learners to achieve their potential.

Woodfield focuses on one of the dominant themes that emerged from a series of interviews that he conducted – the tension between elements of the Government's current agenda for schools as expressed through policy initiatives such as *Every Child Matters* and the emphasis placed on personalisation and inclusion, on the one hand, and the competitive culture of performativity inherent in the neo-liberal basis of the education policies of both New Labour and previous Conservative administrations, on the other. Woodfield discusses the relationship between terms such as 'equality of opportunity' and 'parity of esteem' and the business of education in the 21st century. Is inclusive education for pupils defined at an early age to be of 'below average ability' simply a return to the past prescriptions of the tripartite system, where some prepare for university and others must 'learn to labour'? It is argued that there is a symbiotic relationship between the accelerating inclusion agenda and the need for teachers to adapt successful teaching, learning and behaviour management strategies to suit the needs of *all* learners within an educational environment in which *every* pupil can learn to the maximum.

Mike Cole

Notes

1   'Ist/phobic' is a short-hand term to cover racist; sexist; disablist; classist; homophobic, transphobic, and Islamophobic. Individuals may exhibit one or more 'isms' and/or be homophobic, and/or transphobic, and/or Islamophobic.

2   'Pupils' is used throughout the book to refer to pupils and students. It is acknowledged that in secondary schools and beyond, the common nomenclature is 'student'. However 'pupils' is used in order to avoid the rather clumsy nomenclature of 'pupil/student'. Where chapter authors are referring specifically to the secondary school, they may use 'student'. In addition, the contributors have generally adopted the nomenclatures 'student teacher' and 'teacher education', as opposed to the TDA's 'trainee teacher' and 'teacher training'. This reflects our collective belief that achieving QTS involves much more than mere 'training' (Cole 1999).

References

Boseley, S. (2007) 'British Children: poorer, at greater risk and more insecure', the *Guardian*, 14 February, 2007, pp. 1–2.

Cole, M. (1999) 'Professional Issues and Initial Teacher Education: What Can Be Done and What Should Be Done', *Education and Social Justice*, 2(1): 63–6.

DfES (2004a) *Every Child Matters: Change for Children*. London: DfES.

DfES (2004b) *Every Child Matters: Change for Children in Schools*. London: DfES.

DfES (2005) *Aims and Outcomes* (of *Every Child Matters*). Available at http://www.everychildmatters.gov.uk/aims/ (accessed 14 April, 2007).

Prince, R. (2007) 'Britain Worst for Kid's WellBeing', *The Daily Mirror*, 14 February.

Training and Development Agency (TDA) (2006) *Qualifying to Teach*. London: DfES.

Training and Development Agency (TDA) (2007) *Professional Standards for Teachers: Qualified Teacher Status*. London: TDA. Available at http://www.tda.gov.uk/upload/resources/pdf/s/standards_qts.pdf (accessed 12 September 2007).

UNICEF (2007) UNICEF report on childhood in industrialised countries. News item 14 February 2007. http://www.unicef.org.uk/press/news_detail.asp?news_id=890 (accessed 12 September 2007).

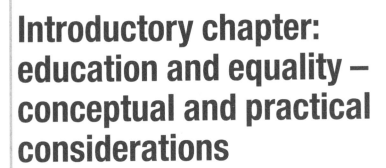

Introductory chapter: education and equality – conceptual and practical considerations

Mike Cole

Learning objectives

To raise awareness of:

- the distinction between equal opportunities and equality;
- conceptual issues relating to 'race' and racism; gender; sexuality; disability and social class, and their relationship to education;
- practical issues related to these identities on a personal level, and their relationship to education.

Part one: conceptual issues

Introduction: equality and equal opportunities

IN ORDER TO BE AWARDED Qualified Teacher Status (QTS) in England and Wales, teachers must demonstrate that they have high expectations of and respect for *all* pupils (S1.1 of Training and Development Agency (TDA) 2006: 8) (my emphasis).[1] If teachers are to do this, then it is self-evident that they need to be aware of the way in which social class, gender, ethnicity, disability and sexuality impact on pupils' lives.[2] Teaching and learning about equality, then, is *not* an optional extra, something to be tagged on to teacher education courses after the important stuff has been dealt with. It is, rather, an integral part of the teaching and learning process.

1

First of all, a distinction needs to be made between equality of opportunity, on the one hand, and equality, on the other. Equal opportunity policies in schools and elsewhere seek to enhance social mobility within structures that are essentially unequal. In other words, they seek a meritocracy, where people rise (or fall) on 'merit', but to grossly unequal levels or strata in society – unequal in terms of income; wealth; lifestyle; life-chances and power. Socialist policies, policies to promote equality, on the other hand, seek to go further. First, socialists, those who believe in equality, attempt to develop a systematic critique of structural inequalities, both in society at large and at the level of the individual school (or other institution). Second, socialists are committed to a transformed economy, and a more socially just society, where wealth and ownership are shared far more equally, and where citizens (whether young citizens or teachers in schools, economic citizens in the workplace or citizens as voters) exercise democratic controls over their lives and over the structures of the societies of which they are part and to which they contribute.

Meritocrats seek equality of opportunity. Socialists seek equality of outcome. While equal opportunity policies in schools (and elsewhere) are clearly essential, it is the socialist view that they need to be advocated within a framework of a longer-term commitment to equality (Cole and Hill 1999: 1–2; Cole 2006).[3]

Equality and equal opportunity issues have been pertinent through history and they are pertinent now (Cole (ed.) 2006; Hill and Cole (eds) 2001). Another of the requirements of TDA (2006) is that those awarded QTS need to 'recognise and respond effectively to equal opportunities issues as they arise in the classroom' (S3.3.14 of TDA 2006: 14). This includes 'challenging stereotyped views', 'challenging bullying or harassment' and 'following relevant policies and procedures' (ibid.). In order to do this, it is necessary to understand equality issues *per se* as well as being able to apply them to education. Theory and practice must be interrelated. For example, in order for us, as teachers (and other educational workers), to deal with racism in schools, we first of all need to understand what is meant by the concept of racism; to challenge homophobic bullying, we need to be conversant with sexuality issues; to deal with gender differentials in achievement, for example, we need to understand what is meant by gender. In order to deal with social class issues, we need to know about theories of social class, and in order to deal with disability issues, we need to be aware of issues of disability rights.

All of these equality issues are dealt with at length in Cole (ed.) (2006) and Hill and Cole (eds) (2001). They are dealt with on a subject-by-subject basis, at the primary level in Cole *et al.* (eds) (1997); and at the secondary level, in Hill and Cole (eds) (1999).

As well as needing to have a sound knowledge of the equality issues both *per se* and in relation to education, beginning teachers and teachers also need to know the current state of play with respect to national and international legislation pertaining to equality and equal opportunity issues (see Chapter 3 for a thorough analysis; see also, for example, the regular editions of the University and College Union's (UCU's) *Equality News* (http://www.ucu.org.uk/index.cfm?articleid=1963).

Equality and equal opportunity issues are interrelated. For example, every human being has multiple identities. To take a case in point: there are, of course, lesbians, gays, bisexuals and transgendered (LGBT) people in all social classes; among the Asian, black and other minority ethnic communities;[4] and among 'white' communities. There are LGBT people with disabilities and special needs. Equality and equal opportunity issues are also discrete. For conceptual clarity, I will deal with each in turn.

'Race' and racism

There is a consensus among certain geneticists and most social scientists that 'race' is a social construct rather than a biological given. That this is the case is explained succinctly by Steven Rose and Hilary Rose (2005), and I will summarise their arguments here. They point out that 'race' is a term with a long history in biological discourse. Given a rigorous definition by the evolutionist Theodosius Dobzhansky in the 1930s, 'race' applied to an inbred population with specific genetic characteristics within a species, resulting from some form of separation that limited interbreeding. 'In the wild', they go on, 'this might be geographical separation, as among finches on the Galapagos islands, or imposed by artificial breeding, as for example between labradors and spaniels among dogs' (ibid.). Early racial theorising also divided humans into either three (white, black, yellow) or five biological 'races' (Caucasian, African, Australasian, American and Asian), supposedly differing in intellect and personality. However, in the aftermath of Nazism, the UNESCO panel of biological and cultural anthropologists challenged the value of this biological concept of 'race', with its social hierarchies. When, in the 1960s and 1970s, genetic technology advanced to the point where it was possible to begin to quantify genetic differences between individuals and groups, it became increasingly clear that these so-called 'races' were far from genetically homogeneous. In 1972, the evolutionary geneticist Richard Lewontin pointed out that 85 per cent of human genetic diversity occurred *within* rather than *between* populations, and only 6 to 10 per cent of diversity is associated with the broadly defined 'races' (*ibid.*). As Rose and Rose explain:

> [m]ost of this difference is accounted for by the readily visible genetic variation of skin colour, hair form and so on. The everyday business of seeing and acknowledging such difference is not the same as the project of genetics.

For genetics and, more importantly, for the prospect of treating genetic diseases, the difference is important, since humans differ in their susceptibility to particular diseases, and genetics can have something to say about this. However, beyond medicine, the use of the invocation of 'race' is increasingly suspect. There has been a growing debate among geneticists about the utility of the term and, in Autumn 2004, an entire issue of the influential journal *Nature Reviews Genetics* was devoted to it. The geneticists agreed with most biological anthropologists that, for human biology, the term 'race' was an unhelpful leftover. Rose and Rose conclude that '[w]hatever arbitrary boundaries one places on any population group for the purposes of genetic research, they do not match those of conventionally defined races'. For example, the DNA of native Britons contains traces of multiple waves of occupiers and migrants. 'Race', as a scientific concept, Rose and Rose conclude, 'is well past its sell-by date' (ibid.). For these reasons, I would argue that 'race' should be put in inverted commas whenever one needs to refer to it.

Racism, however, is, of course, self-evidently real enough and, indeed, like inequalities associated with the other conceptual issues discussed in this chapter, a major worldwide problem. In order for teachers to deal with racism, they need to have an awareness of what it means. My view is that we should adopt a wide-ranging definition of racism, rather than a narrow one based, as it was in the days of Empire, for example, on biology. Racism can be institutional or personal; it can be dominative (direct and oppressive) as opposed to aversive (exclusion and cold-shouldering) (Kovel 1988); it can be overt or covert; intentional or unintentional; biological and/or cultural. Attributes ascribed to ethnic groups can also be seemingly positive, as, for example, when whole groups are stereotyped as having strong cultures or being good at sport. Such stereotypes may well be followed up, respectively, with notions that 'they are taking over', or 'they are not so good academically'. The point is to be wary of attributing any stereotypes to ethnic groups. All stereotypes are *at least potentially* racist.

There can, of course, be permutations among these different forms of racism (Cole 2004a, 2007a).

The implications for education are as follows. Education has played a role in re-producing racism (monocultural and much multicultural education), but also has a major role to play in undermining racism (anti-racist education). Monocultural education is to do with the promotion of so-called British values;[5] multicultural education is about the celebration of diversity and has often been tokenistic and patronising, and anti-racist education focuses on undermining racism (Cole 1998; Cole and Blair 2006). The Stephen Lawrence Inquiry report acknowledged that '[r]acism, institutional or otherwise, is not [only] the prerogative of the Police Service' (Macpherson 1999: 6.54) and that 'other agencies including for example those dealing with . . . education also suffer from [it]' (ibid.). Macpherson went on to argue that '[i]f racism is to be eradicated, there must be specific and co-ordinated action both within the agencies themselves and by society at large, *particularly through the education system*, from pre-primary school upwards and onwards' (ibid.) (my emphasis).

Modern technology has major implications for delivering anti-racist multicultural education, in that it allows people to speak for themselves, via websites and email. This is not an argument in favour of postmodern multivocality, where all voices are equally valid; but rather the flagging of opportunities to avoid speaking on other people's behalf.

To repeat, teachers need a conceptual awareness of what racism is in order to combat the racism endemic in our education system, and in other institutions of society.

Gender

Generally speaking a distinction is made between 'sex' and 'gender', with sex being biological and gender being constructed. These essentialised categories of male and female have important consequences in society, for you are either 'in' the category or 'outside' of it (Woodward 2004). Within a patriarchal society the male is the norm and women are the 'other' (Paechter 1998). However, it is argued that gender roles are learned and are relative to time and place. In other words, what are considered 'acceptable modes of dress' or body language for males and females vary dramatically through history and according to geographical location (this is not to say, of course, that everyone in a given society conforms to such norms – there are many examples throughout history of people who have refused to conform).

Davies (1993) has shown that from their earliest years children hold strong views about their gender positioning and that gender identities are constructed and learned throughout schooling. Schools have traditionally reproduced gender categorisation and as Francis (1998) suggests, children work hard at constructing and maintaining their gender identities. However, she also points out that gender constructions are only one part of the children's identities and that, for example, 'race', ethnicity (e.g. Connolly 1998; Archer 2003) and social class (see Reay 2006) are also part of their identities and these can compete with or reinforce gender stereotypes. For example, there are undoubtedly differences between boys' and girls' development and progress in reading and writing. However, there is sometimes an oversimplification of the debate about gender and achievement in English, as it is not all boys who are underachieving but particularly those from lower socio-economic groups (Coultas 2007; Francis and Skelton 2005).

Many schools today are aware of their role in providing a curriculum free of bias and a curriculum which is emancipatory. Many schools are also aware of the power that the structures, rules and regulations can have in promoting sexism. The curriculum, actual and hidden, can be non-sexist, or it can be anti-sexist (George 1993). In other words, schools can make sure that they do not promote sexism, or they can actively promote anti-sexism. Traditionally, there has been concern among feminists and their supporters about the way in which schooling has reproduced gender inequalities, particularly with respect to female subordination. More recently, now that it has become apparent that many boys are now being outperformed academically by girls, there has been more general media and government concerns about boys. It is important to note that for many years girls had been disadvantaged by the education system with very little media attention being given to the problem. Indeed in the 1950s and 1960s, it was acknowledged that girls' literacy and numeracy skills were superior to those of boys and that, as a consequence, to achieve a grammar school place girls had to score far higher than boys in the 11+ (Gaine and George 1999; George 2004). It has only been with the compulsory assessment and testing following the introduction of the National Curriculum that girls' superior achievement has become visible, provoking a minor 'moral panic'. In fact boys are actually improving year on year. Head (2004) points to a much more serious issue in relation to adolescent boys which is their alienation from not only schooling but from society in general.[6] He notes the disproportionate numbers of boys who are excluded from schools, are deemed dyslexic, suffer from ADHD and attempt suicide. It is not all plain sailing for girls either. Much of the recent work, which focuses on 'girls', indicates that girls are now caught between two competing discourses. They are valued for being caring and selfless, putting the concerns of their friends first, but at the same time they have to be competitive and individualistic in order to maintain their current successes in school (e.g. George 2007).

If many boys are now being out-performed by girls, this is not to say, of course, that schooling does not continue to reproduce other forms of sexism, of which females are at the receiving end. For example, boys often still dominate in mixed-sex classrooms, and schools and university education departments suffer from an over-representation of men in higher positions, which is a reflection of the wider society. Women, despite their 'schooling success', still occupy the low ranks in most areas of work and their earning potential is still far worse than it is for men, with women earning approximately 80 per cent of a man's wage. For discussions on the way in which sexism impacts on schooling, on differential achievement and what can be done about it, see Gaine and George (1999); Hirom (2001); Martin (2006); Skelton *et al.* (eds) (2006); and the Equal Opportunities Commission (http://www.eoc.org.uk).

To repeat, gender roles are not fixed, but are relative to time and place. Boys do not *need* to do badly at school relative to girls. Sexism, where subordinate gender locations are reproduced for females, does not *need* to predominate in schools. Women's structural location in the workforce can be changed and teachers *can* do something about it.

Disability

Richard Rieser has made a distinction between what he calls the 'medical' and 'social models' of disability (see Figures 0.1 and 0.2). The 'medical model' views the disabled person as the problem. Disabled people are to be adapted to fit into the world as it is. Where this is not possible, disabled people have historically been shut away in some specialised institution or isolated at home. Often disabled peoples' lives are handed over to others (Rieser 2006a).

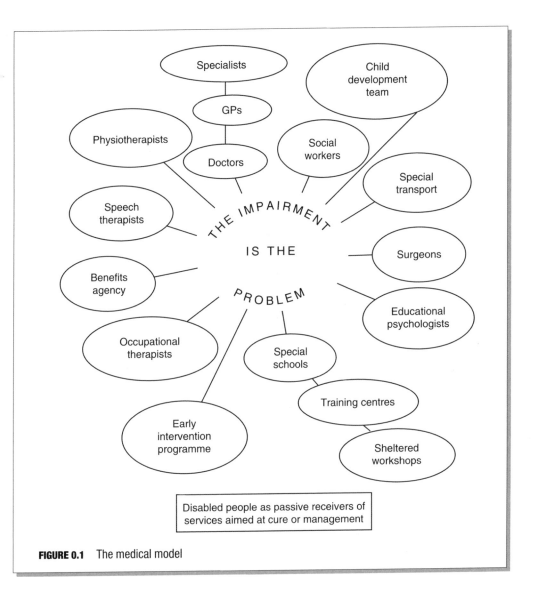

FIGURE 0.1 The medical model

The 'social model' of disability views society as the problem. It is up to institutions in society to adapt to meet the needs of disabled people. This is the model favoured by disabled people.

The educational implications for each of these are the 'fixed continuum of provision' and the 'constellation of services' (see Figures 0.3 and 0.4). Under the former, the disabled person is slotted and moved according to the assessment of (usually non-disabled) assessors. This model is based on segregation (Rieser 2006b). With respect to the 'constellation of services', provision is made for the disabled child in

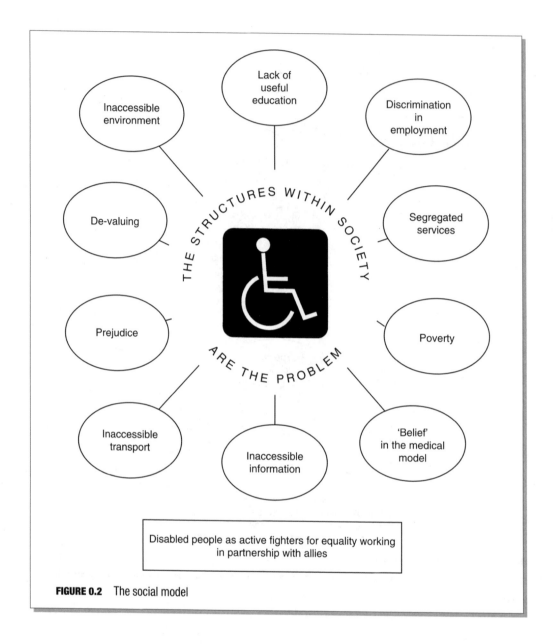

FIGURE 0.2 The social model

mainstream school. The child and teacher are backed up by a variety of support services (ibid.).

Currently, there is a wide consensus among disability activists, many educational institutions and the Government that the way forward is inclusion, which, of course, relates to the 'social model' and the 'constellation of services' (ibid.; see also, Chapter 3 of this volume). There is an urgent need for major investment in all mainstream state schools to make genuine inclusion a reality.

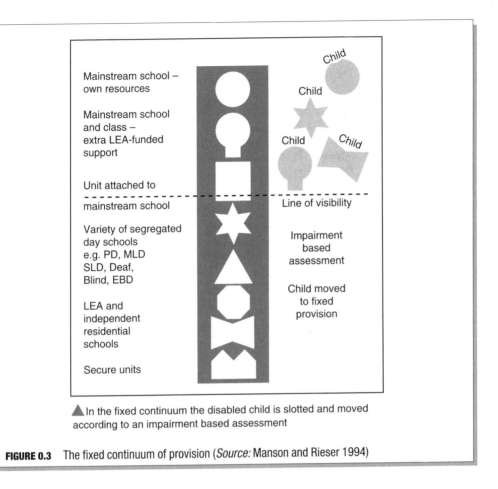

In the fixed continuum the disabled child is slotted and moved according to an impairment based assessment

FIGURE 0.3   The fixed continuum of provision (*Source:* Manson and Rieser 1994)

Sexuality

Sexuality has often been ignored in education. There are a number of reasons why this should not be the case. First, sexuality is an issue for every teacher, primary as well as secondary; for example, there is evidence that some children identify as gay or lesbian in the primary years (NUT 1991: 7; Epstein 1994: 49–56; Letts IV and Sears (eds) 1999). For this reason and to militate against the normalisation of homophobic attitudes, it is important that sexualities education starts at an early age.

Second, in most schools, lesbians, gay men and bisexuals will be members of the teaching and other staff. In some schools, there will be transgendered members of staff. Some parents/carers will lesbian, gay, bisexual or transgendered (LGBT), and some pupils will be open about their sexuality. Virtually all children will be aware of issues of sexuality.

Third, ignoring sexuality and homophobia is unprofessional and illegal. The National Union of Teacher's Code of Professional Conduct, for example, quite rightly deems harassment on the grounds of sexual orientation to be unprofessional

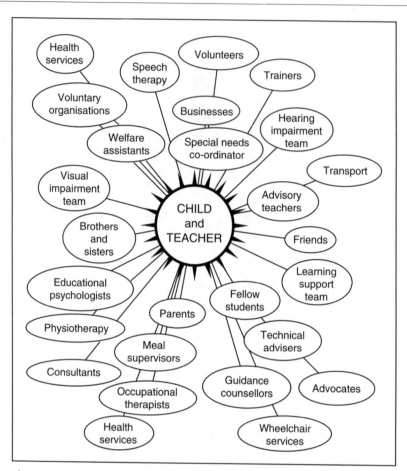

▲ The constellation of services provides what the child and the class teacher need in ordinary schools, from a variety of services, resources and specialists. This conception allows for the development of inclusive schools.

FIGURE 0.4 The constellation of services (*Source:* Manson and Rieser 1994)

conduct. New equalities regulations outlaw discrimination towards LGBT people in the provision of goods and services as well as employment (see Chapter 3).

Homophobia is an unacceptable feature of society and there is evidence that lesbian and gay young people experience bullying at school, including physical acts of aggression, name calling, teasing, isolation and ridicule (see Ellis with High 2004; see also Forrest 2006; and the Stonewall website (http://www.stonewall.org.uk/stonewall)). There is also evidence that young people who experience homophobic violence are likely to turn to truancy, substance abuse, prostitution or even suicide. Lesbian, gay and bisexual pupils should be listened to and should be encouraged to seek parental/carer advice and/or encouraged to refer to other appropriate agencies for advice. Their experiences of homophobia and harassment should not be dismissed as exaggerated or exceptional. Homophobic 'jokes', remarks or insults should always be challenged.

It should be pointed out here that, given growing research into boys, girls and heterosexualities, and the links between homophobia and misogyny, sexual bullying (from homophobia to heterosexual harassment) encompasses more than issues connected to LGBT identities (Renold 2000a, 2000b, 2005, 2006).[7]

In addition to legislative requirements (see Chapter 3) the curriculum should tackle homophobia and transphobia,[8] as well as other forms of discrimination; just to give some examples: in order to promote equality for lesbians, gays, bisexuals and transgendered people, a range of family patterns and lifestyles can be illustrated in fiction used in English lessons, while drama can help to examine feelings and emotions. Reference can be made to famous lesbian, gay, bisexual and transgendered writers, sports personalities, actors, singers and historical figures (see the NUT website at www.teachers.org.uk). For a fuller discussion of sexuality, see Forrest and Ellis (2006); for fuller discussions of sexuality and education, see Williamson (2001) Forrest (2006) and Ellis (2007); for a discussion of transphobia, see Whittle *et al.* (2007).

Social class and capitalism

Social class defines the social system under which we live. For this reason, among others, social class has tended to be left out of teacher education programmes, except in the narrow though nonetheless fundamentally important sense of more opportunities for working-class children. This is because discussion of social class and capitalism poses a threat to the *status quo*, much more profound than the other equality issues discussed in this chapter.

There are two major ways in which social class is classified. First, there is 'social class' as based on the classification of the Office for Population Census Studies (OPCS), first used in the census of 2001. Based on occupation, lifestyle and status, it accords with popular understandings of social class differentiation; in particular, the distinctions between white-collar workers, on the one hand, and blue-collar workers and those classified as long-term unemployed, on the other. However, it is not without its difficulties:

- it masks the existence of the super-rich and the super-powerful (the capitalist class, and the aristocracy);
- it glosses over and hides the antagonistic and exploitative relationship between the two main classes in society (the capitalist class and the working class);
- it segments the working class and thereby disguises the ultimate common interests of white-collar, blue-collar and long-term unemployed workers (Hill and Cole 2001: 151–3).

Thus, while for sociological analyses in general, it has its uses, its problematic nature should not be forgotten.

The other way to conceive social class is the Marxist definition, in which those who have to sell their labour power in order to survive are the working class, *whatever their status or income*, and those who own the means of production and exploit the working class by making profits from their labour are the capitalist class (see Cole 2007a for an analysis; see also Hickey 2006).

In post-World War II Britain, the economic system was generally described as a mixed economy; that is to say, key sectors of the economy (e.g. the railways, gas, water and electricity and the telephones) were owned by the state and other sectors were owned by private capitalist enterprises. This is no longer the case and not only is globalised neo-liberal capitalism nearly universal, it is openly exalted as the only way the world can be run.[9]

With respect to education, business is in schools, in the sense of both influencing the curriculum *and* having an increasing financial stake in schools. There is 'Capital's' agenda *for* 'Education' and 'Capital's' agenda *in* 'Education'. *The Capitalist Agenda for Education* relates to the role of education in producing the kind of workforce that is currently required by global capitalist enterprises. It is thus about making profits *indirectly*. It entails creating the kind of workers that will 'fit in' with capital's needs. In practical terms, the Capitalist Agenda *for* Education means involving the private sector in the running of schools to ensure that government's and capitalism's aims for education correspond to market needs.

The Capitalist Agenda in Education relates to the role of education in providing profits for capitalists *directly*. It centres on setting business 'free' in education, extracting profits from privately controlled/owned schools. This involves privatising either the schools themselves or services to schools (Hatcher 2001; Hill 2005; Cole 2007c).

It is my view that instead of commodifying knowledge in the interests of global capitalism, education should be about empowerment, where visions of an alternative way of running the planet (Venezuela is a good example) become part of the mainstream curriculum. As Peter McLaren (2002) concludes his book, *Life in Schools*, schools should cease to be defined as extensions of the workplace or as frontline institutions in the battle for international markets and foreign competition. Paulo Freire (1972) urged teachers to detach themselves and their pupils from the idea that they are agents of capital, where *banking education* (the teacher deposits information into an empty account) is the norm and to reinvent schools as democratic public spheres where meaningful *dialogue* can take place. There are some positive developments in schools related to globalisation, to world poverty, and to ecology, but no space is provided for a discussion of *alternatives* to neo-liberal global capitalism, such as world democratic socialism (see Cole 2007a for a discussion). Discussing socialism in schools may be seen as one of the last taboos. It is time to move forward and bring such discussions into the classroom.

To summarise Part 1 of this chapter: all equality issues are important, but they all need to be considered in the context of, but not *reduced* to, social class and capitalism. Capitalism is in many ways reliant on the other forms of inequality. Education should not exist for the glorification of capital, of consumption, of commodification. Teachers at all levels of the education system need to foster critical reflection, with a view to transformative action, for a more just and equitable world.

Part two: practical issues

Introduction

Educators, in my view should:

- develop the learning of all pupils without limits rather than entertain vague notions of 'to their full potential';[10]
- reject ideas of fixed ability;
- enable pupils to make rational and informed decisions about their own lives;
- enable pupils to make rational and informed decisions about the lives of others;
- foster critical reflection, with a view to transformative action;
- help empower[11] pupils to be in a position to take transformative action.

Equality and equal opportunity issues have both an institutional and legislative dimension and an individual dimension. Jeff Nixon, in Chapter 3, deals with the institutional and legislative challenge.[12] Here I will deal with the personal challenge.

The personal challenge

It needs to be stressed that people's positions *vis-à-vis* the equality issues outlined in this chapter are not *natural*, but reflect particular social systems. Inequalities are not *inevitable* features of any society; they are social constructs, crucial terrains between conflicting forces in any given society. In other words, societies do not *need* to be class-based; to have racialised hierarchies; to have one sex dominating another. I do not believe that people are *naturally* homophobic or transphobic, or prone to marginalising the needs of disabled people. On the contrary, we are socialised into accepting the norms, values and customs of the social systems in which we grow up. This is a very powerful message for teachers. If we *learn* to accept or to promote inequalities, we can also *learn* to challenge them. Schools have traditionally played an important part in socialising pupils to accept the *status quo*. They have also played and continue to play a major role in undermining that process (Darder 2002; McLaren 2002; Hill 2003; Hill (ed.) forthcoming 2008).

In the personal challenge it is first important to distance oneself from the notion of 'political correctness', a pernicious concept invented by the Radical Right, and which, unfortunately, has become common currency. The term 'political correctness' was coined to imply that there exist (left-wing) political demagogues who seek to impose their views on equality issues, in particular appropriate terminology, on the majority. In reality, nomenclature changes over time. To take the case of ethnicity, in the twenty-first century, terms such as 'negress' or 'negro' or 'coloured', nomenclatures which at one time were considered quite acceptable, are now considered offensive. Anti-racists are concerned with *respect* for others' choice of nomenclature and, therefore, are careful to acknowledge changes in it, changes which are decided by oppressed groups themselves (bearing in mind that there can be differences of opinion among such groups). The same applies to other equality issues. Thus, for example, it has become common practice to use 'working class' rather than 'lower class';[13] 'lesbian, gay, bisexual and transgender' rather than 'sexually deviant'; 'disability' rather than 'handicap'; and 'gender equality' rather than 'a woman's place'. Using current and acceptable nomenclature is about the fostering of a caring and inclusive society, not about 'political correctness' (Cole and Blair 2005).

Haberman (1995: 91–2) suggests five steps which he considers to be essential for beginning teachers to overcome prejudice. I have adapted and considerably expanded Haberman's arguments and replaced his psychological concept of prejudice with the more sociological concept of 'ism/phobia'[14] in order to encompass racism, xeno-racism,[15] sexism, disablism, classism and homophobia/transphobia/Islamophobia/xenophobia. I have also provided my own examples of how each step might develop. It is important to point out that these steps apply to all members of the educational community, as well as beginning teachers, as specified by Haberman. I have also created a sixth step.

The first step is a thorough self-analysis of the content of one's ism/phobia. What form does it take? Is it overt or covert? Is it based on biology or is it cultural? Is it dominative (direct and oppressive) or aversive (excluding and cold-shouldering) (Kovel 1988)? Is it intentional or unintentional?[16] Are my attitudes patronising? This is, of course, a *process* rather than an event. In many ways, this step is the most crucial and difficult of the steps.

The second step is to seek answers to the question of source. How did I learn or come to believe these things? Did I learn to be ist/phobic from my parents/carers? Did I become ist/phobic as a result of experiences at primary school or at secondary school? Was it in further education or in higher education? Did I pick up ism/phobia from my peers; from the media; from newspapers; from magazines; from the internet? Was it a combination of the above? Why was I not equipped to challenge ism/phobia when I came across it?

Step three is to consider to what extent I am on the receiving end of, or how do I benefit from ism/phobia? How does it demean me as a human being to have these beliefs? On the other hand, how do I benefit psychologically and/or materially from holding these beliefs?

Step four is to consider how one's ism/phobia may be affecting one's work in education. Am I making suppositions about young people's behaviour or attitudes to life based on their social class, ethnicity, impairments, gender, sexuality, religion or nationality? Am I making negative or positive presumptions about their academic achievement? If there is evidence of low achievement, am I taking the necessary remedial actions? Am I making assumptions about the parents/carers of the young people in my care? Am I making assumptions about other members of the school community, based on the above?

Step five is the phase in which one lays out a plan explicating what one intends to do about one's ism/phobia. How do I propose to check it, unlearn it, counteract it and get beyond it? This can involve reading a text or texts and/or websites which address the issues. It should mean an ongoing update on equality/equal opportunities legislation. As mentioned in Part One of this chapter, the trade union, UCU, has a very good website on such legislation. It must certainly mean acquainting oneself with differential rates of achievements, and a critical analysis of the various explanations for this, centring on the explanations given by those who are pro-equality. It should mean acquainting oneself with various forms of bullying related to isms/phobia and their effects. It might mean going on a course or courses.

It is not being argued that these five steps will necessarily occur in an individual's psyche (although they might) spontaneously. Indeed, they can often be better addressed in group situations. I am suggesting that, as in this chapter, encouragement should be given for individuals to take these steps. Such encouragement could be done in the form of an introductory lecture to beginning teachers (and other educational workers). Also it is not being suggested that this is *merely* an individual process. It could be followed up with the sharing of questions and answers in groups and publicly. This could then progress (in practice) to an exploration of how a shared analysis of the five steps relates to the work of the school and the community; local, national and international.

The personal and the institutional

After or during these five steps, the sixth step should be to connect the personal with the institutional, in order to undermine isms/phobia, and to promote equality. This might involve becoming active in one's school and/or community and/or becoming a trade union activist.[17] It might involve joining and working for a socialist/Marxist political party. It might also involve becoming active in local, national or international lobby groups. It should involve making the combating of isms/phobia and the promotion of equality central to one's work in educational institutions, in both the actual curriculum (what is on the timetable) and the hidden curriculum (everything else that goes on in educational institutions). It might involve writing and lecturing about isms/phobia and equality.

Conclusion

In this chapter, I have outlined the main conceptual issues with respect to equal opportunity and equality issues in schools. Schools and other educational institutions should be places where personal and group reflection and action on equality issues is central, and an integral part of the institutions' ethos. If we are to relate to and empower our pupils, if we are to engage in meaningful and successful teaching, we need to begin with the pupils' comprehension of their daily life experiences, whether in pre-school or university. From their earliest years, children's self-concepts are tainted by cultures of inequality. By starting from *their* description of these experiences, we are able to ground our teaching in concrete reality, then to transcend common sense and to move towards a critical scientific understanding of the world. This is the process by which teachers can support the process of the self-empowerment of tomorrow's children and young people.

As stressed above, I firmly believe that we are not born ist/phobic. Ism/phobia is a product of the society in which we live.[18] We can make important changes in societies as they are. However, in order to fully eradicate oppression of all forms, we need to change society, and indeed the world. At the beginning of this chapter, I made a distinction between equal opportunities and equality. Socialists support all progressive reforms. Thus, what is happening with respect to the promotion of equality and equal opportunities in the UK, the rest of Europe and elsewhere is to be welcomed. But, in order to achieve real equality, there is a need for a transformed world economy – a world socialist economy. If this all sounds implausibly idealistic, it might be worth considering which is the more utopian: the continued survival of a grossly unequal, imperialistic, destructive and anti-democratic world, capitalist system, en route for ecological disaster, or a democratic, equal world, planned for need and not profit.

I will end with a quote from the Hillcole Group. Whatever the twenty-first century has to offer, the choices will need to be debated:

Each person and group should experience education as contributing to their own self-advancement, but at the same time our education should ensure that at least part of everyone's life activity is also designed to assist in securing the future of the planet we inherit – set in the context of a sustainable and equitable society. Democracy is not possible unless there is a free debate about all the alternatives for running our social and economic system . . . All societies [are] struggling with the same issues in the 21st century. We can prepare by being better armed with war machinery or more competitive international monopolies, both based on consuming ever more of the earth's resources . . . Or we can wipe out poverty . . . altogether. We can decide to approach the future by consciously putting our investment into a massive drive to encourage participation from everyone at every stage in life through training and education that will increase productive, social, cultural and environmental development in ways we have not yet begun to contemplate.

(Hillcole Group 1997: 94–5)

As Alex Callinicos has argued, challenging the current climate requires courage, imagination and will power inspired by the injustice that surrounds us. However, 'these qualities are present in abundance. Once mobilized, they can turn the world upside down' (2000: 129).

Acknowledgements

I would like to thank Viv Ellis, Rosalyn George, Emma Renold and Krishan Sood for their very helpful comments on an earlier draft of this chapter. As always, responsibility for any inadequacies remains mine.

Notes

1   It is significant that, in changing its name from the Teacher Training Agency (TTA) to the Training and Development Agency for Schools (TDA), this body retained the term 'training' rather than 'education'. This is unfortunate but understandable – given the continuity from Thatcher's legacy to Blair – the legacy from Thatcherism to Blairism. Thatcher and the Radical Right of the time believed that teacher education, under the guise of *theory*, was in the grip of Marxists, and that teachers did not need to engage in theory, but needed solely a love of their subject and *training*. As pointed out in endnote 2 of the Preface, the contributors are unanimously of the view that becoming a teacher is very much to do with education, rather than mere training.

2   These five equality issues are not spelt out directly in TDA (2006). Instead, the regulations identify 'social, cultural, linguistic, religious and ethnic backgrounds' (p. 8). Since fulfilling TDA requirements clearly requires attention to all of the five equality issues, I would argue that, to fully ensure inclusion for all, the five issues should be made explicit by the TDA. I have not included a discussion of age and ageism in this chapter. This is not to marginalise its importance, but rather because it is not an issue that impinges on children and young people's lives in their daily interactions with other children and young people. This is not to say that it is not an issue, nor that student teachers and teachers should not be aware of age and ageism and the need to challenge and undermine it (see Chapter 3 of this book).

3   The socialist transition to equality is, in my view, apparent in present-day Venezuela. President Chavez has already instituted a major programme promoting equal opportunities, and massively improved welfare, health and education for the working class. Following a landslide election victory in 2006, Chavez announced a period of 'maximum [socialist] revolution'. Local assemblies have been given money to prioritise their needs – free health, free school meals etc; the curriculum has been changed to promote 'socialist values' and a wealth tax has been imposed on those, for example, with second homes or expensive art collections. Oil, gas and electricity are to be nationalised, and workers in private firms have been given time during the working day to study socialism. The relationship between socialism and Marxism is addressed in Cole 2007a.

4   I prefer the nomenclature, 'Asian, black, and other minority ethnic' to the more common nomenclature, 'black and ethnic minority'. There are four reasons for this. First, the term 'black', once popular as an all-encompassing nomenclature, had ceased to have that purchase from the late 1980s onwards: hence the need for the wider formulation. Second, with respect to this nomenclature, the omission of the word 'other' between 'and' and 'ethnic minority' implies that only 'ethnic minorities' (people of Cypriot and Irish origin, for example) are minority constituencies whereas black people are not. This is, of course, not accurate. Third, the use of the term, 'ethnic minority' has, in practice, meant that members of the dominant majority group are not referred to in terms of their ethnicity, with the implication that they do not have ethnicity (the sequencing of 'minority' before 'ethnic' does not carry this implication, since the creation of a new formulation, together with the prioritising of the former over the latter, facilitates the conceptualisation of a *majority* ethnic group too). Fourth, 'black and ethnic minority' has the effect of excluding people of Asian and other origins who do not consider themselves 'black'. The fact that people of Asian origin form the majority of 'non-white' minority ethnic women and men is masked (Cole 1993: 672–3). Ideally, I believe in 'ethnic' self-definition. I recognise that there can be differences in preferred nomenclature among 'ethnic groups' in opposing certain usages of terms and in defending others (for my views on 'ethnicity', see Cole 2003). Satnam Virdee (forthcoming 2008) has adopted the nomenclature 'racialized minority' as an all-encompassing term. This has the merit of being generally ahistorically applicable, and not confined to a given historical period. 'Asian, black and other minority ethnic' has the advantage of

historic specificity, although this may well need adapting in the light of burgeoning xenoracism and xenoracialisation. In a very real sense, 'Asian, black, and other minority ethnic' is itself a racialised category, albeit an attempt at a *positive* descriptor. Thus Virdee's preferred nomenclature does have an additional merit in avoiding nomenclature that is *itself* racialised. I am aware, of course, that nomenclatures change and I am not attempting to make a definitive statement. If readers can improve on it, this is of course to be welcomed. I would particularly welcome the comments on nomenclature from members of racialised groups.

5   The notion of so-called 'British Values' has recently been extended beyond the usual white middle-class norm by certain politicians and others to imply a shared consensus of values among all British citizens, irrespective of ethnicity. There are a number of problems with this extension. First, it assumes a parity of circumstance for all Britons, whereas the populace is deeply unequal in terms of ethnicity, social class and gender; second, it implies a consensus of values, when in fact these vary considerably according to ethnicity, social class and gender; third, it renders the economic system of global neo-liberal capitalism and imperialism unproblematic – 'we all believe in this, because we are British' (see the discussion on social class below).

6   In a social class-based society, where there is little hope for millions of young working-class people, such alienation often leads to anti-social behaviour. Young people need hope for the future, and expectations of a decent and fulfilling life, something apparent in countries such as Venezuela, but severely lacking in Britain.

7   However, it is not all bad news. Renold (2005) has explored the ways in which some young boys are playing around with homoerotic discourses in fun and pleasurable ways (in contrast to the vast literature on homophobic talk) and girls queering heterosexuality through 'tomboyism'. The ability to queer normative gender and sexuality, however, remains restricted to the middle classes.

8   Transphobia has been defined as 'an emotional disgust towards individuals who do not conform to society's gender expectations' (Hill and Willoughby 2005: 91, cited in Whittle *et al.* 2007: 21).

9   Globalisation is seen as a new epoch, whereas, in fact, the global movement of capital might more accurately be seen as a cumulative process and one that has been going on for a long time – in fact, since capitalism first began four or five centuries ago. Globalisation in the twenty-first century is pre-eminently neo-liberal, that is to say, the market rules; public expenditure is cut; government regulation is reduced; state-owned enterprises, goods and services are privatised; and the concepts of the public good and community are undermined (Martinez and García 2000). (For an extended analysis, see Cole 2007a, Chapter 7.)

10   The book *Learning Without Limits* aims to challenge notions of fixed ability, and 'to build a new agenda for school improvement around the development of effective pedagogies that are free from ability labelling' (Hart *et al.* 2004: 21). For a critical Marxist appraisal of the Learning Without Limits paradigm, see Cole 2007b.

11   'Empowerment' can mean all things to all people. What I have in mind here is something on the lines of Colin Lankshear's (1995) adaptation of Feinberg's notion of 'elliptical' statements. Empowerment, for Lankshear, represents far more than psychologistic notions of 'sensing that one has more power'. Empowerment needs to be situated structurally. The empowered person needs to know who she or he is; where she or he is coming from; what she or he is up against; how she or he can move forward; and what the end result of empowerment might look like. As Lankshear puts it:

> the full version of elliptical statements about empowerment will require attention to at least four variables. Adequate accounts will be required of (1) the SUBJECT of empowerment; (2) the power STRUCTURES in relation to which, or in opposition to which, a person or group is becoming empowered; (3) the PROCESSES or 'achievement' by which empowerment arguably occurs; and (4) the ENDS or OUTCOMES of becoming thus empowered.
>
> (Lankshear 1995: 303)

12   Social class is not part of the swathes of new legislation. For Marxists, social class equality is an oxymoron, since capitalism is fundamentally dependent on the exploitation of one class by another. The end of this exploitation would herald the end of capitalism and its replacement by socialism (see

Cole 2007a for a discussion; see also Hickey 2006). However, it is my view that discrimination with respect to social class origin (classism) should be part of the legislation.

13 As a Marxist, I recognise, of course, that the working class are structurally located in a subordinate position in capitalist societies, and, *in this sense*, are a 'lower class'. However, the nomenclature 'working class' is used to indicate respect for the class as a whole, a class which, as noted above, sells its labour power to produce surplus for capitalists in an exploitative division of labour.

14 For grammatical clarity, I have put 'ism/phobia' in the singular. Clearly, for many people it will be 'isms/phobia'. I also recognise that there are a number of positive 'isms' – Marxism, socialism, feminism, trade unionism among them.

15 Xeno-racism is non colour-coded racism, and has been defined by Sivanandan (2001: 2) as follows:

> [T]he other side of the coin of the 'fear or hatred of strangers' is the defence and preservation of 'our people', our way of life, our standard of living, our 'race'. If it is xenophobia, it is – in the way it denigrates and reifies people before segregating and/or expelling them – a xenophobia that bears all the marks of the old racism, except that it is not colour-coded. It is a racism that is not just directed at those with darker skins, from the former colonial countries, but at the newer categories of the displaced and dispossessed whites, who are beating at western Europe's doors, the Europe that displaced them in the first place. It is racism in substance but xeno in form – a racism that is meted out to impoverished strangers even if they are white. It is xeno-racism (for an extended analysis, see Cole 2007a, Chapter 8).

Xeno-racism has increased considerably in the last few years as Eastern European migrant workers from the expanded European Union have entered the UK (see, for example, Cole 2007a).

16 These considerations are adapted from my definition of racism (see the ' "Race" and racism' section of this chapter and also, for example, Cole 2004a: 37–8, Cole 2007a: pp 117–119).

17 It should be pointed out here that, as a matter of principle, all socialists and Marxists join trade unions, and honour strikes and do not cross any picket lines, believing that industrial action is essentially a struggle over surplus value appropriated from workers' labour (for a discussion, see Cole 2007a, Chapter 8).

18 Having visited Cuba on three occasions, I became even more convinced of the importance of socialisation. Nearly 50 years of socialisation in socialist values has had a dramatic effect all over the island. The selfish Thatcherite values abundant in the West are generally not apparent. They are apparent, however, in the tourist resorts and hotels, and in some of the *casas particulares* (private rented accommodation). With respect to Venezuela, with the projected programme for socialist values to be promoted in schools and workplaces, we are likely to see a further consolidation of socialist values and attitudes in that country.

References

Allen, M., Benn, C., Chitty, C., Cole, M., Hatcher, R., Hirtt, N. and Rikowski, G. (1999) *Business, Business, Business: New Labour's education policy*. London: Tufnell Press.

Archer, L. (2003) *Race, Masculinity and Schooling*. Buckingham: Open University Press.

Callinicos, A. (2000) *Equality*. Oxford: Polity.

Cole, M. (1993) ' "Black and ethnic minority" or "Asian, black and other minority ethnic"; a further note on nomenclature', *Sociology*, 27: 671–3.

Cole, M. (1998) 'Racism, reconstructed multiculturalism and antiracist education', *Cambridge Journal of Education*, 28(1): 37–48.

Cole, M. (2004a) ' "Brutal and stinking" and "difficult to handle": the historical and contemporary manifestations of racialisation, institutional racism, and schooling in Britain', *Race, Ethnicity and Education*, 7(1).

Cole, M. (2004b) ' "Rule Britannia" and the new American Empire: a Marxist analysis of the teaching of imperialism, actual and potential, in the English school curriculum', *Policy Futures in Education*, 2(3).

Cole, M. (2005) 'New Labour, globalization and social justice: the role of education', in Fischman, G., McLaren, P., Sunker, H., and Lankshear, C. (eds) *Critical Theories, Radical Pedagogies and Global Conflicts*. Lanham, Maryland: Rowman and Littlefield.

Cole, M. (2006) 'Human rights, equality and education', in M. Cole (ed.) *Education, Equality and Human Rights: issues of gender, 'race', sexuality, disability and social class*, 2nd edn. London: Routledge.

Cole, M. (ed.) (2006) *Education, Equality and Human Rights: issues of gender, 'race', sexuality, disability and social class*, 2nd edn. London: Routledge.

Cole, M. (2007a) *Marxism and Educational Theory: Origins and Issues*. London: Routledge.

Cole, M. (2007b) 'Learning Without Limits: a Marxist assessment'. Paper presented to the ESRC Learning Without Limits Seminar Series, Bishops Grosseteste University College Lincoln, 18 June 2007.

Cole, M. (2007c) 'Neo-Liberalism and Education: a Marxist critique of New Labour's Five Year Strategy for Education' in A. Green, G. Rikowski and H. Reduntz (eds) *Renewing Dialogues in Marxism and Education: Volume I – Openings*. Basingstoke: Palgrave Macmillan.

Cole, M. and Blair, M. (2006) 'Racism and education: from Empire to New Labour', in M. Cole (ed.) *Education, Equality and Human Rights: issues of gender, 'race', sexuality, disability and social class*, 2nd edn. London: Routledge.

Cole, M. and Hill, D. (1999) 'Equality and secondary education: what are the conceptual issues?', in D. Hill and M. Cole (eds) *Promoting Equality in Secondary Schools*. London: Cassell.

Cole, M. and Stuart, J. M. (2005) ' "Do you ride on elephants?" and "never tell them you're German": the experiences of British Asian and black, and overseas student teachers in south-east England', *British Educational Research Journal*.

Cole, M., Hill, D. and Shan, S. (eds) (1997) *Promoting Equality in Primary Schools*. London: Cassell.

Coultas, V. (2007) *Gender and Constructive Talk in Challenging Classrooms*. London: Routledge.

Connolly, P. (1998) *Racism, Gender Identities and Young Children*. London: Routledge.

Darder, A. (2002) *Reinventing Paulo Freire: a pedagogy of love*. Cambridge, MA: Westview Press.

Davies, B. (1993) *Shards of Glass*. Sydney, Allen Unwin.

East Sussex County Council (2004) *One of Us* (Videotape). Lewes: East Sussex County Council.

Ellis, V. (2007) 'Sexualities and schooling in England after Section 28: measuring and managing "at risk" identities', *Journal of Gay and Lesbian Issues in Education*.

Ellis, V. with High, S. (2004) 'Something more to tell you: gay, lesbian or bisexual young people's experiences of Secondary Schooling', *British Educational Research Journal*, 30(2) April: 213–25.

Epstein, D. (1994) 'Introduction', in D. Epstein (ed.) *Challenging Lesbian and Gay Inequalities in Education*. Buckingham: Open University Press.

Forrest, S. (2006) 'Difficult loves: learning about sexuality and homophobia in schools', in M. Cole, (ed.) *Education, Equality and Human Rights: issues of gender, 'race', sexuality, disability and social class*, 2nd edn. London: Routledge/Falmer.

Forrest, S. and Ellis, V. (2006) 'The Making of Sexualities: sexuality, identity and equality', in M. Cole (ed.) *Education, Equality and Human Rights: issues of gender, 'race', sexuality, disability and social class*, 2nd edn. London: Routledge.

Francis, B. (1998) *Power Plays: Primary School Children's Construction of Gender Power and Adult Work*. Stoke-on-Trent: Trentham Books.

Francis, B. and Skelton, C. (2005) *Reassessing Gender and Achievement: questioning contemporary key debates*. London: Routledge.

Freire, P. (1972) *Pedagogy of the Oppressed*. Harmondsworth: Penguin.

Gaine, C. and George, R. (1999) *Gender, 'Race' and Class in Schooling. A New Introduction*. London: Falmer Press.

George, R. (1993) *Equal Opportunities in Schools. Principles, Policy and Practice*. Harlow: Longman.

George, R. (2004) 'The Importance of Friendship during Primary to Secondary School Transfer' in M. Benn and C. Chitty (eds) *A Tribute to Caroline Benn*. London: Continuum.

George, R. (2007 forthcoming) *Urban Girls Friendships: Complexities and Controversies*. Rotterdam: Sense Publications.

Haberman, M. (1995) *Star Teachers of Children in Poverty*. West Lafayette, Indiana: Kappa Delta Pi.

Hart, S., Dixon, A., Drummond, M. J. and McIntyre, D. (2004) *Learning Without Limits*. Maidenhead: Open University Press.

Hatcher, R. (2001) *The Business of Education: How Business Agendas Drive Labour's Policies for Schools*. Stafford: Socialist Education Association.

Head, J. (2004) *Understanding the Boys. Behaviour and Achievement*. London: Routledge.

Hickey, T. (2006) 'Class and class analysis for the twenty-first century', in M. Cole (ed.) *Education, Equality and Human Rights: issues of gender, 'race', sexuality, disability and social class*, 2nd edn. London: Routledge/Falmer.

Hill, D. (2003) Global Neo-Liberalism, the Deformation of Education and Resistance, *Journal for Critical Education Policy Studies*, 1(1) (http://www.jceps.com/index.php?pageID=article&articleID=7).

Hill, D. (2005) 'Globalisation and its educational discontents: neo-liberalisation and its impacts on access, equality, democracy, critical thought, and education workers' rights pay and conditions', *International Studies in the Sociology of Education*, 15(3): 257–88.

Hill, D. (ed.) (2008 forthcoming) *Contesting Neoliberal Education: Public Resistance and Collective Advance*. London and New York: Routledge.

Hill, D. and Cole, M. (eds) (1999) *Promoting Equality in Secondary Schools*. London: Cassell.

Hill, D. and Cole, M. (eds) (2001) *Schooling and Equality: fact, concept and policy*. London: Routledge.

Hillcole Group (1997) *Rethinking Education and Democracy: a socialist alternative for the twenty-first century*. London: Tufnell Press.

Hirom, K. (2001) 'Gender', in D. Hill and M. Cole (eds) *Schooling and Equality: fact, concept and policy*. London: Routledge.

Kovel, J. (1988) *White Racism: a psychohistory*. London: Free Association Books.

Lankshear, C. (1995) 'Afterword: some reflections on "Empowerment" ', in P. McLaren and J. Giarelli (eds) *Critical Theory and Educational Research*. Albany, NY: State University of New York (SUNY) Press.

Letts IV, W. J. and Sears, J. T. (eds) (1999) *Queering Elementary Education: Advancing the Dialogue about Sexualities and Schooling*. Lanham, MD: Rowman and Littlefield.

McLaren, P. (2002) *Life in Schools*, 4th edn. Boston, MA: Pearson Education.

Macpherson, W. (1999) *The Stephen Lawrence Inquiry, Report of an Inquiry by Sir William Macpherson*. London: The Stationery Office.

Martin, J. (2006) 'Gender, education and the new millennium', in M. Cole (ed) *Education, Equality and Human Rights: issues of gender, 'race', sexuality, disability and social class*, 2nd edn. London: Routledge.

Martinez, E. and García, A. (2000) 'What is "Neo-Liberalism" A Brief Definition', *Economy 101*. Available at: http://www.globalexchange.org/campaigns/econ/01/neoliberalDefined.html.

Mason, M. and Rieser, R. (1994) *Altogether Better*. London: Comic Relief.

National Union of Teachers (NUT) (1991) *Lesbians and Gays in Schools: an issue for every teacher*. London: National Union of Teachers.

Race Relations (Amendment) Act 2000 http://www.homeoffice.gov.uk/comrace/race/raceact/amendact.html (accessed February 2005).

Paechter, C. (1998) *Educating the Other: gender, power and schooling*, London: Routledge.

Reay, D. (2006) 'Gender and Class in Education' in C. Skelton, B. Francis and L. Smulyan, (eds) *The SAGE Handbook of Gender and Education*. London: Sage.

Renold, E. (2000a) 'Coming out: gender, (hetero)sexuality and the primary school, *Gender and Education*', 12(3): 309–27.

Renold, E. (2000b) 'Presumed Innocence: heterosexual, homophobic and heterosexist harassment in the primary school', *Childhood*, 9(4): 415–34.

Renold, E. (2005) *Girls, Boys and Junior Sexualities: Exploring Children's Constructions of Gender and Sexuality in the Primary School*. London: Routledge.

Renold, E. (2006) They won't let us play unless you're going out with one of them: girls, boys and Butler's 'heterosexual matrix' in the primary years, *British Journal of Sociology of Education*, 27(4).

Rieser, R. (2006a) 'Disability discrimination, the final frontier: disablement, history and liberation', in M. Cole (ed.) *Education, Equality and Human Rights: issues of gender, 'race', sexuality, disability and social class*, 2nd edn. London: Routledge/Falmer.

Rieser, R. (2006b) 'Special educational needs or inclusive education: the challenge of disability discrimination in schooling', in M. Cole (ed.) *Education, Equality and Human Rights: issues of gender, 'race', sexuality, disability and social class*, 2nd edn. London: Routledge/Falmer.

Rose, S. and Rose, H. (2005) 'Why we should give up on race: as geneticists and biologists know, the term no longer has any meaning', the *Guardian*, April 9 2005. Available at http://www.guardian.co.uk/comment/story/00,,1455685,00.html (accessed 8 August 2006).

Sivanandan, A. (2001) 'Poverty is the new Black', *Race and Class*, 43(2): 2–5.

Skelton, C., Francis, B. and Smulyan, L. (eds) (2006) *The SAGE Handbook of Gender and Education*. London: Sage.

Training and Development Agency (TDA) (2006) *Qualifying to Teach: professional standards for Qualified Teacher Status and requirements for initial teacher training*. London: Training and Development Agency.

Travis, A. (2004) 'Minister defends new equality body', http://www.guardian.co.uk/guardianpolitics/story/0,,1215402,00.html (accessed January 2005).

Vaz, K. (2004) 'Divided we stand, united we fall', *Guardian*, 21 May.

Williamson, I. (2001) 'Sexuality', in D. Hill and M. Cole (eds) *Schooling and Equality: fact, concept and policy*. London: Routledge.

Virdee, S. (forthcoming 2008) *Racism and Capitalist Modernity*. Oxford: Polity.

Whittle, S., Turner, L., Al-Alami, M. (2007) *The Engendered Penalties: Transgender and Transsexual People's Experience of Inequality and Discrimination*. London: The Equalities Review, http://www.theequalitiesreview.org.uk/upload/assets/www.theequalitiesreview.org.uk/transgender.pdf (accessed 25 April).

Woodward, K. (2004) *Questioning Identity: Gender, Class, Ethnicity*. London: Routledge.

1

High expectations, achieving potential and establishing relationships

Camilla Baker and Maud Blair

Q1 Have high expectations of children and young people including a commitment to ensuring that they can achieve their full educational potential and to establishing fair, respectful, trusting, supportive and constructive relationships with them.

Learning objectives

To raise awareness of:

- the need for cultural sensitivity in the school context;
- the different learning needs of pupils from diverse backgrounds;
- the need for readers to reflect on their own development needs in relation to 'race' and ethnicity.

In addition, this chapter will provide practical examples to support teachers in achieving these standards.

Introduction

THE PHRASE, 'EDUCATION FOR ALL' became a slogan for 1980s' multiculturalism in schools. In Britain, this new ethos was heralded by the Rampton (1981)/Swann Report (1985). For the first time a major official inquiry highlighted the extent of racism that was affecting a significant number of British children in schools. Although multicultural education had been a feature of many schools in the 1970s, this was the first time that an official report recognised the importance of preparing teachers to acknowledge and cater for diverse cultural needs in the classroom. This led to the setting up in local education authorities of centres for multicultural education and the subsequent implementation of anti-racist training initiatives for teachers. Although many mistakes were made in the name of multicultural education (Cole 1989, 1998; Cole and Blair 2006) and anti-racist education (Macdonald *et al.* 1989) and severe critiques were levelled at some of the training initiatives (see Sivanandan 1985), the Swann Report could be said to have been the first official document to set standards for a more inclusive system of education.

Two recent high profile cases have prompted the Government's move toward expectations of schools to ensure equality and provision for the 'whole' child. First, the racially motivated murder in 1993 of Stephen Lawrence, a black teenager living in south-east London, and the subsequent lack of a conviction prompted an inquiry into the police. MacPherson's report cited institutional racism as a principal cause. His official definition was included as part of the Race Relations Amendment Act 2000, which requires all schools to have a Race Equality Policy which is acted on and regularly monitored. Second, Victoria Climbié, a Nigerian girl in the legal care of her aunt, died in 2000 after suffering a series of traumatic child abuses. Lord Laming headed a far-reaching inquiry which found that public services had failed in their duty of care.

Consequently, local authorities are required to work together to ensure all public bodies are communicating clearly so other cases such as this do not slip through the net. This new move to encompass the 'whole child' is given the banner 'Every Child Matters' and has required local authorities to work towards integration of social services, health and education provision for children and families. The new standards reflect this change.

There is of course an assumption behind the setting of standards that teaching is a moral enterprise underpinned by a set of commonly accepted truths. Although there are some who would question the validity of such an assumption and indeed whether there can ever be agreement about what these standards should be, an increasing number of writers and commentators endorse the need to identify a set of working principles which guide teachers and other professionals in their work, especially in relation to work with children (Soltis 1986; Halpin 2000; DfES 2004a). The relativism that surrounds debates about ethics, values and standards has been dismissed as ignoring the real need for teachers to have guidance in an increasingly complex profession (Campbell 2000). Teachers, it is argued, need to work within a set of common principles not only to safeguard their own professional identities, but in order also to protect children's rightful entitlement to education.

The Standards for the Award of Qualified Teacher Status (TDA 2006) can be seen as building on the *Every Child Matters* agenda. Under the 2004 Standards, beginning teachers were expected to provide evidence that: 'they have high expectations of all pupils; *respect their social, cultural, linguistic, religious and ethnic backgrounds*; and are committed to raising their educational achievement' (emphasis added). Two aspects of the 2004 Standards remain largely unchanged, and we believe the third is inferred within the last phrase of the new wording. Where previously teachers were expected to show 'commitment to raising achievement', teachers now must provide evidence of 'a commitment to ensuring that [pupils] can achieve their *full* educational potential' (emphasis added). This alteration reflects the recent statistics which show that, while the achievement gap is narrowing, progress is too slow (DfES 2006a). Total equality would be proven only when the gap is fully closed, so schools and staff should strive for 'maximum learning' (see Cole's introductory chapter to this book).

The most dramatic change in the 2006 Standards is the removal of the phrase which expects beginning teachers to 'respect (pupils') social, culture, linguistic, religious and ethnic backgrounds'. The need for respect of pupils' backgrounds has not evaporated, but has been incorporated in a more generalised standard of 'establishing fair, respecting, trustful, supportive and constructive relationships with (pupils)'. Teachers are implicitly expected to understand, respect and value their pupils' backgrounds but also to act on these principles constructively. Shifting from a passive 'reflection' to more active 'relationship building' moves the focus for teachers away from the details of their teaching and instead concentrates on the product of their work: the learning they effect in their students. Ofsted lesson observations now parallel this shift, by looking at progress made by the students, not only a 'ticklist' of technical skills.

It could be argued that standards are particularly important in an ethnically diverse and changing context. The historical experiences of pupils from minority ethnic groups within the British school system would indicate that a code of practice is essential. The last 50 years have not delivered the educational successes on which Asian, black and other minority ethnic families had built their hopes when they left their homes in various parts of the diaspora to come to Britain. At the time of writing, black (Caribbean heritage) pupils and pupils of Pakistani and Bangladeshi heritage, still occupy the bottom end of achievement tables (Gillborn and Gipps 1996; Gillborn and Mirza 2000; Bhattacharyya *et al.* 2001; Ison 2005). The over-representation of black pupils in exclusions from school highlights the tenacity of problems faced by black pupils and the official malaise in dealing with these difficulties.

The proportion of children from minority ethnic backgrounds is likely to increase.[1] Issues around respecting different backgrounds should be seen as an issue for all educational institutions, not only those with traditionally diverse student populations (e.g. urban schools, settings and certain universities). A report on supporting minority ethnic pupils in 'mainly white' schools states that 'the great majority of teachers across the country may now expect to work with minority ethnic pupils at some point in their career'. Social and religious backgrounds will vary between and within communities, and isms/phobia (see the introductory chapter to this book) around sexuality may also impact teachers' relationships with their students. The picture is made more complex by the presence of children from diverse refugee and asylum-seeking families (Myers and Grosvenor 2001), the differing yet related issues surrounding second and third generation pupils (Gregory and Williams 2001), and those from dual-heritage backgrounds. Then there are local education contexts which reveal difficulties faced by certain white minority ethnic groups such as Turks and Portuguese (Peters 2002).

How are teachers, and in particular beginning teachers, to fulfil these requirements in the face of such complexity? This chapter is written for them and is an attempt to provide some pointers as to how best one can translate these abstract requirements into practice.

Self-reflection – coming to grips with professional values

In discussing the standards set out by the DfES above, we explicitly accept their validity, but do not shy away from acknowledging the difficulties faced by beginning teachers in their attempt to comply with them as a basis for obtaining their teaching qualifications. Indeed, pupils in schools would undoubtedly benefit from all teachers at any point in their careers reflecting on their practice in the light of this new wording.

The idea that teachers need to reflect on what they do is by no means new (Stenhouse 1983). Reflection is a powerful tool, but one normally only used for when things are going badly. Beginning teachers have structured opportunities to reflect on their practice both during their student days and whilst a NQT, with the support of a mentor. Some reflection of why one is in teaching, particularly where a teacher's experience is different from the pupils they meet in the class, is essential for a starting point which might reveal areas of potential change that might help the individual take control of their situation. Moreover, reflection should be not only about methods of teaching but also be concerned with the 'being' of teaching. The 'being' of teaching requires an examination of one's values in relation to a range of factors to do with one's world view and whether one is equipped mentally and emotionally for the job. With the shift from teaching to learning, self-reflection needs to include the ways in which we as teachers identify and relate to our pupils.

In the introductory chapter Mike Cole adapts and expands, at length, Haberman's (1995) five steps in overcoming our 'isms/phobia'. He explains that 'step five is the phase in which one lays out a plan explicating what one plans to do about one's ism/phobia. How do I propose to check it, unlearn it, counteract it and get beyond it?' His step six is a commitment to sharing what one has learnt in a public forum. In the following sections, we examine the issues for reflective teachers to address and practical ideas to support these last important steps in developing one's own pedagogy for equality.

High expectations

It is widely accepted that underachievement in pupils is related, among other things, to the level of expectation the teacher has of them (Blair 2001; Blair and Bourne 1998). How does a teacher check his or her own expectations of pupils? It is important to know the social class, ethnic, linguistic, gender and special needs profile of one's pupils and to ask questions, such as:

What attitudes do I have towards people of this or that background?

On what are my beliefs and attitudes based?

Dependent on age and disclosure, this also applies to sexuality.

The history of racism, social class, gender, disability and sexuality is imbued with notions of inferiority (Cole 2006). That teachers are no less affected by ist/phobic attitudes than other members of society is stating the obvious. In order to check such attitudes one has to acknowledge them. One method in this process is to ask the above questions, and reflect either alone or with colleagues on the common-sense understandings or stereotypes about this group and to what extent these stereotypes are taken for granted. Feeding one's guilt about these feelings is at best pointless and at worst counterproductive. It would be better to acknowledge the presence of normative and often unsubstantiated beliefs in society and in oneself, and resolve to move on from there.

In practical terms this means getting to know pupils as individuals and not assuming that their behaviour or performance is somehow caused by their particular class, gender or minority status. Various aspects of their experience may be caused by the social and political circumstances or dominant understandings of 'race' or ethnicity or gender, disability, sexuality or social class, namely, the way they are positioned in society, but not by the fact of difference. To this end, teachers would benefit from asking more individually specific questions, such as:

What do I know about each of the children and young people I work with?

Where did I get my knowledge?

How do I use this knowledge to support and maximise their learning?

Teachers need to know each pupil well by knowing the circumstances of that young person's life and how these realities may lead to fluctuations in behaviour or in performance on a day-to-day basis. We are asking teachers to reflect not only on their general attitudes and beliefs to groups as a whole, but also to consider the complexities of individual children. The truly reflective and practitioner will ask:

To what extent is my action influenced by realistic knowledge of the individual child and not by 'prior knowledge' of the ethnic group, special needs, gender or economic status/ social class of the child?

How am I identifying the barriers to learning faced by this individual?

How can I support each student to overcome these?

It is becoming increasingly accepted that having a clear picture of whether differential achievement occurs along ethnic, class, gender, disability or other lines, monitoring by ethnicity, class etc. is important. A school's self-evaluation forms the central tenet of the new Ofsted inspections, and achievement data (with contextual factors taken into account) is used as the starting point. The annual School Census requires schools to collect and update information on their pupils and report it centrally. For example, one is able to take attendance information about pupils from different groups and examine it against gender, special educational needs (SEN) and free school meals (as an indicator of social class) in order to provide a more refined picture of truancy in the school.[2] It may indicate that further work is needed to be done by educational welfare officers with appropriate interpreters, perhaps in explaining the importance of attendance and government's expectations and laws concerning parental/carer responsibility.

When examining an issue such as the disproportionate number of excluded black males (DfES 2006c), free school meals are, however, a crude measure of social class especially as some pupils (especially in secondary school) who qualify may not take up this service for fear of being ridiculed. It might be necessary therefore to take exclusion, set that against free school meals but also against knowledge of the pupil's family circumstances (single parent, poverty, housing, street code or address) and their previous achievement in school in order to get a better understanding of which black boys are most affected by exclusion. A similar exercise can be carried out in relation to information about other groups, such as truancy levels among white boys.

Schools are also supported with accessing their data through a new online resource, RAISEonline (www.raiseonline.org). This website gives password-controlled access for all schools and local authorities to the latest end of Key Stage achievement data for their pupils. Contextual factors (free school meals, ethnicity, first language other than English etc.) have been controlled for through a complex formula based on national statistics. Differential achievement must therefore be caused by aspects of the individual school's provision, such as teaching and learning and ethos. This gives schools with low context value-added achievement less chance to attribute the low attainment to the social situation of their pupils, instead forcing practitioners to re-assess the learning environment they have created and how this may inhibit their pupils' learning.

Schools are set numeric targets for achievement which are filtered down to year groups, phases and particular groups, cohorts and classes at the discretion of the management. In some cases, one's expectations of pupils are influenced by the culture and ethos of the school in which one works. In one school which had changed from a white middle-class grammar school to a comprehensive school catering for a largely working-class population of Pakistani and Bangladeshi origin, the head teacher realised that the only way to tackle the culture of low expectations of the staff was to create a system of accountability which made each teacher responsible for the level of achievement of their pupils. Teachers had to explain to the head of their department why pupils performed at particular levels, and heads of departments in turn had to explain the performance of their department to a deputy head. Teachers were thus forced to look closely at the nature of their explanations and to re-think their methods of supporting their pupils. This itself became a system of support for the teachers who were able to identify areas of personal and professional development. Departments that followed this conscientiously experienced a large shift in the performance levels of their pupils (Blair and Bourne 1998). The difference was that instead of teachers blaming the pupils' cultures, or languages or social class positions for their performance, they asked a different set of questions, namely, 'What do I know about this pupil and what am I doing to help and support him or her?'

Opportunities for holding teachers to account, such as the meetings outlined above, provide formative discussions around the impact of specific interventions, by either teacher, teaching assistant or outside agency. These can then be altered, repeated or ended depending on results. As primary schools move to map their provision for SEN support, such discussions enable the school as an organisation to share responsibility for children's achievement with all staff involved.

Important here is the need to understand the barriers to learning for one's pupils. For example, having an afternoon homework club or revision class may be an important strategy. However, unless one monitors take-up of such provision, there is no guarantee that those who need such provision make the most of such opportunities. Boys will often not take advantage of these resources for fear of being labelled swots or nerds. The teacher or school needs to engage with these fears and find ways of encouraging boys to take up such opportunities. Where particular pupils never seem to take advantage of extra resources provided by the school, it is worth investigating the personal circumstances of the pupil to see whether there are factors in the home or in the school which might be creating difficulties for the pupil. Crucial within the process of self-reflection proposed at the beginning of this chapter is the understanding that the barriers are not inherent to the child but are located within the social constructs and physical environment around them. Where a pupil's homework is consistently poor, is it possible they do not have facilities at home for homework? This can be a real issue for refugees or asylum seekers who might live in inadequate temporary homes where a simple item such as a table is a luxury (Virani 2002). There could be many other factors. For example:

Is it possible that the pupil is being bullied?

Are pupils of Gypsy/Traveller background afraid to come to after-school activities for fear of harassment?

Do some pupils live too far from the school to take advantage of what is on offer?

Do such opportunities clash with other commitments beyond school: helping parents/carers or involvement in community or religious activities (e.g. such as visits to the Mosque)?

Were students admitted mid-term given the list of clubs, and were the procedures for applying and the benefits fully explained and supported (in first language where necessary)?

This practice of looking inwards towards our professional practice and school culture rather than outwards towards the child and his/her family for explanations of failure or low performance is an important step in unlearning previously held assumptions. The teacher's concerns must be for *all* pupils so that one is motivated, not by a charitable attitude which in effect renders different ethnic groups 'Other'. The standards require a professional approach which recognises, via honest self-reflection, the equality of all pupils within your realm of responsibility and the need to do everything within one's professional capacity to support the maximum learning of each child. Thus teachers have high expectations for their students, but also for themselves and the impact they can have as professionals.

Commitment to achieving full educational potential

It would probably be unusual to find a teacher who was not committed to ensuring his or her students achieve their full educational potential. Why then would such a condition exist in the standards for Qualified Teacher Status? The probable reason lies, once again, in the racial and ethnic dimensions of academic achievement. Reviews of research by Gillborn and Gipps (1996), Gillborn and Mirza (2000), Bhattacharyya *et al.* (2001) and Ison (2005) have shown the persistence of underachievement among some minority ethnic groups over the years. Patterns vary between boys and girls, with for example Caribbean-heritage boys underachieving in literacy, while girls of Caribbean heritage attain considerably lower than expected grades in maths. There is no single explanation for this. Writers have variously pointed to issues of language acquisition, to social class, gender, racism and to an interplay of all these, as significant factors in pupil achievement. An important point made by many social analysts and educators is that teaching is a middle-class profession perpetuating middle-class values and therefore excluding in its processes and underlying assumptions, pupils from working-class backgrounds (Sharp and Green 1984). Furthermore, in a society where the bulk of the teaching profession is white, then the interaction of 'race' and class mediates in a powerful way the relationships between minority ethnic group pupils and their teachers (Sleeter 1993).

The exhortation that teachers should be committed to the achievement of their pupils is rooted in an implicit acknowledgement of the role of stereotypes in influencing teachers' beliefs, attitudes and actions. Research shows that such stereotypes affect teachers' relationships with very young children. Connolly (1995), for example, details the ways in which six-year-old boys of Caribbean background are labelled and the effects of this labelling on teachers' attitudes towards them. Stereotypes of black men prevalent in the wider society are just as likely to be used against these boys so that they are constructed not only as sexually deviant, but as having behaviour problems needing and deserving more stringent control than their white and/or Asian peers.

There is another, deeper, concern here about the chosen terminology of the new standards. Within the phrase 'their full educational potential' there exists the possibility of different potential for different children. There are of course children with specific educational and medical needs whose potential is limited by precise diagnoses. However, for broader groups of children, who and what is deciding the limit of that child's potential? Teachers, as outlined above, just like all people, will bring to this reflection assumption about groups. With the well-documented evidence of particular groups achieving less well, it could be easy to forget that individual children within that group will far exceed average expectations (Gillborn and Mirza 2000). The persistent underachievement of black (Caribbean-heritage) children has prompted the Government to pilot a Black Children's Achievement Project which states very specifically there is *no inherent reason for this discrepancy* (emphasis added, DfES 2006a). Well-informed teachers need to ask themselves how much the data further supports their assumptions of potential achievement for groups within their class. How they challenge those assumptions through their actions is vital. Cole in his introductory chapter supports the idea of achieving 'maximum' learning, not just the potential of each child, and we have used the same phrase in this chapter to remind readers not to limit their expectations to the achievement levels they associate with a particular group.

No matter how the process of examining data and target-setting occurs in a school, each teacher needs to set challenges for him- or herself by setting targets for each pupil, based on the highest expectation of attainment and progress. With a target to achieve, teachers will be creative in devising programmes to help that pupil reach those targets or in appropriating the support within or beyond school that is necessary. Outside agencies have expertise and advice to provide, but need teacher referral and input so they are not just brought in when it is too late. For example, behaviour experts are brought in to school to discuss a pupil's permanent exclusion, whereas an earlier request for support could have provided intervention that prevented the exclusion in the first place.

Within the *Every Child Matters* agenda is a strong move to look at the whole of the child, and this also requires teachers throughout education to look at potential in a broad sense, not only within the limited realm of academic prowess in that teacher's subject. As schools extend their provision by hours, they must also extend the content and style of provision. The time spent in that institution is therefore likely to grow for individual children. Thus the need to give pupils a range of opportunities, and largely positive ones, within the same building presents an increasing challenge for schools.

Individual teachers and schools use many strategies for raising achievement generally and some have developed imaginative and innovative ways to engage their pupils from different social and ethnic backgrounds. Researchers have found that an important method for motivating and encouraging students is to investigate the social and cultural interests of pupils and to incorporate these into one's teaching. Teachers use folk tales, histories, pop and football stars, hip hop music and whatever is topical among pupils or in their communities to engage their pupils and provide a relevant context for the learning they wish to accomplish in various subjects (Ofsted 2002; Blair and Bourne 1998; Ladson-Billings 1994).

The effective school or teacher goes further to find out about the various displays and what they mean to the communities whose histories they tell and to incorporate this into the teaching and learning process. This can be led by staff in the school or by a combined synergy of parents and community. A primary school in London had a group of parents/carers concerned that the representation of black history was tokenistic, even going so far as accusing the school of institutional racism. The head of humanities was brought in to meet with them, and through a series of occasionally 'quite painful' meetings, they developed a term's work under an overarching theme of 'Why does one group oppress another?' Younger children looked at the journey of exotic fruits and African printed materials (actually made in China) to a local market. Upper Key Stage 2 children interviewed one of the Caribbean grandparents about coming to England and raising her daughter here, which the class then turned into a poem set to rhythm. They can recite it from memory even months later. The same grandparent was willing to come and speak at a borough-wide event, showing how far the relationship had grown, through investment of time and willingness to answer each other's legitimate concerns and find a mutual way forward. The final display and performance were of equal importance to the process by which they were created. The teachers were fully committed to giving the time needed to deal with the concerns raised by the parents. Furthermore, they were willing to rethink their assumptions of their provision, and go to extra lengths to engage with the challenge set by the parents/carers. Pupils benefited from clearer communication between parents/carers, community and school, and also achieved the 'maximum' academically due to strong identification with the content of their learning. Such school projects are not only effective and important in challenging stereotypical and tokenistic views of black history, but more importantly in building a mutually respecting and trustful relationship between those once angry parents/carers and the school (O'Kelly, 2007). Relationships will be examined in more depth in the next section.

Commitment to ensuring children and young people achieve to the maximum is therefore about going one step further in one's efforts to make sure that all pupils are given an equal chance to succeed and given whatever scaffolding (that is, the provision of sufficient supports to promote learning when concepts and skills are being first introduced to students) and other help that they need to access learning. Providing equality of opportunity is not only about neutral provision of access but ensuring that the outcomes are also fair.

Establishing fair, respecting, trustful, supportive and constructive relationships with students

Relationships are at the heart of the learning process. Education hinges on positive and productive interactions between teacher and pupil. Throughout this section issues around the new standards will be discussed, but also consideration will be given to the inferred expectation that teachers respect the varying social, cultural, ethnic, religious and linguistic backgrounds of their students.

From the introduction of mass education in the 1870s to the present day, educational provision has reflected divisions of class in different ways, but generally in ways which have benefited those with middle-class cultural capital (Bowles and Gintis 1976). Social class is, as a result, one of the significant indicators of pupil performance (Hatcher 2005; Hill and Cole 2001).

Social class interacts with ethnicity, gender and other indicators of identity in the experiences that pupils have. An important watchpoint for the teacher is not to assume that ethnicity is the sum total of the identities of pupils from minority ethnic groups. This may appear to be stating the obvious. However, research evidence shows that teachers do sometimes seek remedies for problems based on pupils' ethnicity alone, disregarding other factors that make up the pupils' identities, such as their social class position, gender or their age (Blair 2001). This has the effect of blocking the teacher's ability to think through imaginative ways of helping them (Wright *et al.* 2000).

Relevant questions to reflect upon here might be:

How much do I understand the need for children and in particular young people to establish a sense of their own identity?

How is this process manifesting itself among the young people of (this) school?

What is the ethos and social environment of the school and how does it support pupils?

What can I do to change things?

What is my own relationship with pupils and how far do I attempt to communicate with them in ways that confirm their sense of self?

The importance of these questions lies in the practice of thinking critically about issues that affect one's attitudes and beliefs and by extension, one's relationships with pupils of different faiths. It is only on the basis of such critical understanding and questioning that one can assess whether one accepts and not merely tolerates different faiths (Bhavnani 2002), and can respond properly to the needs of pupils of faiths other than one's own.

Learning is situated in a particular context and environment. It has long been argued that teaching is not just transferring facts and information from teacher to students. Friere (1972: 53) described this notion as 'banking', where teachers would deposit ideas into an otherwise empty 'account'. He argued that education was better seen as dialogue. This theory has mainstream acceptance now, as the DfES document 'Excellence and Enjoyment' supports the constructivist view of learning as assisting the process of enquiry. This has moved teachers' roles away from the delivery of skills towards facilitating the class's learning. Central to a teacher's responsibility now is making individuals active participants in their learning. A simple activity is to ask students to close their eyes and point to the person responsible for their learning. Truly active learners would point to themselves, not the teachers, their friends or the head. While individuals are responsible for their own learning, it is also true to say that learning is a social process that cannot be achieved alone. It is understood that the relationship between teacher and pupil is paramount in that young person's educational achievement and development. To build these relationships, teachers will need to be aware of how they are positioned, and what their grounding/founding principles are in terms of the social, cultural, ethnic, religious and linguistic backgrounds of their students.

Fair

Students have a strong sense of justice, but they also know that not all pupils get the same treatment. Ladson-Billings described successful teachers having relationships with their class (together with community and parents/carers) that were 'humanely equitable' (1994: 55). The conundrum for any beginning teacher to consider is how to treat students fairly but not just treat them the same. The data over the years shows an inequitable access to exam grades. This is not a 'fair' relationship between the school system and pupils from different ethnicities, cultures, religions, social classes and sexes.

To what extent might the fact of being working class and black and male be leading to unfair treatment of some pupils and therefore to behavioural and academic difficulties? It has been known for individual difficulties have been attributed to a pupil's 'racial' or cultural background and not to the fact of, for example, racism or adolescence, leading inevitably to mishandling of problems to the detriment of the pupils concerned. We have already discussed above how the high expectations held by a teacher can positively impact achievement. To be fair, teachers should have equally high expectations of *all* their learners.

An area of social interaction that has been the subject of much discussion and debate is that of black boys and teachers. Black boys of Caribbean heritage have been and are, at the time of writing, unfairly over-represented among those who are excluded from school. Explanations proffered vary from racism (Gillborn 1990, 1995), the strong pull of the peer group on black boys (Sewell 1997), to the over-representation of middle-class white women in primary schools and the absence of black male role models (Abbott 2002). Again, the importance of reflecting on one's own attitudes cannot be overemphasised. Gillborn (1990) writes that black boys are sometimes regarded by white teachers as threatening. The result has been either an unfair level of discipline imposed on black boys, or a fear of reprimanding them leading to an absence of clear boundaries for the pupils in question and consequent deterioration in their behaviour. Every teacher therefore needs to examine his or her fears and anxieties about 'race'. What are these fears and where do they come from? How can they be overcome? How are they affecting relationships in the classroom or in the school?

A fair teacher is one whose decisions are transparent and rigorous, and who does not base decisions (especially disciplinary ones) on pre-judged beliefs about a child's actions based on assumptions about a group to which they belong. Generating fair relationships means creating an ethos that is just and consistent. Citizenship and PSHE lessons provide a space to discuss issues of rights and responsibilities, at a local as well as a global level. Other subjects can also provide opportunities for discussions of justice. In history, for example, studying the abolition of slavery allows pupils opportunities to consider how individuals and groups have acted to overturn unjust situations. Ideas from distant contexts can be related to the immediate contexts of their lives. Guidelines can be drawn within such conversations of how students would like their classes to be run and why. Teachers are right to be nervous of allowing students this opportunity to comment and suggest. It is part of the shift of control from teacher as the sole mode of delivery to learning as an experience co-created by everyone in the class. By requiring students to lead their own learning they are being trusted to take on this responsibility. Moreover, empowering pupils to voice their opinions can also build confidence in these young people that their actions will prompt change.[3] As Parekh (2004) observes: 'The fundamental need is to treat people equally *and* to treat them with due respect for difference; to treasure the rights and freedoms of individuals *and* to cherish belonging, cohesion and solidarity' (original emphasis, p. 3).

Respecting

Respect is about recognising our common humanity and accepting our differences. The history of racism and of colonialism is a history of hierarchy where people's languages, among other things, were placed, both implicitly and explicitly, in order of importance. The languages of colonised countries were inevitably placed in positions of least importance (Cole and Blair 2006). This situation was often perpetuated in British schools where children who spoke one or more languages from non-European countries were regarded in some schools as having 'language problems', while the teaching of languages such as German or French to English speakers was considered as improving children's language skills. This often led to children who spoke non-European languages being forbidden to speak their home languages and for these to be considered an impediment to learning English. The recently arrived Eastern European pupils are not entirely immune to this hierarchy: while GCSEs are offered in Polish, for example, parents are reluctant to speak their languages at home in case their children are held back by their mother tongue. Research evidence contributed in large part to a re-assessment of this approach at institutional level. Evidence that use of the child's mother tongue enhanced the acquisition of a second language helped to shift the perception that these languages were a hindrance rather than a help (Cummins 1991).

However, the acceptance of the logic of language acquisition is not necessarily an indicator of using languages constructively within the teacher/student relationship. The teacher needs to demonstrate his or her acceptance and regard for languages other than his or her own, and in particular those languages which have been subject to inferiorisation. Each practitioner has their own relationship with languages, and their own experience of learning one or more. A new Polish teacher working in London did not feel comfortable speaking Polish to a Polish child in her class, and had to be assured that not only was it acceptable, but actually it provided a possibility to support that child's learning. Practitioners may need also to discuss with parents methods and reasons for supporting their children develop sophisticated levels of their home language.

Schools use a range of strategies for including the languages of the pupils they teach. One north London school has developed 'Language of the Month' over the years, which all teachers use to greet their class and take the register. Key greetings are introduced in assemblies and posters displayed in the main entrance hall of the school. Native speakers are asked to record the phrases on a language master card so all classes can hear the correct pronunciation. It is a useful way to incorporate languages of the school and involve parents/carers and community in high profile but simple activities. Asking parents/carers to provide translations of key words around topics shows that the teacher values home language.

More important than just having signs up, languages are not meant just as 'wallpaper' but should be used, useful and related to the topic. With the move to using 'working walls' instead of just 'wallpaper' displays which contain end product work, key words should be put up in classes where they can be seen by the children, taken down and used in lessons as reference.

We often take the meaning of the term 'respect' for granted. Do teachers and pupils share the same meanings? Among the most widely reported concerns of black pupils, especially in secondary schools, is the concern that teachers do not respect them (Blair 2001; Blair and Bourne 1998; Sewell 1997; Wright *et al.* 2000). All pupils wish to be treated with respect, but how do teachers demonstrate this? It is by understanding and then putting into practice the ways in which pupils wish to be respected. A simple questionnaire about what pupils like and do not like about the school will soon reveal many areas in which they do not feel respected. A small study conducted with Year 10 students in a London school exposed widespread unhappiness with the way they felt they were treated by teachers. Statements such as:

'Their body language. It's just rude. And the way they talk to you, man, it's just so rude.'

'It's the tone of voice which they use in front of the whole class.'

'Say you're talking, yeah, and they say things like, "shut up".'

(Blair 2001: 54)

This is, of course, not to deny that pupils are rude to teachers, but what is being underlined here is the importance of teachers always setting the example and being role models for pupils.

When the term 'respect' is extended to cultural differences, this poses a particular challenge to teachers and to schools. Misunderstandings can occur very easily, and are an increasing challenge to schools the more diverse the society becomes. When parents/carers do not respond to situations in expected ways; for example, they respond negatively or do not turn up to a meeting about the behaviour of a child, this is a sign that the school or the teacher needs to delve deeper in order to understand where miscommunication or misunderstanding may have taken place. It is not a sign that the parents/carers are not interested in their children's education. In the example above, they may have been shy and anxious about the response they would receive. It is often the case that schools do not take the initiative to open up avenues of communication with parents/carers because they feel hampered by language differences, or by a negative interaction with parents/carers from a particular ethnic group, which then translates into suspicion or lack of trust for the whole group.

This is a basic understanding of 'respect' – namely, not operating on the basis of stereotypes and being able to put things right when they go wrong. An example was given above of a school taking parents/carers' concerns as legitimate, and providing the time, energy and resources to confront and deal with the issues raised. It is worth noting that this was a school which already had a very positive, inclusive atmosphere. In fact it is arguable that without that ethos, the parents/carers would not have felt comfortable in coming forward in the first instance. Ethos is an intangible concept, yet holds a great power in creating a school in which parents/carers and pupils feel comfortable, and have a sense of belonging. All teachers need to work to create such a feeling in their classes, and by extension throughout the school.

Trustful

After many attempts, a rural village school persuaded some mothers of their Nepali pupils to lead small groups of reception children in cooking traditional food with a bilingual lady translating. The afternoon timetable ran over time. When the other parents/carers came in to collect their children, not one of them was concerned by the curry stains down their boy's T-shirts or the fact we were late. They were keen instead to sample the leftovers and wanted to know if they could have the recipes. The Nepali mums were surprised by the strong positive response. It transpired that these women did not think English people would like their food, and this had contributed to their reluctance in leading the event. A teacher that asks parents/carers, or children, to share from their lives beyond school, is asking that person to reveal a part of themselves that they perhaps do not associate with school. It requires trust to share something of yourself and assume that the other person will not demean or devalue your contribution. Parents/carers and pupils are the best resource available for making learning culturally relevant and meaningful. Once they see that the school or the teacher is interested in them and in their cultures, they will go out of their way to help with time, ideas and resources (Blair and Bourne 1998).

It is well recognised that teachers need to build relationships between themselves and their pupils (and also between the class members) that make children 'safe, valued and secure' (DfES 2004c). Learning occurs by risk-taking and making mistakes. Pupils must trust their teacher and classmates enough to know that they will be given the time and support they need, and that mistakes will not be derided. An environment that encourages any pupils to show vulnerability by making errors in order to learn from them is an environment in which all children can thrive.

Relationships are continuously re-engineered and redrawn. Teachers can only build a relationship given time, contact and clear communication with their pupils. Trust is built gradually through respect and the sharing of positive moments before it can be tested. Children only spoken to in a negative manner will not want to engage with the class learning again.

The same is true when speaking with parents/carers. When interacting with parents/carers, especially of older children, tone and manner of communication is very important. Consider the anxieties these parents/carers may have, and the potential frustration and embarrassment of having to speak in an unfamiliar language. It is important to remember that language differences do not necessarily denote different values or different human needs. An attempt to greet in a language that is not one's own is a respectful beginning and shows a willingness to recognise their skills.

Equally, where negative interactions have occurred, it is important that the school or teacher find out what went wrong and re-establish positive channels of communication and build up some of the lost trust. It is after all, the school, or it could be the individual teacher, who is providing a service to the student, and not the other way around.

Supportive

Within *Every Child Matters*, each child needs to be seen as both whole and individual. Teachers may build supportive relationships with boys from minority ethnic groups and their white working-class counterparts through similar methods, but find that in a particular class the girls from different ethnic groups respond to varying approaches. The DfES states that 'most teachers and practitioners would readily agree that helping children develop as confident, enthusiastic and effective learners is one of their major aims' (2004c: 6). We have discussed above how creating a learning environment that is fair, respecting and trustful is important because it will enable students to achieve their maximum learning.

The peer group is where young adolescents have their identities affirmed and where they feel their sense of belonging confirmed (Cullingford and Morrison 1997; Hargreaves *et al.* 1996). It is a time in a young person's life that teachers need to properly understand. This is particularly important in situations where young people from particular groups feel alienated and/or rejected by the society. The peer group in these circumstances is for young people a refuge and place of safety. It is easy, in circumstances where the peer group constitutes a powerful alternative culture for young people, for teachers to feel that their efforts are in vain, to conclude that the fault lies in the young people themselves and that there is no more that they can do. However, research shows that some teachers succeed with even the most difficult of pupils if one attempts to understand them and their world views, to empathise with what they are going through, to include them in decisions and to take account of their interests and concerns in one's teaching so that what they learn has relevance in their lives (Fine 1991; Ladson-Billings 1994).

We have argued that the role of the teacher is to maximise their pupils' learning. Language is a significant limiting factor in children accessing ideas and expressing what they know. Through an examination of issues surrounding students for whom English is an additional language (EAL), we will provide methods of supporting the language development of all pupils.[4] Nationally more than 10 per cent of UK pupils learn to hear and speak a language other than English at home and in their community during the first few years of their life (DfES 2004d). Although they may be exposed to some English at preschool age from watching television or from older siblings, their extensive exposure to English effectively begins when they enter the education system.

Early exposure to more than one language has been found to provide a cognitive advantage (Petitto *et al.* 2001), yet, as we note above, teachers have not always approached the teaching of English as an additional language in this way. It is important that teachers ensure that bilingual pupils understand that their first language is valued. Negative attitudes towards a young child's first language will quickly lead to discontinuation of usage in academic contexts and, for some pupils, this will eventually lead to a plateau of achievement. Crucial in this is for both teachers and parents to truly value the home language as a medium for learning. Reading books and work sent home may be in English but should be discussed with parents/carers in the home language wherever possible. In class this dialogue should also occur. It is not necessary for teachers to share the first language to do this; in some cases, pupils can discuss with peers in their first language and then report back to the teacher in English. This allows pupils to develop concepts in their strongest language without being limited by their lack of proficiency in English. Children need to be given opportunities to learn new words but also the phrases to express more sophisticated cognitive ideas. A science lesson where children are allowed to explore practically what happens between magnets and other materials will allow open access for the child who does not know the names of the items in English. Provide that child with labels on the items (e.g. magnet, coin, plastic) and a translated part of a sentence (e.g. 'is attracted to') and the child will have their learning supported by the language cues he or she has been given. This 'scaffolding' supports pupils' development of the appropriate language structures and vocabulary to explain and apply their knowledge. Ultimately children will need to do this in English if they are to show their skills within our exam system.

Within the context and language-rich curriculum of the Foundation Stage and the physical context of playground games, many EAL learners quickly develop the ability to communicate verbally in English with their peers. Within two years, most pupils learning EAL have acquired a good level of conversational fluency in English.

However, as the language demands of the curriculum increase in complexity, higher order skills such as the language of hypothesising, evaluating, predicting and classifying are fundamental to the development of thinking skills and progress in the National Curriculum. Exposure to target language alone without explicit teaching of the academic language required will not usually be sufficient to ensure continued progress in English beyond the initial stages (Ofsted 2003a; DfES 2004e). Teachers of all subjects therefore need to consider the language demands of the curriculum and employ specific strategies to ensure access for EAL learners, including those who appear orally fluent. Language support is best provided within the curriculum wherever possible, as time out of subject lessons for additional language tuition will ultimately cause the learner to fall further behind in the curriculum. Rather, teachers of all subjects should employ strategies to enable access for these pupils such as the use of visual cues to promote understanding, allowing opportunities for oral rehearsal of concepts and providing templates as a support for writing. Tasks requiring formal recording are not likely to be indicative of ability or understanding. It is useful to remember that in the long term, bilingualism is an asset, as pupils working in two languages have greater general cognitive capacity and their writing, for example, has been found specifically to contain a wider range of idioms and figurative language at KS4 (DfES 2004e; CILT 2006).

For both UK-born EAL learners and recent arrivals, accurate identification of cognitive ability as well as language proficiency is vital. The dilemma which faces education professionals when assessing EAL learners is the danger of diagnosing a learning difficulty when none is present, or the failure to identify a learning difficulty because poor progress is wrongly attributed to language development needs (Hall 2001). Teachers should take great care in interpreting the results of standardised tests since the results have invariably been standardised for a monolingual population (Cline and Shamsi 2000). Hall (2001) describes a model of hypothesis testing where it is necessary to consider a range of complex social, linguistic and medical factors involved in making an accurate diagnosis of special educational needs for pupils learning English as an additional language.

Constructive

A constructive teacher–student relationship is one in which learning occurs successfully. In her study of successful teachers of minority ethnic students, Ladson-Billings described them as demonstrating 'a connectedness with all students' and encouraging 'a community of learners' (1994: 55). This culture or ethos within a class is a mainstay of recent DfES guidelines on supporting learning. 'Children are more likely to learn successfully if they feel unthreatened, secure, safe and valued, feel a sense of belonging to the group' (DfES 2006c: 7). The building of constructive relationships is considered here in two parts – first, by a brief look at assessment for learning and second, by examining how to build on what children already know.

Black and Wiliam's summary of research found that assessment *for* learning, as opposed to assessment *of* learning (i.e. formative not summative) was the biggest contributing factor to improvements of achievement (2006). Key aspects of successful assessment for learning include modelling what is expected of children, and making overt the criteria by which their work will be assessed. Once these criteria are established, they can be continuously referred to during the process of a lesson. Instead of praising a child for 'being clever' (a fixed state), they are praised instead for achieving a particular aspect. This transfers across to constructive marking of work very easily. Against a set of criteria, pieces of work can be marked so that evidence of meeting those criteria is highlighted, and a comment at the end suggests ways for students to improve their work. It is crucial then that students have time to read these comments, attempt what they have been asked, and comment in return. Books are another place where relationships are built, and constructive comment-based marking should be both positive and useful.

Religious backgrounds are an area not yet considered in this chapter. All children live in a context where diverse religious affiliations are expressed in overlapping global, political and social contexts. The media recently has published much debate over whether faith schools should be supported by the state. Column inches have been given to views that disrespect faiths not of a Christian denomination. Faith schools have existed in Britain since before the introduction of mass education, and have often been extolled for the positive service they render both educationally and morally to the society. The media objection to faith schools which are mainly Islamic (notwithstanding September 11) would have to be considered very carefully. The teacher needs first of all to examine the historical relationship between Christianity and Islam, the political context of Islamophobia in the West specifically and in Britain in particular (Commission on British Muslims and Islamophobia 2002; Cole and Virdee 2006), and the hierarchical positioning of religions within the education system and in society generally.

These beliefs are reinforced by social divisions and violent strife between specific ethnic groups such as those that occurred in Bradford and Oldham between Asian and white people in the summer of 2000. They are also endorsed by political state-ments about the need to integrate minorities in order to avoid such problems in the future (see Parekh (2004) cited above).

Where pupils are supported to choose subjects appropriately, children from minority ethnic backgrounds can draw on their first-hand knowledge of practices and beliefs. Portuguese students in a GCSE group were able to identify with Chris-tians taking pilgrimages and believing in the power of prayer as one had a devout mother whose Catholicism prompted her to visit a shrine for support at a difficult time. Such understanding enhanced their essays beyond those of the indigenous population of this particular majority white, rural school. It is important to remem-ber that each child is negotiating a complex interplay of attitudes and assumptions. An Iraqi Kurdish boy in the same school had friends in Iraq who were surprised that Islam was even discussed in school. They assumed he would be persecuted as their media led them to believe.

Pupils raised into a particular religion may not have 'textbook' knowledge of their religion as an entity but will have experienced a rich variety of practical experience. A teacher reported that her Hindu pupils could not explain or did not know many facts about why Hindus did certain things. She had hoped their knowledge would be help-ful with the class RE curriculum. A different approach was then tried. A small group of Hindu children were taken out together. They were shown a range of pictures (gathered from an internet search of Hindu temples in Nepal) and the discussion was unstructured and led by the children. Pictures which generated discussion were added to a PowerPoint presentation and notes were written. This eventually turned into a virtual book on Hinduism, complete with recordings of songs and captions in both home language and English, which the class read as a text in their next RE lesson.[5]

Why did the teacher need to alter her approach? She had not considered that children may be fluent in the social practice of their religion but unable to express that knowledge as abstract ideas. While British Christian children may struggle to explain the connections between Easter and the crucifix, all could associate Easter with chocolate eggs and bunnies. In the second situation, the pupils felt safer because they worked as a group. Also, there was time to value the experiences they wanted to share. In addition, by asking open questions, such as 'What do you know about this picture?' instead of closed ones, such as 'Why do Hindus revere cows?' there was no way in which students could fail. As they gained confidence that what they were sharing was valid, they were able to extend themselves and each other. Having experienced themselves as experts on a particular subject, they were then able to share it with the class confidently.

Assemblies held to mark high days and holidays are an important part of valuing children's background, culture and religion, and a potential for building relationships with parents/carers. Teachers need to find prompts that can reach what children already know, and need to go outside the comfort of a provided curriculum to find the current reality of children in their class. A school in east London celebrated a 'Festival of Light' where traditions from Christmas, Diwali, Eid, Hanukkah and Kwanzaa were all represented. By asking everyone to share something, a teacher develops a sense of trust among all groups towards each other. Learning respect, tolerance and trust of different groups of people will support social cohesion, a notion that has been given recent attention by organisations concerned with Britain's future as a thriving multi-ethnic nation (Parekh 2004). For true social cohesion to become a realistic possibility, however, class conflicts need to be addressed, and here we concur with Cole that class conflict can only disappear in a world socialist economy, based on planning for need and not profit (see the introductory chapter to this book).

Having established this kind of ethos, it becomes easier to introduce activities that are inclusive of the different cultural heritages of the pupils. While some groups have called for 'Britishness' to be on the curriculum, we would argue that all culture needs to be taught as a flexible, evolving entity. Fixed notions of 'Britishness' not only alienate pupils in school with non-white skin colour but also more generally contribute to the xeno-racist notions of 'other' as threatening and alien. As a way to expand the canon of stories read, the English department of one school collected folk tales from the children (and this, of course, meant that the parents/carers were involved). With the rich source of tales from diverse countries, they were able to draw parallels with stories around the world and show the commonalities that exist in humankind and to draw on these parallels in their teaching of literature. It is, however, important not to single out minority students for this information, but to involve all pupils, including those from dominant cultures. People around the world show, through their stories, that they share the same concerns, the same desires, the same ambitions. Finding global themes within religion, and indeed outside religion can allow for collective celebration of diversity and similarities.

Conclusion

Technical competencies in teaching are important but not sufficient in a diverse, class-based, gender-based, multi-ethnic, multi-faith, multilingual society. The authors of this chapter welcome the theoretical move of focus from teaching to learning, and the respective shift in the standards from passive understanding and valuing of pupils' background, to the active building of constructive relationships. Teachers now need to think in more complex multi-dimensional ways in order to build relationships with classes in schools where justice respect, trust and support are central factors, which in turn construct a positive, effective learning environment for all. This is necessary if one is to fulfil the requirements of QTS set out above.

A 'colour blind' approach, that is, an approach that assumes that all pupils are the same and require the same treatment or provision, overlooks the needs and learning requirements of many pupils. In addition, an approach which does not recognise non colour-coded racism or xeno-racism (see the introductory chapter to this book; see also Cole and Virdee 2006) does not accommodate the needs of an increasing number of pupils in British schools.

On the other hand, an approach which overemphasises difference between pupils is in danger of creating fixed ethnic or other enclaves which construct groups as 'other' and, in the process, marginalises or excludes them. How is the teacher to achieve the balance of perspective that promotes social justice and fairness for all pupils?

This chapter has sought to underline the importance of taking time to think and reflect upon the demands brought about by this diversity. Pupils are not 'the same' because the dynamics of class, gender, sexuality, disability, ethnicity/culture, to name but a few, position people differently and lead to different experiences. The promotion of justice and fairness for all pupils requires an understanding of history, namely Britain's relationship with former colonial subjects, in addition to earlier and more recent immigration patterns (Cole and Blair 2006; Cole and Virdee 2006). The processes of globalisation and their general impact with respect to ethnicity, class and gender on different groups around the world extends the need for a global as well as a local awareness of policies and politics, if justice and fairness are to prevail.

The classroom is often a good starting place for this kind of personal growth and development for the teacher. Faced with pupils from diverse backgrounds, this is a rich source of information and knowledge about the world, provided one is open and willing to investigate and challenge one's own strongly held beliefs and opinions. It is the inward focus, the examination of one's own world view that is the starting point for high expectations, commitment and establishing fair, respecting, trustful, supportive and constructive relationships with one's pupils. It can be a challenging place to be, but is nevertheless essential. Haberman (1995) advises that one examines the source of one's beliefs and prejudices, understands how one came to see the world in this way and then finds ways of moving forward in a direction which is always reflective and seeks to take responsibility, rather than blames others for problems.

The ability to do this provides a strong foundation for fulfilling one's duties towards pupils from all backgrounds to enable them to reach their maximum learning, as Cole aims for in the introductory chapter to this book. The self-reflective process Haberman describes might help to strengthen one's feelings for social justice and thereby influence one's ability to be fair, respecting, trustful and supportive of all pupils in one's care. The demands of constructing such relationships require all teachers to think imaginatively about the learning in their classroom and about creative ways of providing an overt and covert curriculum that is inclusive of all pupils. Each individually constructed relationship can thereby promote social justice in the wider society.

Notes

1   Nationally, approximately 10 per cent of primary school children and 8 per cent of secondary school children have English as an additional language (EAL). The higher primary proportion suggests that the number is set to rise in the future (DfES 2004c).

2   The 2007 School Census was the first to include data on pupils' first language. The new language categories allow schools to investigate attainment by ethnicity in a more meaningful way. Now, for example, a school can identify Somali or Twi speakers separately rather than having them always grouped as 'Black African'. This provides a more realistic method for considering children from separate countries of origin, with differing politics, social structures and religions.

3   There are excellent resources for teachers of all ages in the Social and Emotional Aspects of Learning pack (DfES 2005).

4   An analysis of the DfES primary EAL programme showed that the largest group of children to benefit from the successful implementation of the methods suggested by the initiative were white working-class English speakers. This shows that good practice for EAL students is good practice for language development generally. The full 'EAL toolkit' is now available for all schools to order (DfES 2006b).

5   This work and other ideas for supporting pupils can be found in *Aiming High: Understanding the Educational needs of Minority Ethnic Pupils in Mainly White Schools, A Guide to Good Practice* (DfES 2004f).

References

Abbott, D. (2002) 'Teachers are failing black boys', *Observer*, 6 January.

Bhattacharyya, G., Gabriel, J. and Small, S. (2001) *Race and Power: global racism in the twenty-first century*. London: Routledge.

Bhavnani, R. (2002) *Rethinking Interventions in Racism*. London: CRE with Trentham Books.

Black, P. and Wiliam, D. (2006) *Inside the Black Box: Raising Standards Through Classroom Assessment*. London: NFER Nelson Publishing.

Blair, M. (2001) *Why Pick on Me? School Exclusion and Black Youth*. Stoke-on-Trent: Trentham Books.

Blair, M. and Bourne, J. (1998) *Making the Difference: teaching and learning in successful multi-ethnic schools*. London: DfEE.

Bowles, S. and Gintis, H. (1976) *Schooling in Capitalist America: educational reform and the contradictions of economic life*. London: Routledge and Kegan Paul.

Campbell, E. (2000) 'Professional ethics in teaching: towards the development of a code of practice', *Cambridge Journal of Education*, 30(2): 203–21.

CILT (2006) *Positively Plurilingual*. London: The National Centre for Languages Publications.

Cline, T. and Shamsi, T. (2000) *Language Needs or Special Needs?* London HMSO: DfEE.

Cole, M. (1989) 'Monocultural, multicultural and anti-racist education', in M. Cole (ed.) *The Social Contexts of Schooling*. Lewes: Falmer Press.

Cole, M. (1998) 'Racism, reconstructed multiculturalism and anti-racist education', *Cambridge Journal of Education*, 28(1): 37–48.

Cole, M. (ed.) (2006) *Education, Equality and Human Rights: issues of gender, 'race', sexuality, disability and social class*, 2nd edn. London: Routledge/Falmer.

Cole, M. and Blair, M. (2006) 'Racism and education: from Empire to New Labour', in M. Cole (ed.) *Education, Equality and Human Rights: issues of gender, 'race', sexuality, disability and social class*, 2nd edn. London: Routledge/Falmer.

Cole, M. and Virdee, S. (2006) 'Racism and Resistance: from Empire to New Labour' in M. Cole (ed.) *Education, Equality and Human Rights: issues of gender, 'race', sexuality, disability and social class*, 2nd edn. London: Routledge/Falmer.

Commission on British Muslims and Islamophobia (2002) *Changing Race Relations: race equality schemes and policies*. London: CBMI with Runnymede Trust.

Connolly, P. (1995) 'Boys will be boys? Racism, sexuality and the construction of masculine identities amongst infant boys', in J. Holland and M. Blair (eds) *Debates and Issues in Feminist Research and Pedagogy*. Clevedon: Multilingual Matters.

Cullingford, C. and Morrison, J. (1997) 'Peer group pressure within and without school', *British Educational Research Journal*, 23(1): 61–80.

Cummins, J. (1991) 'Inter-dependence of first and second language proficiency in bilingual children', in E. Bialystock (ed.) *Language Processing of Bilingual Children*. Cambridge: Cambridge University Press.

DfES (2004) *Aiming High: Understanding the Educational needs of Minority Ethnic Pupils in Mainly White Schools. A Guide to Good Practice*. London: The Stationery Office.

DfES (2004a) *Every Child Matters*. London: The Stationery Office.

DfES (2004b) *Excellence and Enjoyment: Supporting the needs of bilingual students*. London: DfES Publications.

DfES (2004c) *Excellence and Enjoyment: Creating a learning culture*. London: DfES Publications.

DfES (2004d) *Pupil Characteristics and Class Sizes in Maintained Schools in England*. London: The Stationery Office.

DfES (2004e) *More Advanced Learners of English as an Additional Language at Key Stage 2*. London: The Stationery Office.

DfES (2004f) *Aiming High: Understanding the Educational Needs of Minority Ethnic Pupils in Mainly White Schools, A Guide to Good Practice*. London: The Stationery Office.

DfES (2005) *Excellence and Enjoyment: Social and Emotional Aspects of Learning*. London: DfES Publications.

DfES (2006a) *African-Caribbean Achievement Pilot*. London: DfES Publications.

DfES (2006b) *Excellence and Enjoyment: Supporting the needs of bilingual students*. London: DfES Publications.

DfES (2006c) *Getting it, Getting it Right*. London: DfES Publications.

Fine, M. (1991) *Framing Dropouts: notes on the politics of an urban public high school*. New York: Suny Press.

Freire, P. (1972) *Pedagogy of the Oppressed*. Harmondsworth: Penguin.

Gillborn, D. (1990) *'Race', Ethnicity and Education*. London: Unwin Hyman.

Gillborn, D. (1995) *Racism and Anti-racism in Real Schools*. Buckingham: Open University Press.

Gillborn, D. and Gipps, C. (1996) *Recent Research on the Achievement of Ethnic Minority Pupils*. London: Ofsted.

Gillborn, D. and Mirza, H. (2000) *Educational Inequality: mapping race, class and gender*. London: Ofsted.

Gregory, E and Williams, A. (2001) 'Siblings bridging literacies in multilingual contexts', *Journal of Research in Reading*, 24(3).

Haberman, M. (1995) *Star Teachers of Children in Poverty*. West Lafayette, Indiana: Kappa Delta Pi.

Hall, D. (2001) *Assessing the Needs of Bilingual Pupils: living in two languages*. London: David Fulton.

Halpin, D. (2000) 'Hope, utopianism and educational management', *Cambridge Journal of Education*, 31(1): 103–18.

Hargreaves, A., Earl, L. and Ryan, J. (1996) *Schooling for Change: re-inventing education for early adolescents*. London: Falmer.

Hatcher, R. (2005) 'Social class and school: relations to knowledge', in M. Cole (ed.) *Education, Equality and Human Rights: issues of gender, 'race', sexuality, disability and social class*, 2nd edn. London: Routledge/Falmer.

Hill, D. and Cole, M. (2001) 'Social class', in D. Hill and M. Cole (eds) *Schooling and Equality: fact, concept and policy*. London: Kogan Page.

Ison, L. (2005) *Ethnicity and Education: the evidence on minority ethnic pupils*. London: DfES.

Ladson-Billings, G. (1994) *The Dreamkeepers: successful teachers of African American children*. San Francisco: Jossey-Bass Publishers.

Macdonald, I., Bhavnani, R., Khan, L. and John, G. (1989) *Murder in the Playground: the Burnage Report*. London: Longsight Press.

Maylor, U. (1996) 'The experiences of African, Caribbean and South Asian women in initial teacher education'. PhD thesis, Open University.

Myers, K. and Grosvenor, I. (2001) 'Policy, equality and inequality: from the past to the future', in D. Hill, and M. Cole (eds) *Schooling and Equality: fact, concept and policy*. London: Kogan Page.

Office for Standards in Education (Ofsted) (2002) *The Achievement of Black Caribbean Pupils: good practice in secondary schools*. London: Ofsted.

Office for Standards in Education (Ofsted) (2003a) *More Advanced Learners of English as an Additional Language in Secondary Schools and Colleges*. London: Ofsted.

Office for Standards in Education (Ofsted) (2003b) *The Education of Asylum-seeker Pupils*. London: Ofsted.

O'Kelly, A. (2007) *Developing a scheme of work with Parents*. Unpublished presentation to Hackney EMA and Humanities Coordinators' Forum, London.

Parekh, B. (2004) *Realising the Vision: The report of the Commission on the Future of Multi-Ethnic Birtain (2000) revisited in 2004*. Runnymede Trust Briefing Paper, London: Runnymede Trust.

Peters, M. (2002) Paper presented to DfES conference on the collection of ethnic background data and ethnic monitoring, 6 February.

Petitto, L.A., Katerelos, M., Levy, B., Gauna, K., Tétrault, K. and Ferraro, V. (2001) 'Bilingual signed and spoken language acquisition from birth: implications for mechanisms underlying bilingual language acquisition', *Journal of Child Language*, 28(2): 1–44.

Rampton, A. (1981) *West Indian Children in our Schools*. London: HMSO.

Sewell, T. (1997) *Black Masculinity and Schooling*. Stoke-on-Trent: Trentham Books.

Sharp, R. and Green, A. (1984) 'Social stratification in the classroom', in A. Hargreaves, and P. Woods (eds) *Classrooms and Staffrooms: the sociology of teachers and teaching*. Milton Keynes: Open University Press.

Sivanandan, A. (1985) 'RAT and the degradation of the black struggle', *Race and Class*, 22: 1–33.

Sleeter, C. (1993) 'How white teachers construct race', in C. McCarthy and W. Crichlow (eds) *Race, Identity and Representation in Education*. New York: Routledge.

Soltis, J. F. (1986) 'Teaching professional ethics', *Journal of Teacher Education*, 37(3): 2–4.

Stenhouse, L. (1983) *Authority, Education and Emancipation: a collection of papers*. London: Heinemann.

Swann Report (1985) *Education for All: report of the Committee of Inquiry into the Education of Children from Minority Ethnic Groups*. London: HMSO.

Training and Development Agency (TDA) (2006) *Qualifying to Teach: professional standards for Qualified Teacher Status and requirements for initial teacher training*. London: TDA.

Virani, Z. (2002) *Listening to Somali Pupils and Parents: a research project*. London Borough of Harrow.

Wright, C., Weekes, D., McGlaughlin, A. and Webb, D. (2000) *Race, Class and Gender in Exclusions from School*. London: Falmer.

Demonstrating positive values

Carol Smith

Q2 demonstrate the positive values, attitudes and behaviour they expect from children and young people.

Learning objectives

To encourage teachers to:

- develop an understanding of the complexity of, and overlap between, beliefs, values, attitudes and behaviour;

- develop an awareness of the influence of culture and experience on values, beliefs, attitudes and behaviour;

- understand the importance of reflecting critically on their own values and those of others within the education system;

- consider the practical issues involved in promoting inclusion in their routine classroom teaching.

Introduction

THE TERM 'POSITIVE VALUES' is open to interpretation. Individuals' values, beliefs and attitudes are shaped by their past experiences, and therefore by the influences of 'significant' others in their lives. The first part of this chapter discusses the complex nature of values and beliefs. It identifies some core values that should pervade our teaching in a democratic society, and discusses how these shape our attitudes to the pupils we teach and the framework within which we work. Student teachers are encouraged to reflect on their teaching through evaluation of their planning and the effectiveness of the delivery of individual lessons. However, to become truly reflective practitioners, it is important that they go beyond this and consider how legislation, central initiatives and school policies should be interpreted and put into practice. This involves an awareness of the values underpinning current educational policy and an understanding of some of the tensions involved in their implementation.

The second part of the chapter focuses on more practical issues. With a continuing move towards inclusive schools and the implementation of the *Every Child Matters* (DfES 2004a) agenda, teachers will need to develop inclusive approaches and a class-room environment where all children are valued as individuals and in which there are high expectations for all. This section considers some strategies for achieving these goals. However, this is a complex task as success will only be achieved by lis-tening to pupils, valuing their opinions and reflecting on how these should inform practice.

Defining beliefs, values and attitudes

In my early years of teaching I clearly remember my confusion, at times, in trying to understand the difference between 'beliefs' and 'values', though 'attitudes' always seemed less problematic. Raths and McAninch (2003) state that evidence from teacher cognition studies suggests a lack of differentiation between the concepts of belief and knowledge, but their definition of beliefs as 'psychologically held under-standings, premises or propositions about the world that are felt to be true' clarifies this, as the emphasis with beliefs is on what is 'felt' rather than 'known'.

Values have been defined in many ways, but Halstead and Taylor's (2000) defini-tion is both clear and comprehensive, stating that they are:

> principles and fundamental convictions which act as general guides to behaviour, endur-ing beliefs about what is worthwhile, ideals for which one strives, standards by which particular beliefs and actions are judged to be good or desirable.
>
> (Halstead and Taylor 2000: 3)

Examples of values that are particularly pertinent to teaching are justice, equal-ity and fairness, all of which underpin recent legislation and should guide our approaches to the delivery of the curriculum and to the individuals we teach.

My own definition of attitudes is that they are ways of thinking, or feeling, that de-termine the behaviours we demonstrate towards others, and that they are shaped by the beliefs and values that we hold. So, in valuing equality or inclusion, our attitudes towards the children we teach, would, for example, include respect, tolerance and openness to their comments and points of view. But, equally, they would guide us to challenge negative stereotypes and, for example, racist or sexist views. These are also attitudes that children should be encouraged to demonstrate towards each other.

It is important that student teachers and teachers reflect on the extent to which their positive values permeate their daily teaching, so that they routinely guide and change their practice (Ghaye and Ghaye 1998). Also, unless they reflect on their beliefs, values and attitudes, and how these both influence and are influenced by their practice, they will be unable to challenge their own thinking and that of others. They have a responsibility to 'clarify their own values and attitudes, and to articulate them, in order to be able to enter into a reasoned debate when confronted with opposing views' (Rice 2005: 56).

The influence of experience on values, beliefs and attitudes

In order to have a clear understanding of their values, to articulate them, to challenge them and to recognise how they guide their provision for, and interactions with, pupils within the classroom, teachers also need an awareness of where their values come from. It is important to acknowledge that an individual's values and beliefs originate from the shared understandings of the cultures and subcultures to which we belong and 'reflect our social position, previous experience and historical location' (Pollard 2002: 93). However, it is equally important to be aware that the children we teach also have values and beliefs based on their social positions and experience, and that at some times these will be in agreement with the teacher's, but at other times they will conflict.

Social influences on the values of both teachers and pupils come from the family, the neighbourhood and, often significantly, the media. Children are influenced by the views of parents/carers, siblings and extended family. Religion and religious practices, 'race' and ethnicity, as well as gender, sexuality, disability and social class, can also be significant in the way people perceive themselves in relation to others. My own experience, as one of a minority of working-class pupils at a selective secondary school, was characterised by feelings of inferiority, which on reflection were engendered by the different perceptions of social class that were held by me as well as by others. Today's children also experience the wider social influences of the media. Television is possibly the most pervasive of these media influences, but cinema, comics, children's magazines, the internet and the advertising media have a considerable impact on children's views too.

Schools have an impact on pupils' perceptions of self and their developing values at several levels. The culture of the playground and peer subcultures based on, for example, gender, age, ethnicity, sexuality, disability and social class help shape their views and attitudes towards others. Also, the type of school will provide different experiences. A small rural school with 50 pupils and mixed-age classes will have a different ethos to a city school which has twice this number in one year group. Whether a school is linked to the Church, is multi-faith and multicultural, or is independent from the state system will also lead to different pupil experiences.

The way in which schools and individual teachers implement government policy, which itself is value-laden, will reflect their values and shape those of the pupils. While the introduction of the National Curriculum was welcomed as an entitlement curriculum which promoted equal opportunities for all children, it was also introduced at a time of rising concern about standards in teaching and pupils' levels of achievement, and the raising of standards was one of its main aims. Children's levels of achievement have since been measured against attainment targets and level descriptors. They are also assessed through Standardised Assessment Tasks (SATs) at the end of Key Stages 1 and 2 in primary schools and Key Stage 3 in secondary schools. As school performance data, based on SATs results, are published and therefore available to parents/carers in and beyond the individual school, this has led to considerable pressure on teachers to achieve good results in order to compete for pupils with other schools (Smith 2006). For this reason, the dimension of inclusion has been overshadowed by the need for accountability.

While the use of school improvement data is now beginning to have an increasing influence on teaching, these data are partly based on the National Curriculum SATs and the 'marketisation' of education is still a significant influence (see the introductory chapter to this book). This is reflected in the way that the curriculum is delivered and that pupils are frequently placed in groups according to their ability and anticipated levels of attainment. Test results label children and allow them to develop labels for themselves and peers from an early age, and the placing of children in ability groups, even when used flexibly as a means of differentiation, can still contribute to pupils' development of self-image. Also, while this de-motivating, target-driven approach has been softened by the introduction of *Excellence and Enjoyment* (DfES 2003), as a result of the Government's recognition that children achieve more highly if they enjoy the learning experience, and personalised learning is being encouraged as a means of meeting the learning needs of the individual, there is still a considerable focus on levels of attainment. This leads to the question of whether excellence (which is a standard) and enjoyment (which is an emotion) can be achieved together (Hartley 2005), and teachers' values will determine how this strategy is interpreted and implemented.

A further issue related to the pressure on teachers to ensure that their pupils achieve high academic standards and that they themselves meet the requirements of Ofsted inspections to a high standard is the amount of time spent in planning, delivering and assessing learning. While teachers should translate such values as democracy, justice and human rights into their everyday practice, and model these as positive values that our future citizens should adopt, Wilkins (2003) found that teachers were finding it difficult to reflect on and incorporate this 'social dimension' into their teaching when their time was already committed to other dimensions. It will be interesting to see whether the new formula for inspections relieves teachers of some of these pressures or simply changes the pressures, and whether the implementation of non-contact time for teachers to plan, prepare and assess, commonly known as PPA time (see Chapter 3 of this book) reduces their workload sufficiently for them to give more attention to these dimensions. Perhaps PPA time could, at times, be used by teachers to consider issues such as the transmission of these values within the curriculum.

Educational policy, inclusion and values

Although the National Curriculum promotes inclusion as an entitlement curriculum for all children, asserting all children' rights to a broad, balanced and differentiated curriculum, and emphasising this through its underpinning principles of inclusion, it has been seen, in the previous section, that there are tensions in its implementation that hinder the development of inclusion. However, more recent legislation has introduced initiatives that fostered, first of all, the inclusion of children with special needs and disabilities, and second, has been extended to incorporate the inclusion of all children who belong to marginalised groups.

The introduction of a Special Needs Code of Practice in 1994 was the Government's response to the demands of Human Rights movements for an end to the segregation of children in special schools and the provision of equal opportunities in mainstream settings. Two influential documents were the 'UN Convention on the Rights of the Child' (1989) and the UNESCO Salamanca Statement (1994). Rustemier (2002) stresses the importance of these documents on government policy:

> These international human rights texts are not simply guidelines but place obligations on governments to reform education. One of the main strengths of a human rights approach to education is the recognition that the rights of children and young people to enjoy inclusive education are accompanied by the responsibilities of the government to provide it.
>
> (Rustemier 2002: 10)

The Code of Practice (1994) provided guidance to schools for including children with special needs, identifying eight categories of need and setting out a five-stage approach to provision. Individual Education Plans (IEPs) were introduced to support the identification of need and subsequent provision. While Mittler (2000) described this as a 'landmark document' as it set out schools' responsibilities to adapt provision to meet the needs of all children, which reflects the social model of disability, the processes of assessment, identification and then provision though the use of IEPs continued to reflect a medical or deficit model. (See the introductory chapter of this book for a discussion of the social and medical models of disability.)

To meet the requirements of the Special Needs and Disability Act (2001), a revised Code of Practice on Special Educational Needs (DfES 2001) was introduced to schools in 2002, followed by a Disability Code of Practice (2002). While the Special Needs Code of Practice is less complicated to implement than its predecessor, it continues to reflect a deficit model, locating difficulties within the child. However, the way in which teachers provide for children to achieve their IEP targets should reflect values of genuine inclusion and the extent to which this occurs will depend on the individual teachers' values and their attitude to children experiencing learning difficulties.

The disability legislation places an obligation on teachers to ensure that pupils with disabilities are not treated 'less favourably' than their peers because of their disability, and also that 'reasonable adjustments' are made to the delivery of the curriculum and the school environment to avoid disadvantaging disabled pupils. The vagueness of these terms caused anxiety for teachers as they were concerned with breaking the law if appropriate provision was not put in place. However, unlike the special needs code, the strength of this legislation is that it is based on the social model of disability and provision, which locates a child's difficulties within the barriers created by society and by the education system, and it also extends to include not only pupils with disabilities, but all pupils from marginalised groups. Although many teachers were initially resistant to this model, and some still are, if schools are going truly to reflect the values of rights, inclusion and respect for the individual, then inclusive practices must be embraced fully by all teachers and modelled to pupils. The 'Index for Inclusion for Schools' (CSIE 2000) and the later 'early years' version encourage teachers to reflect on their values and attitudes as they collaborate in developing inclusive cultures and practices, not only for children with special educational needs or disabilities, but for *all children*. By doing this, teachers may develop ways of supporting children in meeting their IEP targets that minimise the adverse effects of the medical model. At the same time, through the guidance in the 'Index for Inclusion', they will be developing practices that include children from *all marginalised groups,* and therefore including those whose associated needs may previously have been overlooked.

The introduction of *Every Child Matters: Change for Children* (DfES 2004a) and *Every Child Matters: Change for Children in Schools* (DfES 2004b) was the Government's response to criticism of the way in which the country's most vulnerable children were failed because of a lack of communication between services such as education, health and social services. The five outcomes listed in *Every Child Matters* (ECM) aimed at achieving well-being for all children, reflect positive values of caring about the well-being of others, respect children's rights to stay safe and to achieve their potential, and the right to be listened to in decisions about themselves and their school. How these values can be translated into classroom practice will be discussed in subsequent sections. At this point it is relevant to note concerns expressed by colleagues in education about the continuing and unresolved policy contradictions of the ECM agenda and the standards agenda, both of which have to be balanced by teachers, with the outcome dependent on reconciling their own values with the values underpinning policy.

Removing Barriers to Achievement (DfES 2004c) is frequently described as the Education Department's response to *Every Child Matters*. If this is so, then it appears to send out mixed messages about its underpinning values. Its strategy focuses on four key areas:

- Early intervention.
- Removing barriers to learning.
- Raising expectations and achievement.
- Delivering improvements in partnership.

The title of the document, and repeated reference to 'removing barriers' within the text, suggest that a social model is being adopted, rather than viewing children negatively from a deficit model, and the introduction reflects a 'rights' perspective:

> All children have the right to a good education and the opportunity to fulfil their potential. All teachers should expect to teach children with special educational needs (SEN) and all schools should play their part in educating children from their local community, whatever their background.
>
> (DfES 2004c)

While the first sentence refers to 'all children', the statement continues by referring to 'all children with special needs'. Furthermore, the main focus throughout the document, and also reflected in the title, is on children with special needs. If one considers the categories of need set out in the SEN Code of Practice (2002), then this excludes many children from marginalised or disadvantaged groups who may be underachieving, unless they have an additional special need. Strategies to support these groups can evolve through the commitment of whole-school staff to developing inclusive practices through the use of the materials in the 'Index for Inclusion' or other forms of staff development. However, it is for individual schools to decide on the extent to which they do this, which raises the issue of whether all children are equally valued. Therefore, again, teachers must reflect on these conflicting values and how they will interpret and implement the strategy in their own classrooms in a manner which is socially just.

The need to raise expectations and achievement reflects one of the five outcomes of *Every Child Matters* and is discussed in *Removing Barriers to Achievement* in relation to children with special needs. However, the focus on the use of personalised learning 'that brings out the best in every child, that builds on their strengths, enables them to develop a love of learning, and helps them to grow into confident and independent citizens, valued for the contribution they make' (DfES 2004c: 16) introduces valued individual attributes that are equally important and empowering for all children, and that can be promoted through personalised learning for all. Westcott (2005), however, expresses a very realistic concern that personalised learning 'could also further undermine the notion of an entitlement curriculum'. If the emphasis in teaching is on meeting the needs of each individual, then there is a risk that this will have a higher priority than providing a common curriculum for all. A similar concern has also been expressed by teaching colleagues, in that the emphasis placed on meeting children's wider personal and social needs, as a response to the *Every Child Matters* agenda, could also overshadow the provision of a broad and balanced curriculum. Teachers, therefore, have a duty to reflect on how personalised learning and an increased emphasis on the personal and social dimensions can be implemented within, and additional to, the National Curriculum if they are going to maintain the rights of all individuals to a broad and balanced curriculum, while also using personalised learning to enable them to fulfil their learning potential.

Developing inclusive practice

So far, in this chapter, the focus has been on the dilemmas teachers face when deciding how best to implement strategies that have conflicting values, or strategies where the implicit values conflict with the needs of the individual, or with those values underpinning the promotion of inclusion and celebrating of diversity. This section considers some of the steps teachers can take that will motivate children to learn and to achieve their potential through the use of good inclusive practice, while working within the framework of government legislation.

Teachers frequently use the terms 'well-motivated' or 'lacking in motivation' when discussing children, and these suggest that motivation lies within the child. If children appear not to be inspired by well-planned lessons presented in ways that interest and enthuse others, then their lack of motivation is seen as 'within child' and thus reflects a deficit model. However, if children have care needs that are unmet, a negative self-image, are being bullied, or feel that they are discriminated against by peers on, for example, grounds of 'race', disability, gender, sexuality or social class, then these factors will prevent them from becoming well-motivated by the subject that is being taught, regardless of the way it is taught or the activities used to reinforce learning. Therefore, for children to become well-motivated they must feel safe, cared for and included. To this end, inclusive classroom practices, which value diversity, challenge isms/phobia (see the introductory chapter to this book) and encourage respect between peers will enable children to engage with the curriculum and become better motivated learners.

For children to feel included it is important that they know that teachers take an interest in them. Teachers can be proactive in creating opportunities to show an interest informally in children and their families at break times. They can also, for example, use the time when children are lining up to come into school at the start of the day to smile at them or speak to them individually as this is welcoming and signals to children that the teacher is looking forward to working with them (BASS, date unknown). Positive relationships developed between teachers and learners will also encourage a positive sense of self within the learner (McLaughlin and Byers 2001). When this is combined with positive peer attitudes as a result of promoting respect and the valuing of diversity, a classroom climate will be fostered that improves behaviour and increases levels of motivation, and there is a strong likelihood that an individual's self-esteem will be enhanced (Jacques and Hyland 2000).

By taking time to listen to pupils and reflect on what they say, teachers can reach a better understanding of pupils' perspectives and behaviour. Teachers need to have empathy 'to get behind the often baffling behaviour that children can confront them with, and start to work out what it may mean' (Weare 2004: 45). And, by showing sensitivity, tolerance, respect and concern for others, teachers are modelling this skill to their pupils, and the ability to empathise is a crucial aspect to their social success (Webster-Stratton 1999) and for developing sound relationships with classroom peers.

To be an inclusive teacher is to ensure the inclusion and motivation of all pupils through the development of their self-image, raising their self-esteem and providing an emotionally secure environment. 'Teachers who provide emotional support for their pupils understand the vital links between feelings and the motivation to learn' (Rice 2005). After a period in which considerable value had been placed on learning the skills of literacy and numeracy, the development of 'emotional literacy' for schools reintroduced the importance of emotional competence for enabling pupils to achieve. Developing an emotionally literate school is a complex task and, to be successful, will permeate all areas of the school day. However, its importance to teachers and pupils alike is summarised by Sharp:

- We need to *understand* our emotions in order to be effective learners.
- We need to *manage* our emotions in order to develop positive and wholesome relationships.
- We need to *appropriately express* our emotions in order to develop as rounded people capable of helping ourselves, and so to become emotionally healthy. In turn we will be better able to help others.

(Sharp 2001: 12)

These three statements contain many of the positive values that teachers should be demonstrating to and encouraging in children throughout their contact time.

However, demonstrating positive values goes beyond wider teacher–pupil relationships and should be reflected in the way teaching is organised and learning is discussed. If teachers value the inclusion of all children in the learning process and accept that not all children learn best in the same way, this will be taken into account when planning learning. A variety of learning styles will be accounted for and opportunities for children to develop independence as learners will be provided, as well as opportunities to work collaboratively in groups to enable peer support and develop skills of cooperation. Rather than encouraging pupils to label themselves negatively through the use of inflexible ability grouping, if ability grouping must be used then this must be flexible, allowing children to move between groups. However, there is still the danger of negative labelling if some pupils are in the 'bottom set' for everything. While ability grouping may be seen as the easiest way of teaching to meet the targets of the National Curriculum, 'the more flexible the teaching style, the more likely to include a wider variety of pupil/student needs' (Rieser 2006: 174). In the introductory chapter to this book, Cole argues against notions of fixed ability and for developing the learning of all pupils *to the maximum* rather than entertaining vague notions of 'to their full potential'.

The way teachers interact with pupils about their work and to assess their understanding is of considerable significance, both in demonstrating how pupils are valued and contributing to the development of their self-image. Teachers' beliefs about children's attitudes to learning can be evident in the comments they make to them during lessons, which means that it is particularly important that negative comments are guarded against. To this end, it is essential that teachers are positive in their comments, encouraging a 'can-do' attitude in pupils, making verbal comments and comments through marking children's work constructive – to raise achievement – and positive – to motivate them to learn. Similarly, when asking pupils questions, it is important not to put them in a position of being seen to fail because the level of questioning is inappropriate or the process of questioning is insensitive. While closed questions are the most frequently used to assess children's understanding, open-ended ones can be used to challenge, to stimulate curiosity and to develop enquiring minds. However, not all pupils will be able to succeed in answering complex questions, the language used in asking the question may need to be simplified to enable understanding and 'thinking time' may need to be built in so that pupils can process the question and plan an answer.

So, the language teachers use is a key factor in demonstrating positive values. Pollard's (1985) research found that teachers use comments that can demonstrate negative attitudes towards children when attempting to encourage positive attitudes within them ('I don't think you're trying today', 'Stop being silly!' 'Is that your best writing?'). Children label themselves from the remarks teachers make about them. Also, using labels to describe pupils' needs, when talking to parents/carers or colleagues, can lead to pupils being seen from a negative point of view. However, educational labels (e.g. 'is experiencing difficulty with reading') which indicate where pupils need support, rather than categorisation labels (e.g. 'has ADHD and dyslexia') which reflects a deficit model, 'lead to more inclusive responses to pupils' learning needs' (Clough and Garner 2003: 79).

Finally, there are often children within a class who are overlooked. These tend to be quiet children who appear to be achieving 'satisfactorily' and do not cause any problems in class. Teachers will frequently realise who these children are when writing class lists, as there will be one name that cannot be recalled and the class register has to be consulted. These 'invisible children' (Hughes 2000) need to be identified as they may not feel included, have low self-esteem, have unmet needs and it is therefore very possible that they are not achieving their potential.

The importance of the pupil's voice

Many of the strategies discussed so far are based on interaction between teacher and pupil. However, there is traditionally a power relationship between them, in that the teacher has control of the extent and quality of interaction. It can be argued that this replicates the power relationships of wider society and the workplace and prepares children for their place within that system (see the introductory chapter to this book; for extended analyses see also, for example, Bowles and Gintis 1976; Cole 2007a, 2007b; Ribowski 2005; Hatcher 2006a, 2006b). Freire (1993) has described this as the 'banking' concept of education, where the teacher deposits information with the pupils, and proposes an alternative where the teacher is 'taught in dialogue with the students' and they become 'jointly responsible for a process in which all grow' (p. 61). This approach respects principles such as an awareness of the condition of learners and respecting the freedom and rights of learners, and it is dependent on dialogue between teacher and learner based on more equal relationships (Matheson and Matheson 2000).

While this approach has not been embraced by the English education system, the importance of children having a voice in decisions about their education has been introduced into recent policy as a result of lobbying from human rights groups and a realisation that a social model of inclusion can only work if children are able to express their views on what they see as barriers to their learning and inclusion in the school environment.

The SEN Code of Practice (2002) strengthens the rights of pupils to be involved in any decision making about their provision. Children now have the right to be involved not only in target-setting and the reviews to assess the extent to which targets have been met, but also in any other decision making regarding their provision. The extent to which this is carried out varies considerably between schools, as teachers frequently voice concerns about children's ability or level of maturity and the resulting quality of dialogue. However, research has shown that without listening to children, teachers cannot be fully aware of the extent to which their needs are being met.

Rose and Shevlin's (2004) research findings illustrate the dissatisfaction of participants with their schooling arising from an unwillingness to consult them in decision making about their education. This research aimed to investigate the degree to which young people from marginalised groups, such as minority ethnic groups, young people with disabilities, members of Gypsy Traveller groups and refugees, felt included in school. The results of the research found that physical access and access to the curriculum continued to be a difficulty for pupils with disabilities. Negative peer attitudes and low teacher expectations were also a concern. Although this research was conducted with pupils of secondary school age, it identifies a number of common issues which could apply equally across phases. But the real concern, from my point of view, is that either the participants were not being consulted or that the 'listening' was tokenistic. Also, if this age group felt that an assumed lack of competence or immaturity was behind the lack of consultation, this view may be more prevalent with those working with children of primary-school age.

Quicke (2003) argues that individuals need to be taught how to contribute to the decision-making process, but that before Years 5 or 6 pupils have insufficient experience of learning to have developed an understanding of what 'good learning' is. This view is not shared by Hoard and Clark (1992), who feel that even very young children have some metacognitive understanding, but both views suggest that strategies to encourage participation must consider the individual's level of maturity. Nevertheless, Quicke's (2003) emphasis on the importance of older children developing an understanding of how they learn and fostering this through interactionism is very relevant to the upper primary phase. Without this understanding they are likely to focus on their own difficulties rather than social barriers.

For primary school pupils who find it difficult to, or are unable to, express their individual views or concerns, either because they have communication difficulties or because they are still in the Foundation Stage or early Key Stage 1, teachers must find alternative ways of accessing children's voices. They may be able to express their opinions through writing or drawing. However, all children use body language to make their feelings known. As Mortimer (2004) points out, 'expressions or emotions are . . . the earliest form of communication'. Through observation (and recording) of these, teachers and support assistants can build up a picture of what children enjoy, find frustrating or painful, and what they dislike doing.

In addition to listening to the voices of individual children, it is important to show that the views of all children are valued, but that negative views are challenged, and this can be achieved by employing strategies to listen to larger groups of children through circle time and school councils. These give all children the opportunity to raise issues they want to discuss. However, there is a danger with circle time that, unless children's feelings and spoken contributions are handled sensitively, they may have a negative impact. Two of the aims of circle time are to raise self-esteem and solve emotional problems, but if children are learning a negative vocabulary about their moods and feelings, it is possible that the opposite will be achieved. Therefore, it is important that teachers are aware of this and that it is reflected in their own use of words and the way in which the sessions are led.

The purpose of a school council is to give pupils the opportunity to participate in decisions about the school ethos and the way their school is run. It presents pupils with an opportunity:

For increased understanding of management issues, enhancing problem-solving abilities by taking into account the perspectives of others, and improving behaviour through an increased consideration of the rights of others and commensurate responsibilities.

(Rice 2005)

School councils provide opportunities for children to participate in democratic activity, develop confidence through feeling that their opinions are valued, promote inclusion and challenge discriminatory practices. However, as with previous examples of pupil involvement in decision making, it is possible that children's views may not be considered with sufficient thought once expressed to staff and that these therefore become tokenistic.

In order to participate in these activities children need to learn how to make their voices count. Ground rules should be laid down for discussion sessions about turn-taking, not interrupting and being sensitive to the needs of others through the use of generalisation rather than commenting directly about an individual.

With the development of pupil participation through circle time and school councils, listening cultures can evolve in schools, where children know their views will be heard and valued, and that they will receive feedback as to why their initiatives cannot be implemented if it is not possible. Listening to pupils must be a genuine activity if it is to promote inclusion and positive values.

Conclusion

Values are at the heart of all the decisions that teachers make in the school and classroom. The values of others also underpin the legislative framework within which teachers work. Teachers, therefore, need to be aware of their own values, beliefs and attitudes and to reflect whether they promote inclusion, democracy and social justice. They also need to identify the values implicit in educational policy, any conflicting values between policies and where these values conflict with their own, as this will determine how they are interpreted and implemented.

Children's values are socially constructed and reflect their culture, family values and social influences of their local community. To include children fully in the school and classroom community, and to ensure positive learning experiences, teachers must understand the values children bring to school, and work with these to promote a positive attitude to learning, to themselves and to others, and encourage the valuing of diversity.

The importance of listening to children cannot be overemphasised. It is through the listening process that teachers become aware of pupils' values and attitudes, of how their own values impact on the pupils' learning and self-image and whether the pupils feel fully included in the learning environment. Only when children feel included and valued will they be able to enjoy the school experience and be able to learn to the maximum.

References

Birmingham Advisory and Support Services (BASS) (date unknown) *Behaviour: Getting It Right.* (Videotape) Birmingham: BASS Publications.

Bowles, S. and Gintis, H. (1976) *Schooling in Capitalist America.* London: Routledge and Kegan Paul.

Cole, M. (2007a) 'Correspondence Theory', in G. McCulloch (ed.) *International Encyclopedia of Education.* London: Routledge.

Cole, M. (2007b) 'Neo-liberalism and Education: a Marxist critique of New Labour's Five Year Strategy for Education', in A. Green and H. Raduntz (eds) *Renewing Dialogues in Marxism and Education: Volume 1 – Openings.* Basingstoke: Palgrave Macmillan.

CSIE (2000) *Index for Inclusion for Schools.* Bristol: CSIE.

Clough, P. and Garner, P. (2003) 'Special Educational Needs and Inclusive Education: Origins and Current Issues', in S. Bartlett and D. Burton (eds) *Education Studies: Essential Issues.* London: Sage.

DfEE (1994) *Code of Practice on the Identification and Assessment of Special Educational Needs.* London: DfEE.

DfES (2001) *Code of Practice on the Identification and Assessment of Children with Special Educational Needs* London: HMSO.

DfES (2003) *Excellence and Enjoyment: a Strategy for Primary Schools.* London: DfES.

DfES (2004a) *Every Child Matters: Change for Children.* London: DfES.

DfES (2004b) *Every Child Matters: Change for Children in Schools.* London: DfES.

DfES (2004c) *Removing Barriers to Achievement: The Government's Strategy for SEN.* London: DfES.

Disability Rights Commission (2002a) *Code of Practice for Schools – Disability Discrimination Act 1995; Part 4.* London: Disability Rights Commission.

Freire, P. (1993) *Pedagogy of the Oppressed.* London: Penguin Books.

Ghaye, A. and Ghaye, K. (1998) *Teaching and Learning Through Critical Reflective Practice.* London: David Fulton.

Halstead, J.M. and Taylor, M.J. (2000) *The Development of Values, Attitudes and Personal Qualities: A Review of Recent Research.* Slough: NFER.

Hartley, D. (2005) 'Excellence and Enjoyment: The Logic of a "Contradiction" ', *British Journal of Education Studies*, 54(1): 3–14.

Hatcher, R. (2006a) 'Privatisation and Sponsorship: the re-agenting of the school system in England', *Journal of Educational Policy*, 21(5): 599–619.

Hatcher, R. (2006b) 'Academies, Building Schools for the Future and the 14–19 vocational agenda'. Talk given at Anti-Academies Alliance conference, London, 25 November. Available at www.socialist-teacher.org.

Hoard, C. and Clark, H. (1992) *Self-Regulatory Behaviours in Preschool Children: Fact or Fantasy?* in J. Quicke 'Educating the pupil voice', *Support for Learning*, 18(2): 51–7.

Hughes, P. (2000) *Principles of Primary Education Study Guide.* London: David Fulton.

Jacques, K. and Hyland, R. (2000) *Professional Studies: Primary Phase.* Exeter: Learning Matters.

Matheson, C. and Matheson, D. (2000) *Educational Issues in the Learning Age.* London: Continuum.

McLaughlin, C. and Byers, R. (2001) *Personal and Social Development for All.* London: David Fulton.

Mittler, P. (2000) *Working Towards Inclusive Education: Social Contexts.* London: David Fulton.

Mortimer, H. (2004) 'Hearing children's voices in the early years', *Support for Learning*, 19(4): 169–74.

Pollard, A. (1985) *The Social World of the Primary School.* London: Holt Education.

Pollard, A. (2002) *Reflective Teaching: Effective and Evidence-informed Professional Practice.* London: Continuum.

Quicke, J. (2003) 'Educating the pupil voice', *Support for Learning*, 18(2): 51–7.

Raths, J. and McAninch, A.C. (2003) *Teacher Beliefs and Classroom Performance: The Impact of Teacher Education*. Greenwich (USA): Information Age Publishing.

Rice, L. (2005) *Promoting Positive Values*, in M. Cole (ed.) *Professional Values and Practice: Meeting the Standards*. London: David Fulton.

Rieser, R. (2006) *Inclusive Education or Special Educational Needs*, in: M. Cole (ed.) *Education, Equality and Human Rights: Issues of Gender, 'Race', Sexuality, Disability and Social Class*. London: Routledge/Falmer.

Rikowski, G. (2005) *Silence on the Wolves*. Education Research Centre, University of Brighton Occasional Paper (Brighton: University of Brighton). Available from the Education Research Centre, University of Brighton, Room 242, Mayfield House, Falmer, Brighton, BN1 9PH, email: Education.Research@brighton.ac.uk.

Rose, R. and Shevlin, M. (2004) 'Encouraging Voices: listening to young people who have been marginalised', *Support for Learning*, 19(4): 155–61.

Rustemier, S. (2002) *Social and educational justice: the human rights framework for inclusion*. Bristol: CSIE.

Sharp, P. (2001) *Nurturing Emotional Literacy: A Practical Guide for Teachers, Parents and those in the Caring Professions*. London: David Fulton.

Smith, C. (2006) *From Special Needs Provision to Inclusive Education*, in J. Sharp, S. Ward and L. Hankin (eds) *Education Studies: An issues-based approach*. Exeter: Learning Matters.

Special Educational Needs and Disability Act (2001). London: The Stationery Office.

Training and Development Agency (TDA) (2007) *Professional Standards for Teachers: Qualified Teacher Status*. Available at http:www.tda.gov.uk/upload/resources/pdf/s/standards_qts.pdf (accessed 13 September 2007).

UNESCO (1994) *Salamanca Statement*, World Conference on Special Educational Needs. Paris: UNESCO.

United Nations (1989) *Convention on the rights of the Child*. New York: United Nations.

Weare, K. (2004) *Developing the Emotionally Literate School*. London: Paul Chapman.

Webster-Stratton, C. (1999) *How to Promote Children's Social and Emotional Competence*. London: Paul Chapman.

Westcott, E. (2005) 'Equality of opportunity and inclusion', *Journal of Education for Teaching*, 31(4): 273–4.

Wilkins, C. (2003) 'Teaching for equality and diversity: putting values into practice', in A. Ostler (ed.) *Teachers, Human Rights and Diversity*. Stoke on Trent: Trentham Books.

Statutory frameworks relating to teachers' responsibilities

Jeff Nixon

Q3 (a) Be aware of the professional duties of teachers and the statutory framework within which they work.

(b) Be aware of the policies and practices of the workplace and share in collective responsibility for their implementation.

Learning objectives

To raise awareness and understanding of:

- the concept of a teacher's duty of care;
- the statutory framework relating to teachers' conditions of service;
- regulations/guidance on the welfare of the child, special needs and health and safety;
- legislation relating to equality and equal opportunity issues.

Introduction

THERE ARE THREE ELEMENTS TO the concept of a teachers' duty of care: the common law aspect, the statutory consideration and the contractual obligation. The 'common law duty' was highlighted in *Lyes v Middlesex County Council* in 1962 (Local Government Review 1963) where the 'standard of care' expected of a teacher was held to be that of a person exhibiting the responsible mental qualities of a prudent parent in the circumstances of the school, rather than the home. It has been acknowledged that a teacher's duty of care to individual pupils is influenced by the subject or the activity being taught, the age of the children, the available resources and the size of the class. This can be clarified further by adding the proviso that, even though others may disagree, if it can be shown that the teacher acted in accordance with the views of a reputable body of opinion within the profession, the duty of care will have been discharged. The definition of the 'common law' duty of care may become even more sharply focused as progress is made to reduce the size of classes and with the establishment of the General Teaching Councils (GTCs) for England and Wales.

Since September 2000 there has been established a GTC for England and a separate one for Wales; Scotland has had one since 1965. The GTCs have key powers over entry to the profession and the manner in which the profession conducts itself, which will clearly impact upon individual teachers in relation to any issues that would fall into the category of misconduct. The GTCs do not have the powers that relate to pay and conditions; these issues will continue to be dealt with by the Review Body procedures.

With respect to the 'statutory duty of care', the Children Act 1989, Section 3; subsection 5 defined the duty of care as doing 'what is reasonable in all circumstances of the case for the purpose of safeguarding and promoting the child's welfare'. Teachers who are entrusted with the care of children during the school day have this statutory duty. The Children Act stresses the paramount importance of the wishes and needs of the child, reflecting the law's current more child-focused approach. Rather than the old-fashioned idea that a child was owned by its parents and this parental authority of property rights was delegated to teachers during the school day, the child's ascertainable needs and wishes should be taken into account by the teacher and considered in the light of the child's age and level of understanding. The teacher needs to assess the risk of harm that could arise to a child in particular circumstances, and to consider the safeguarding of the child and the promotion of the child's welfare and interest. This approach is clearly much more complex than the simplistic doctrine of the child as the property of the parents and demonstrates again how outmoded the term *in loco parentis* has become.

The new Children Act following the publication of the White Paper, *Every Child Matters* (DfES 2004a) will undoubtedly increase this trend. It is changing the way local authorities (LAs) provide services for children and their parents/carers. Some local authorities reorganised their provision prior to the new Act and new departments have emerged from the previous education and social services departments; more and more we will see the development of Children, Families and Schools departments and the establishment of Children's Commissioners. Indeed, the Central Government Education Department was re-named in June 2007 from the DfES to the Department for Children, Schools and Families (DCSF) when Ed Balls became the first Secretary of State for the new department. Much of this legislation was motivated by the tragic case of Victoria Climbié. The legislation seeks to ensure that children like Victoria do not slip through any holes in local authority provision.

If the concept of the 'duty of care' appears to be a complicated matter when it refers to activities within the school, it becomes ever more complex when a teacher is engaged in leading or assisting with activities off the school site, such as educational visits, school outings or field trips. The law on negligence is particularly significant here; the legal liability of a teacher or head teacher for any injury which is sustained by a pupil on a school journey or excursion would be dependent upon the tests for negligence. If a child suffered an injury as a direct result of some negligence or failure to fulfil the duty of care, the employer of the teacher or head teacher would be legally liable. This is because employers have vicarious liability for the negligence of employees at work. Consequently, where legal claims arise following an accident to a pupil, and there is a suggestion of negligence on the part of the teacher, the claim will most likely be made against the LA as the employer of the teacher (or the governing body in the case of Voluntary Aided, Foundation Schools, sixth form colleges or independent schools), if the teacher was, at the time of the accident to the pupil, working in the course of employment. It is possible, however, for teachers to be fined and, as recent cases have demonstrated, be subjected to custodial sentences particularly in relation to the breach of trust provisions of legislation.

Schoolteachers' conditions of service

What do we mean by conditions of service? In the 1920s and 1930s, for example, a woman teacher could be dismissed if she got married or even kept company with men. She was not allowed to ride in a carriage or automobile with any man except her brother or father. She had to be home between the hours of 8 p.m. and 6 a.m., unless in attendance at a school function, and could not leave town without first obtaining the permission of the Board of Trustees. The contract also laid down a non-negotiable dress code which included the prohibition of make-up and stipulated that she should not be seen in places such as ice-cream stores (Teacher's Contract 1923: Women In Education).

Eighty years later, for those teachers employed in Local Authority (LA) maintained schools, national conditions of service are derived from two basic sources. The first is the *Schoolteachers' Pay and Conditions Document* (DfES 2006), often referred to as the 'Blue Book'. This sets out working time, professional duties and conditions of service. The second is *Conditions of Service for Schoolteachers in England and Wales* (Council of Local Education Authorities/Schoolteacher Committee (CLEA/ST) 1985; revised edition, August 2000) (the 'Burgundy Book'). This covers national agreements between local education authorities and the teachers' organisations, including such issues as sick pay, sick leave, maternity pay and periods of notice.

Much of what happens in schools is, however, subject to local interpretation. In addition, initiatives may occur either at local or national level which change certain aspects of the teacher's job or may simply emphasise one or a number of items in the conditions of service package at a particular time; for example, the administration in different schools of in-service education and training (INSET) days – the so-called 'Baker Days'. These are named after Kenneth Baker who, as Secretary of State for Education and Science, introduced them in the Teachers' Pay and Conditions Act of 1987 (DES 1987). The Act does not specify where or when the INSET days need to be taken, so some schools have operated sessions known as 'twilight training', whereby INSET is carried out during the school's academic year. This is often with the agreement of the staff concerned, with some schools converting days designated as 'Baker Days' into days of school closure. However, if this is the case the school must provide the statutory 190 days of education for all pupils. Teachers are required to be available for work in school for 195 days in any school year, although during the Golden Jubilee Year in 2002 this was reduced by one day for both pupils and teachers.

There may also be local agreements, on issues not covered elsewhere. These may be better or worse than conditions agreed nationally. On the positive side, for example, some LAs operate a maternity leave and maternity pay agreement that is better than the national one. On the negative side, there exist in the aided or voluntary sector and now in Foundation Schools – formerly Grant Maintained Schools (where the governing body is the employer of teachers) – conditions of service that may not be in teachers' best interests. In Church schools, for example, it is not uncommon to see a clause in the contract of employment that states that the employee should not engage in any activity that may bring the Church into disrepute. This is frequently subject to interpretation at local level within the parish. Here one can see shades of the 1920s contract, with teachers in such schools rarely realising the position they are in until the local parish notable starts asking questions. Beginning teachers should also bear in mind that there are three different types of contract: permanent,[1] temporary and fixed term. In addition, during the induction year the beginning teacher's contract only becomes permanent once the year has been successfully completed.

The 'Blue Book': *Schoolteachers' Pay and Conditions Document* *(STPACD)* in England and Wales

Prior to this system being introduced, negotiations on pay and conditions of service took place in the Burnham Committee and the Council of Local Education Authorities/Schoolteacher Committee (CLEA/ST), respectively. The Burnham Committee was abolished under the provision of the Teachers' Pay and Conditions Act 1987, whereas CLEA/ST still exists but rarely meets. An Order that provided for conditions of employment to be incorporated into teachers' contracts also came into force in 1987 (HM Government 1987) and is reviewed annually.

The conditions of service elements of the 1987 Order dealt with teachers' duties and working time only. They contained little safeguard against the excessive workload that was being imposed upon teachers. The Order set down a contractual requirement that teachers can reasonably be directed to perform certain duties by the head teacher for up to 1265 hours across the 195 days of service in any one year. It also specified a list of required professional duties. These cover teaching, related activities, assessments and reports, consultation sessions with parents/carers, appraisal, review of further training and development, educational methods, discipline, health and safety, staff meetings, cover for absent teachers, public examinations, management and administration.

The Workforce Reform agenda

As part of the remodelling agenda outlined in the Government's White Paper *A Time for Standards* (HM Government 2002), a number of significant changes have been incorporated into the Blue Book; these were introduced progressively over the period 2003–2005. The parties to these amendments to the conditions of service element of the Blue Book make claims that the workload of teachers will be dramatically reduced; however, the largest teachers' organisation, the National Union of Teachers (NUT), has remained outside these discussions and has been excluded from discussions on Upper Pay Spine (UPS 3) progression and the Rewards and Incentive Group (RIG) proposals on Teaching and Learning Responsibilities (TLRs). The debate on all of this continues and the major stumbling block centres on whether schools should be able to employ non-qualified staff to supervise/teach whole classes. The NUT's principled approach has remained consistent throughout the implementation of TLRs, with some schools taking industrial action because teachers were facing cuts in salary in the transition from management allowances to TLRs.

The introduction of new Performance Management Schemes in schools from September 2007 has been as controversial as the implementation of TLRs. Heralded under the banner of New Professionalism, those parties to RIG (and there can never have been a more appropriate acronym!) have devised a system for performance management that will increase the burdens on teachers and see closer links between pay progression and the outcome of meeting targets set by either the headteacher or line manager. The manner in which teachers are rewarded for their work in education is now closer to those Victorian days when payments by results was the order of the day. It is remarkable that the Government has had such an easy ride with this; however, those parties to RIG will undoubtedly see this coming back to haunt them as the profession realises exactly what has happened.

The changes in the Blue Book stemming from the remodelling agenda are outlined in Section 4 of the 2006 edition of the STPACD (DfES 2006b). In 2003 a list of administrative tasks was drawn up which teachers could no longer be 'routinely required' to perform. Three tests are outlined to assist schools in determining whether teachers should carry out such tasks. These are:

Does it need to be done at all?
Is the task of an administrative or clerical nature?
Does it call for the exercise of a teacher's professional skills or judgement?

If the answers to the first two questions is yes and the answer to the third is no, then the task should be transferred away from teachers.

A Work/Life Balance section has been added to the Blue Book; this is about helping teachers combine work with their personal interests outside school. The section emphasises the aim of reducing bureaucracy, limiting the time outside 1265 hours to what is regarded as reasonable, keeping a check on the number and length of after-school meetings and encouraging schools to develop Work/Life Balance policies. The evidence on this element would suggest schools and teachers have a long way to go in making significant reductions in the average working week, currently in excess of 50 hours during term time. Indeed, the 2006 Report into Teachers' Workload produced by the Office of Manpower Economics concluded that there had been 'no statistically significant reduction in teachers working time'.

From September 2004 two new contractual changes on providing cover for absent teachers came into effect:

- A limit on the amount of cover that can be provided by an individual teacher (38 hours per year per teacher).

- An amended duty on head teachers to ensure cover is shared equitably . . . and of the desirability of not using a teacher at the school until all other reasonable means of providing cover have been exhausted (this would include the use of non-qualified cover supervisors).

A no detriment clause is included in this part of the Blue Book to cover those schools and teachers where the amount of cover provided is already fixed at less than the 38 hours. The interpretation of how this clause works in practice is currently the subject of intensive debate in staffrooms.

From September 2005 every school had to introduce a minimum of 10 per cent planning, preparation and assessment (PPA) time for all teachers. Again a no detriment clause is provided to protect teachers who are already in receipt of more than this amount. The consequence of this provision has meant greater strain on over-stretched school budgets. While welcome, PPA time will only work effectively if schools are given extra resources to pay for the extra staff that will need to be employed. Head teachers are also entitled to guaranteed PPA time commensurate with their teaching time.

Finally, from September 2005 teachers have no longer been required routinely to invigilate external examinations including SATs (Standard Assessment Tests). The opening sentence of this section of the Blue Book boldly announces that invigilating examinations is not a productive use of teachers' time. As with the other elements of the remodelling agenda, the aims are ambitious and far reaching; however, there are elements within this that are very worrying, encapsulated in the question many parents and carers will pose: Is my child being taught by a qualified teacher today?

The 'Burgundy Book': *Conditions of Service for Schoolteachers in England and Wales*

The 'Burgundy Book' deals with sick pay and sick leave, maternity pay and maternity leave and notice. It also refers to legislation affecting teachers' conditions of service with respect to redundancy payments, unfair dismissal, sex discrimination, trade union membership and activities, time off work, race relations, health and safety at work, premature retirement and medical fitness to teach (including those medical conditions when teachers would be suspended from teaching duties on the grounds of ill-health).

Three other sections of the 'Burgundy Book' are also worthy of note. These are the model procedure to resolve collective disputes, facilities for trade union representatives and the 1968 School Meals Agreement. This agreement was a major breakthrough for teachers in that it allowed teachers the freedom to take a lunch break away from the children and the school. Teachers could no longer be required to undertake supervision at lunchtime and that aspect of the conditions of service package remains intact to the present day. There is not much employment law beneficial to the workforce that has survived almost 40 years. The 1968 School Meals Agreement was thus an historic landmark for teachers and, in my view, remains so.

Grievance and disciplinary procedures

The 'Burgundy Book' places an obligation on employers (LAs and governing bodies in relation to Foundation Schools, Voluntary Aided Schools, sixth form colleges and City Technology Colleges, and schools in the independent sector) to provide teachers with copies of procedures governing the resolution of grievances and discipline. Since Local Management of Schools (LMS), governing bodies have usually adopted procedures recommended by the personnel sections of LAs. It can be argued that all such procedures form part of a teacher's contract of employment and if they are not followed, this could readily give rise to a claim for breach of contract.

Since new regulations on making claims to Employment Tribunals (ETs) were introduced from the beginning of October 2004, the use of grievance procedures and disciplinary appeal procedures have played an increasingly significant role prior to cases ever coming before an ET. In short, an applicant will have to demonstrate that all existing internal procedures have been exhausted before the case is listed for a hearing in tribunal. The aim of these new regulations was to reduce the number of claims ever reaching an ET hearing; however, evidence suggests that the backlog of cases in the ET system is still as bad as it was before the changes in the regulations were introduced.

Local agreements

The third component of the conditions of service package for teachers is contained within whatever local agreements have been negotiated within the LA or the school (e.g. Foundation school, Voluntary Aided school or sixth form college); it is unlikely that negotiated local agreements will exist in the independent sector, as recognition of the teaching unions and associations is likely to be problematic. However, since the introduction of the right for unions to be recognised under certain specific circumstances, there have been a few instances of union recognition developing in the independent sector. In addition, as the Employment Relations Act 1999 gave workers a statutory right to be accompanied by a trade union official at a disciplinary or grievance hearing, this has been used to establish a foothold in schools in the independent sector where, for example, the unions have not been recognised or where representation rights have been limited to employees within the school or college. Local agreements normally cover matters not covered in the 'Burgundy Book', such as time off other than for sickness and maternity leave. Entitlements or guidance to head teachers and governing bodies in exercising discretion on leave of absence covering bereavement, a relative's illness, weddings, study leave, moving house and other circumstances are all dependent on local agreements. There will not always be a right to time off for these matters and it may not always be paid leave. The decision on leave of absence may be delegated to the head teacher. This has particularly been the case since the introduction of LMS. However, the ultimate decision on the right to leave of absence will rest with the employer, which in most cases will be the LA.

Other aspects of teachers' conditions of service that are determined locally are the precise timings of the school day. There are considerable variations between the Key Stages. The amount of contact time in an infant school, for example, may be around five hours per day, whereas in a secondary school it may be up to five hours 45 minutes. It is left to the school to decide the precise timings of the day, the timing of breaks, the length of morning and afternoon sessions and the length of the lunchtime.

The changing face of conditions of service

Market forces applied to the education service have had a serious effect on the conditions of service of schoolteachers and on their salaries. It inevitably means local variations within the national framework; sometimes this local interpretation at school level can work to the advantage of teachers, sometimes not. However, the evidence would suggest that the workload of teachers is still excessive.

What is specifically required is a limitation on the current paragraph 78.7 within the STPACD 2006. This paragraph effectively means that a teacher's working time is open-ended in terms of performing the professional duties of the job. In practice, this means that teachers regularly work on average in excess of 50 hours per week during term time. The whole aim of the remodelling agenda is to assist serving teachers to reduce their workload; however, an equally important aim is to make teaching as a profession more attractive to prospective teachers. As the age profile of teachers becomes older this increasingly takes on a greater significance. Within the next five years a huge number of teachers will be eligible for retirement when they reach 60 years of age. The question for the Government both then and now is whether those who retire will be replaced easily by another generation of teachers; the evidence suggests that a severe teacher shortage is almost upon us so it is essential people are attracted to the profession and, what is more, once in it they stay in it for a significant period of time.

The Education Reform Act of 1988 (HM Government 1988) changed conditions of service considerably. This provided for local management of schools (LMS), giving governing bodies much more control and seriously eroding the power of the head teacher and the LAs. The Act also made provisions for schools to opt out of LA control and become grant maintained. This has subsequently been amended within the Schools Standards and Framework Act (HM Government 1998); so that former grant maintained schools are now back under the umbrella of the LA although as most are Foundation Schools, the governors are still the employer. The overall effect was to loosen the influence LAs had on schools and consequently potentially worsen the conditions of service of teachers at local level.

More recently in 2004 there has been an attempt to worsen the sick leave and sick pay provisions for teachers. The National Employers' Organisation for School Teachers (NEOST), in discussions with the teacher unions, failed to reach a negotiated agreement even after the matter was referred to the Advisory, Conciliation and Arbitration Service (ACAS). Subsequently, the assistant secretary of NEOST issued Bulletin No 493 in October 2004 to all education authorities covered by the Burgundy Book. This bulletin encouraged LAs and other employers to introduce the proposed changes into the contracts for all newly appointed teachers, thereby creating a two-tier system within the national framework. To their credit several LAs did not agree to do this; however, this does demonstrate the level to which the employers are prepared to descend in order to worsen certain aspects of teachers' conditions that are regarded as generous.

The profession needs the confidence to take control of its own destiny. The role of the recently established General Teaching Council (GTC) will need to be seen in the context of an education system, which a number of commentators (e.g. Cole 2005, 2007; Hatcher 2005, 2006a, 2006b; Rikowski 2005) have suggested is witnessing burgeoning privatisation. In order to protect and advance the conditions of service of schoolteachers, a major role of GTCs and, of course, the teacher unions, should be to resist this trend.

The welfare of the child

The new guidance issued in 2006 (TDA 2006: 9) specifically mentions confidentiality and states that beginning teachers need to develop an ability to judge when they may need to seek advice. Two specific examples are cited: child protection and confidentiality. It is important for all teachers to be aware that it is frequently not possible to give a pupil an undertaking that everything that is said in a conversation between a teacher and a pupil can remain confidential. Should the teacher be given information by a pupil that would be covered by child protection procedures, then the teacher would have to pass on that information either to the head teacher or the designated child protection officer. If the teacher remained unsure about any aspect of such a conversation with a pupil, then, clearly, advice should be sought from an appropriate colleague. Teachers may also need to seek advice when requests are made for formal assessments or when providing information under the *Special Educational Needs Code of Practice* (DfES 2001b).

Appropriate physical contact and restraint

DfEE *Circular 10/95, Protecting Children from Abuse* (DfEE 1995) provides guidance about physical contact with pupils. Appropriate points of that guidance have now been incorporated into Section 550A of the Education Act 1996 (discussed later in this chapter). The relevant paragraphs of the circular are quoted here. These were drawn up after consultation with the teacher organisations.

It is unnecessary and unrealistic to suggest that teachers should touch pupils only in emergencies. Particularly with younger pupils, touching them is inevitable and can give welcome reassurance to the child. However, teachers must bear in mind that even perfectly innocent actions can sometimes be misconstrued. Children may find being touched uncomfortable or distressing for a variety of reasons. It is important for teachers to be sensitive to a child's reaction to physical contact and to act appropriately. It is also important not to touch pupils, however casually, in ways or on parts of the body that might be considered indecent.

Employers and senior staff have a responsibility to ensure that professional behaviour applies to relationships between staff and pupils, that all staff are clear about what constitutes appropriate behaviour and professional boundaries, and that those boundaries are maintained with the sensitive support and supervision required. That is important in all schools, but residential institutions need to be particularly mindful of this responsibility, as do individuals in circumstances where there is one to one contact with pupils, for example, in the teaching of music or extra-curricular activities.

Teachers are considered to occupy a position of trust in relation to pupils and this may appear to be an obvious point to make; however, under the terms of the Sexual Offences (Amendment) Act 2000, a criminal offence is committed when a teacher embarks upon a relationship of a sexual nature with a pupil who is under the age of 18 years (DfEE 2000). The offence can result in a custodial sentence upon conviction; any teacher who was convicted of such an offence would undoubtedly be placed on List 99, which is maintained by the DCSF, and which contains the names of all those people who have been prohibited from working with children and young people. In December 2004 schoolteacher Justine Rowe was sentenced to 12 months imprisonment, banned from working with children and put on the Sex Offenders Register for ten years for having a lesbian relationship with a girl of 16.

Schools may find it helpful to agree in consultation with the LA or Area Child Protection Committee (ACPC) a code of conduct for staff to reduce the risk of allegations being made. Some LAs have already drawn up such codes that are recommended to schools. Where a school agrees such a code, it should be made known to parents/carers to help avoid any misunderstandings. There have been recently a number of well-publicised cases that relate to teachers, child protection and misconduct. Some of these have concentrated on teachers being the subject of false or malicious allegations made by parents/carers and/or children. The length of time teachers are suspended from duty while child protection procedures are applied has also given cause for concern, so much so that a number of Regional Coordinators were appointed during 2001 to ensure procedures are not subject to any unnecessary delay to avoid teachers who are under investigation being left in a state of 'limbo'. Clearly, LAs and governing bodies have responsibilities to protect children from harm and they need to be vigilant in their approach to these responsibilities. However, there is also a duty of care towards the individual teacher who is the subject of any enquiry and LAs, head teachers and governing bodies must not forget this. All too often the needs of the teacher, who is away from the school community because of the suspension while the investigation is conducted, are considered not to be a priority, furthermore the teacher's absence from the school community leads to rumour, gossip and often unfounded speculation. This frequently makes it very difficult indeed to reintegrate the teacher even when the investigation either exonerates the individual or permits a return to the school community after the disciplinary procedures have concluded.

The GTCs also have roles to play in relation to teacher misconduct and competence issues. The establishment of the GTCs means that the teaching profession is much more self-regulatory although for certain serious criminal convictions, and being placed on the Sex Offenders Register would be one such example, a person's right to teach can be taken away directly by the DCSF. Whereas before the introduction of the GTCs all misconduct cases were referred to the Teacher Misconduct Unit and decisions about whether a teacher could continue to practise were taken by that Unit, in consultation with the Secretary of State, now less serious cases of misconduct and appeals relating to the failure of the induction period are dealt with by the Professional Conduct Committee of the GTC. In much the same way as doctors and lawyers can be 'struck off' by their professional bodies, the GTCs have the power to de-register a teacher, subject, of course, to the usual rights of the teacher concerned making representations to the GTC.

Since 1998, provisions contained in Section 4 of the Education Act 1996 have clarified the position in relation to the use of physical force by teachers. The relevant section of the Act, S550A, defines the powers of members of staff to restrain pupils or students. Staff can use such force as is reasonable in the circumstances for the purpose of preventing the pupil from doing or continuing to do any of the following:

(a) committing any offence;
(b) causing personal injury to or damage to the property of any person (including him or herself); or
(c) engaging in any behaviour prejudicial to the maintenance of good order and discipline at the school or among any of its pupils, whether that behaviour occurs in a teaching session or elsewhere.

These circumstances apply where a member of staff of a school is:

(a) on the premises of the school; or
(b) elsewhere at a time when, as a member of staff, he or she has lawful control or charge of the pupil concerned.

(DfEE 1998: para. 10, p. 4)

The use of corporal punishment is excepted from these provisions as it was abolished in the maintained sector in August 1986.

The term 'member of staff' is defined as any teacher who works at the school, and any other person who, with the authority of the head teacher, has lawful control or charge of pupils at the school. 'Offence' is qualified by the caveat that under a certain age a child may not be capable of committing an offence.[2] The interpretation of this section of the law, therefore, is open to conjecture; the initial assessment and judgement of the teacher and the subsequent course of action adopted will be critical in assessing whether the amount of force used is reasonable. This will also be dependent upon a number of variables such as the age and size of the pupil and how much the teacher knows about the pupil. Other variables may be relevant: for example, whether the pupil concerned suffers from any pre-existing medical condition that may or may not have been known to the member of staff concerned. Restraining, by use of physical force, a pupil who suffers from brittle bone disease, for example, may not be considered a reasonable option in the circumstances.

Before the implementation of the Act, force was allowed in an emergency only: where pupils placed themselves at risk of physical injury, where pupil actions placed others at risk of physical injury and where damage to property could be limited by the use of restraint, without endangering the physical safety of pupils, staff or members of the public. The new provisions make clear that teachers and other authorised members of staff are entitled to intervene in other, less extreme, situations.

There is no definition in the Act of what constitutes 'reasonable force'. The interpretation of this is crucial for teachers and others defending their actions. It must be emphasised that the use of any degree of force is unlawful if the particular circumstances do not warrant it. The degree of force should be in proportion to the circumstances and seriousness of the behaviour or consequences it is intended to prevent. The level and duration of the force used should be the minimum necessary to achieve the desired result, such as to restore safety.

In some circumstances it will, of course, be inadvisable for a teacher to intervene without help, particularly where a number of pupils are involved and where pupils are older and more physically mature. Unless this was considered, the teacher might be at risk of injury and clearly this should be avoided.

Although the provisions do not specifically mention any apparent failure to take some appropriate action, in circumstances which merit the use of reasonable force, such a failure could be regarded as a serious matter; a teacher could well find disciplinary action ensues if an incident which merited physical intervention was simply ignored. This means that it is not possible to argue that it is a safer option for a member of staff to do nothing or to take very limited action, when to take some action would restore safety. As far as a teacher's duty of care is concerned, an omission can be significant if there were to be a subsequent claim for negligence. Having said that, a teacher would not be expected to intervene to restore safety, at all costs, to the personal safety of the teacher concerned. It is a matter for professional judgement that may need to stand up to detailed analysis and justification at a later time.

In 1994, the DfEE provided specific guidance on the physical restraint and education of children with emotional and behavioural difficulties (EBD) contained in Circular 9/94 (DfEE 1994). Schools are required to have clear written policies on controls, restrictions and sanctions that can be used in dealing with EBD pupils and a positive approach is encouraged where intervention by teachers is based upon reward rather than punishment.

There is an acknowledgement in the circular, however, that difficulties in relation to EBD pupils are likely to be more severe and occur more frequently than with other children. Circular 9/94 advises:

> Physical contact and restraint should never be used in anger, and teachers should seek to avoid any injury to the child. They are not expected to restrain a child if by doing so they will put themselves at risk. Brief periods of withdrawal away from the point of conflict into a calmer environment may be more effective for an agitated child than holding or physical restraint. Parents with children in special schools should be told how restraint is being exercised. Children who require complex or repeated physical management should have a prescribed, written handling policy. Staff dealing with them should be trained in proper and safe methods of restraint.

> (DfEE 1994: 37, 38)

Section 550A of the Education Act 1996 applies equally to EBD children.

The NUT recommends that all incidents of restraint should be logged in a record book provided for that purpose and regularly monitored by a senior member of staff. The record should be contemporaneous and sufficiently detailed to help in any later investigation or complaint. It is advisable to inform parents/carers of any recorded incident. Since September 1998, all schools are required to have a behaviour policy which may well include guidance on the use of physical restraint involving touching, pushing, pulling and holding. Teachers will need to be made familiar with the school's policy and ensure they act within its terms at all times.

Training in methods of restraint may be considered appropriate for some staff and for certain types of school; however, the training provided should be appropriate and suitable people should be involved in its provision. A few years ago a residential special school that had encountered a number of students, mainly adolescent boys, exhibiting aggressive and challenging behaviour, brought in some prison officers on a training day to give instruction in physical restraint. The whole staff, teaching and support, received the training. Afterwards the incidence of restraint increased dramatically and the injuries to students also gave cause for concern. Physical restraint and punishment almost became synonymous in the school and it is not surprising that shortly after an LA inquiry into the school and its climate of indiscipline, it was recommended for closure.

The Special Educational Needs and Disability Act 2001

In its advice to beginning teachers (NUT 2004), the NUT summarises the provisions of this Act (DfES 2001a), concentrating on the *Special Educational Needs Code of Practice* (DfES 2001b). It suggests that relevant teachers, in consultation with the Special Educational Needs Coordinator (SENCo), should devise interventions, additional or different to those provided by the school's usual curriculum. The Code of Practice established two straightforward levels of intervention: school action and school action plus. Only the latter category requires agencies from outside the school. The purpose of the legislation was to streamline the provision of education for children with special needs, and the parents/carers of those children. Time will tell how successful this has been.

The Health and Safety at Work Act 1974

The Health and Safety at Work Act 1974 (HM Government 1974) is one of the major pieces of legislation of the 1970s. It was and still is 'enabling legislation' and, since the onset of more and more Directives from Europe, the whole health and safety arena has become more and more crowded with regulation, codes of practice and written recording of such matters as substances that are hazardous to health, dangerous occurrences and risk assessments. It would be impossible for teachers to be familiar with everything connected with the Act; it is far too extensive a field. However, certain elements of the legislation are very important for teachers, particularly Sections 7 and 8 of the Act. The main responsibility under the 1974 Act rests with the employer, who has to take reasonable care for the health and safety of employees and others who are on their premises. This includes not only the children, teachers and support staff, but also parents/carers and other visitors to the school, in particular, those making deliveries.

However, all employees have a duty under the Act to take reasonable care for the health and safety of themselves and others who may be affected by their acts or omissions at work. Consequently, teachers have a duty to take reasonable care of their own and their pupils' health and safety at school. The law also requires employees to act in a cooperative manner with respect to any guidance provided by the employer to assist in maintaining a safe working environment. For teachers, this means following carefully school-based or LA guidance on policy and procedure, and ensuring they are familiar with such practices. It means, in practice, that teachers should act with reasonable care at all times and apply good sense to everything they do, including not taking any unnecessary risks or doing anything that is potentially dangerous to themselves, the children and parents/carers who may be helping out either in school or on out-of-school activities. There is a duty on all employees to report any hazards and potentially dangerous incidents at work; teachers should make themselves familiar with the reporting and recording system in their school (e.g. the accident report book). There may also be a need to report certain types of accident to the Health and Safety Executive for possible investigation, consideration of prosecution and recommendations to be implemented to avoid a similar occurrence. Occupational injuries should also be reported to the local Benefits Office; delay in reporting such injuries could result in any benefits being lost in the short and long term. To facilitate all this, each school should have a trained and well-informed health and safety representative. The unions do encourage members to take on such a role, and provide comprehensive training in the rights and responsibilities associated with such a role. However, the unions discourage members becoming health and safety officers as, under the Act, such individuals are much more liable legally for their acts and omissions; representatives are not liable for the things they do or do not do as representatives.

Health and safety representatives' responsibilities are towards the trade union members they represent only and their job is to ensure that information is made available, accidents and the aftermath are properly recorded and acted upon, investigations are carried out, where appropriate, and inspections of the premises are undertaken on a regular basis (at least once a term in school time). It is important for health and safety representatives to encourage everyone to report even what might seem to be a minor matter that may simply require cleaning up, or a small inexpensive repair. Seemingly minor matters can cause serious accidents. The most frequently recorded accidents in schools involve slipping, tripping and falling – usually because of a patch of wet or because rubbish on the floor has not been cleared away. Teachers themselves can contribute to their own accidents; the most common problem tends to be piling up furniture, attempting to mount displays or to change broken light bulbs on wobbly chairs or wobbly tables. The first questions anyone investigating such accidents will ask are why did the teacher not use proper equipment and, with respect to the light bulb, why, when it is not their responsibility, was a teacher changing a light bulb in the first place?

Teachers who undertake particular specialist activities, such as the instruction or teaching of swimming, trampolining, canoeing and rock climbing, are required to hold particular qualifications. There may also be a requirement within the qualification to update regularly the skills required in order to continue teaching and supervising the activity. Should there be any doubt about the need for an extra qualification or the need for updating, teachers should not take on the activity until the appropriate professional body or association concerned has been consulted. The health, safety and welfare of children in the care of teachers are a fundamental requirement. Parents/carers entrust their children to the schools and to teachers in particular; they do not expect children to come to any harm there.

Satisfying the duty of care absolves teachers from legal liability. However, sometimes accidents occur as a result of the fault of someone with no organising or supervising responsibility for the activity: for example, the bus company used for the trip. Should an accident occur where pupils and/or teachers sustain injury as a result of some defect in the vehicle, the bus company would of course be liable.

Some accidents are pure accidents, not reasonably foreseen and not the result of negligence on anyone's part, if no one is responsible then there can be no liability. Consequently, liability goes with fault. In the case of a pure accident no one bears liability. Schools and LAs will be covered in this eventuality by 'no-fault insurance'. Some LAs act as loss adjusters for their own insurance procedures and settlement of a particular claim does not carry with it a notion of liability on the part of the LA as employer. Recently an Appeal Court judge, deliberating on a case for damages following an accident, said something quite profound given the type of 'blame culture' we now encounter relentlessly in society. She said, 'Sometimes, some things happen that are, quite simply, nobody's fault.' We would all do well to heed these words of wisdom before rushing to the law to attempt to apportion blame.

Equality and equal opportunities

Sex, 'race' and disability discrimination

Under the Sex Discrimination Act 1975 (HM Government 1975) and the Race Relations Act 1976 (HM Government 1976), it is unlawful to discriminate against a person on grounds of sex or marital status, or on racial grounds. The latter includes 'race', colour, nationality, citizenship, ethnic or national origins. It is unlawful to discriminate against a person directly or indirectly.

Direct discrimination

Direct discrimination is where, in similar circumstances, a person is treated less favourably, because of his or her 'race' or sex than the way in which another person of the opposite sex or different 'race' would be treated. Direct discrimination takes many forms. In the treatment of pupils and students, for example, it may vary from crude remarks to subtle differences in assessment, expectation, provision and treatment. It may be unconscious or even well meaning; however, it is still unlawful. Racial or sexual harassment is also a form of direct discrimination. Rights exist on 'race' and sex discrimination when candidates apply for posts and during the interview and other selection processes. This means that short-listing and questions at interview must not contravene the legislation. The woman candidate who was asked at interview for the Head of Technology Department how she would deal with all the reactionary men who currently worked in the department suffered an incidence of sex discrimination on two counts: first, the terms of the question itself and second, the woman claimed that the question was discriminatory and sexist because the same question could not be put to a man and because it challenged her as a woman, rather than as a professional. She was the only candidate who was asked the question, as all the other candidates were men (NUT 1991a: 25).

Indirect discrimination

Indirect discrimination is more complex. It occurs when a requirement or condition, although applied equally, is such that a considerably smaller proportion of a particular racial group or sex can comply with it and when this cannot be objectively justified. The phrase 'objectively justifiable' means in an educational context that the condition or requirement cannot be justifiable on educational or other grounds. It has to be a question of examining the facts and the reason for the objective justification put forward in each and every case. An example of this is a case that reached the House of Lords (*Mandla and Mandla v Lee and Park Grove Private School Limited* (1983) *Industrial Relations Law Reports* 109 HL) and involved the requirement to wear a cap as part of a school uniform. Although applied equally to all pupils, it had the effect of excluding Sikh boys who are required by their religion to wear a turban and this was not justifiable on educational grounds and, therefore, constituted unlawful indirect racial discrimination.

In schools, discrimination is specifically unlawful with respect to the terms of admission. Schools must not refuse to admit pupils or to employ staff on grounds of 'race' or sex. In addition, any arrangement that does not afford pupils equal access to benefits, facilities or services is also unlawful. Finally, it is against the law to exclude pupils from school or to subject them to any other detriment on grounds of sex or 'race'. The law makes an exception for single-sex schools although in doing so, it stipulates that the facilities available should be no less favourable than those in any other school in a given LA.

The Commission for Racial Equality and the Equal Opportunities Commission have both issued Codes of Practice on the elimination of discrimination, and organisations such as the NUT publish, from time to time, pamphlets and research findings on a variety of equal opportunities issues (see, for example, NUT 1988, 1989a, b, c, 1991a, b, 1992, 1995, 2002). Any complaints against schools or LAs concerning discrimination can be made to the Secretary of State for Education and Skills or, if a legal redress is sought, one can go to the county court. Complaints by employees or potential employees can be brought, without any need for a qualifying period, to Employment Tribunals in cases that relate to sex and race discrimination.

The Race Relations (Amendment) Act 2000

Following the Stephen Lawrence Inquiry, the Race Relations Act 1976 was amended to assist public authorities in promoting race equality in all aspects of their work. The Commission for Race Equality (CRE) sent to all schools a guide to the Act and *Race Equality Standards (Learning for All)* (Commission for Racial Equality 2000) providing advice on how schools are able to meet their statutory duties.

The General Duty section of the Act (Home Office 2000) has three parts:

- eliminate unlawful racial discrimination;
- promote equality of opportunity;
- promote good relations between people from different racial backgrounds.

In relation to schools this means that policies and statements covering admissions, assessments, raising attainment levels, curriculum matters, discipline, guidance and support, and staff selection and recruitment, should all have elements which address the three parts of the General Duty. Schools have to bear in mind that the size of the minority ethnic population does not matter; racial equality is important even when there are no minority ethnic pupils or staff in a school or local community.

Schools must have a written statement of policy for promoting 'race' equality and arrangements for assessing the impact of policies on pupils, staff and parents/carers, and a system of monitoring the operation of the policies paying particular attention to the levels of attainment of pupils from minority ethnic groups. The Race Equality Policy must be a clearly identifiable and easily available part of the school's policy on equal opportunities or its policy on inclusion; there should also be a clear link between the policy and the school's action plan or the School Improvement Plan. All racist incidents, whoever perceives them to be racist, irrespective of whether they are on the receiving end, must be investigated and reported to the governing body every school term.

Such policies and planning should become an integral part of the development of the school and its existing decision-making processes; the governing body, therefore, plays a vital role in ensuring that the school meets its statutory duties in relation to promoting racial equality. Parents/carers, pupils and staff need to know what the policy says and what it means for them. The questions that schools need to ask on this legislation would include:

Does the school help all its pupils to achieve as much as they can and do pupils gain the most from what is on offer?

Which groups of pupils are underachieving and what are the reasons for this?

Are the policies of the school having a positive impact on pupils, parents/carers and staff from different racial groups?

How are differences explained and justified? Are there explanations and justifications that have a basis in non-racial grounds like difficulties in the English language?

Are the aims of each policy addressing the different needs of different groups? Do these aims lead to action on specific points like extra tuition or preventative measures to obviate racist incidents?

Does the school prepare pupils for living in a multicultural society, promoting racial equality and harmony, and preventing and dealing with racism?

In attempting to address these questions the school will at least begin the process of complying with the General Duty contained within the Act. More importantly, the school and the community it serves will be laying down guiding principles which will hopefully become the firm foundations for a more tolerant and fair society committed to equal opportunities for all.

The Disability Discrimination Act 1995

The Disability Discrimination Act (DDA) (HM Government 1995), introduced in 1995, addresses discrimination in employment and in the provision of goods and services. It abolishes the employment quota of 3 per cent for disabled people established under the Disabled Persons (Employment) Act 1944 (HM Government 1944). This quota system, whereby employers had to employ a minimum percentage of registered disabled people, was introduced towards the end of the World War II when many service men and women were returning to the labour market and some had suffered disabling injuries during wartime service. The 1995 Act covers temporary and part-time staff as well as permanent and full-time staff.

Section 5 sub-section 1 of the Act states that:

an employer discriminates against a disabled person if, for any reason relating to their disability, the employer treats them less favourably than he treats or would treat others not having the disability and he cannot show that the treatment is justified.

(DDA 1995, cited in TUC 1996: 2)

Teachers need to be aware of this not only in relation to disabled pupils in their care and in the interests of fostering greater awareness on the part of all the children about the needs, perceptions and feelings of disabled people, but also in relation to the employment of disabled young people when they leave school and enter the world of work.

Moreover, schools need to be regarded as places of work for disabled people (both children and adults) and the 'reasonable adjustments' section of the legislation is particularly relevant in this regard. Employers have a duty to make such reasonable adjustments to the workplace, work equipment or organisation of work where disabled employees or applicants need them because of their disability. Victimisation is also unlawful under the Act and employers must not take action against any person (disabled or not) who uses the provisions of the Act or appears as a witness at a tribunal hearing or gives evidence during an internal hearing.

A disability is defined as 'a physical or mental impairment that has a substantial and long term adverse effect on the ability to carry out normal day-to-day activities' (DDA 1995, cited in TUC 1996: 3). An impairment is one that has existed for 12 months or more, can reasonably be expected to last 12 months or more, or can reasonably be expected to last for the rest of a person's life. The impairment can be related to mobility, manual dexterity, physical coordination, continence, and the ability to lift, carry or move everyday objects. It can also be connected to speech, hearing or eyesight, memory, ability to concentrate, learn or understand. Some impairments will need medication or specific equipment. People with a learning or mental disability are covered by the DDA particularly when there is a substantial or long-term effect on the ability to carry out normal day-to-day activities.

The Act does not apply to employers with fewer than 20 employees, so the only schools which are not covered by the provisions are very small Church schools or very small Foundation Schools where the governing body is the employer and the total number of employees who work at the school is less than 20.

Employment discrimination under the terms of the Act takes place when an employer treats a disabled person less favourably than others for a reason that relates to the disability of the disabled person. If the reason for less favourable treatment was not related to the disability, then that would prevent a claim being pursued. However, the reason does not have to be the disability itself; if it is related to the person's disability, it is discrimination. For example, refusing to appoint a teacher with a facial disfigurement, not because of the disfigurement, but because it is claimed children might be frightened or upset, would still count as discriminatory.

Probably the most controversial area in the definition of discrimination is the part that deals with justifiable discrimination. This is when an employer is able to argue within employment tribunal (ET) proceedings that it was necessary to take some form of action against a member of staff, albeit discriminatory, because to take no action may have been even worse. For example, it has been held in an ET that an employer who dismissed a teacher because she suffered from bipolar disorder did act in a discriminatory manner but the discrimination was justifiable because of the potential consequences for children in the care of that teacher. The TUC is extremely unhappy about this concept and believes such discrimination can never be justified. As case law develops on this point and others, it may become clearer how this part of the legislation is interpreted by ETs. It is for the unions to enter into negotiation with employers to establish agreements on good equal opportunities policies, procedures and practices which will need to highlight sufficient safeguards against employers who use this part of the legislation to abrogate their responsibilities. The TUC, for example, is encouraging unions to negotiate agreements on disability leave to avoid a disabled employee having to use sick leave provisions. Sometimes it may be possible for a disabled employee to work from home for the day if driving into work causes a problem from time to time and this is just the type of circumstance covered by disability leave agreements.

The Act applies to disabled applicants for jobs as well as to disabled employees. So the recruitment practices of governing bodies must be in keeping with the legislation. The selection of the best candidate must be based on an objective assessment of the candidate's ability to do the job and in many, if not all, cases the disability of any candidate will be irrelevant unless, of course, the 'reasonable adjustments' section of the legislation is relevant. Indeed this may only become applicable when an employer takes on an employee who is disabled in some way or an existing employee reports an impairment that has lasted 12 months or is expected to last 12 months or longer. Examples that are given about reasonable adjustments include:

making alterations to premises	providing training
reallocation of work	modifying or acquiring equipment
transfer to another job or site	or providing special instruction manuals
changing a disabled person's working hours	providing a reader or interpreter
permitting reasonable absence from work for rehabilitation assessment or treatment	providing a disabled person with supervision and guidance in fulfilling the requirements of the job

All these examples cover all employment, not just teaching.

The DDA is enforced by the employer's grievance procedure, and the employment tribunal system. Cases are beginning to be reported where disabled employees have successfully won several thousands of pounds in compensation, when tribunals have accepted that discrimination has occurred in terms of the provisions of the DDA. Much of the legislation is subject to interpretation, so teachers will need to seek advice and support in pursuing claims under the Act and will undoubtedly look to the unions for assistance with this as they do with other issues that relate to employment, conditions of service, educational and professional matters.

The Human Rights Act 1998

All workers in the UK have been covered by the Human Rights Act 1998 (HM Government 1998) with the incorporation into domestic legislation of the European Convention on Human Rights (ECHR). This Convention and the legislation will develop over time so that account can be taken of case law precedents and the way societies across the European Community change and evolve; those who wrote the Convention were keen for it to become 'a living instrument' which would act as a benchmark for making judgements about human rights issues. This would cover a wider range of discrimination issues than we have been used to in UK legislation and that is why it has been added to the list of legislation that beginning teachers should be familiar with and hopefully understand.

Part-time worker regulations

Since regulations were introduced covering part-time workers (October 2000), it has been unlawful to treat a part-time employee less favourably than a full-time employee. This has made a tremendous difference to the teaching profession which has a significant number of part-time teachers many of whom are women. It has forced the Review Body which makes recommendations on teachers' pay and conditions to look carefully at the way a part-time teacher's pay is calculated. It has also helped in terms of the amount of non-contact time part-time teachers are permitted when comparisons are drawn with full-time staff. Similarly, part-time staff employed on temporary, fixed term or variable hours contracts have been helped enormously by these regulations and almost overnight the type of abuses associated with such contracts have been eliminated. There is still a need for vigilance in this area of contract and employment law; however, the part-time worker regulations have made the policing of the abuses of different types of contracts for teachers a good deal easier.

Age discrimination

Since 1 October 2006 discrimination on grounds of age has been included in regulations similar to those covering gender, 'race' and disability. However, concern has been expressed about the concept of a default retirement age of 65 years. This would permit an employer to dismiss employees once they reach that age as long as particular procedures are carried out. This concept was challenged in December 2006 in the High Court by Age Concern and others. The decision of the High Court was to refer the case to the European Court of Justice because the basis of the claim brought by Age Concern was that the Government has failed to implement the European Directive (2000/78/EC) in breach of its obligations under European law. If the challenge is successful, forced retirement of teachers and other workers at age 65 may be deemed to be unlawful. So at the very outset of ground-breaking legislation on age discrimination, the Government has run into difficulties. The problem with the referral to the European Court of Justice is the length of time it will take for a decision to be reached, so this aspect of the law will need to be addressed in a further edition of this book.

Equality Act 2006 and equality issues for the future

The Equality Act 2006 has gained royal assent, and will eventually put expertise on equality, diversity and human rights all in one place. The Act establishes the Commission for Equality and Human Rights (CEHR) that will come into being on 31 October 2007. The CEHR will bring together the expertise and resources to promote equality and tackle discrimination in relation to gender, gender reassignment, disability, sexual orientation, religion or belief, age, 'race' and also promote human rights.

The Act also pushes the agenda forward, not only in establishing this new body but also banning discrimination in the provision of services on grounds of belief and sexuality. Hard on the heels of the Disability Equality Duty (DED), in force since 4 December 2006, comes the Gender Equality Duty (GED) which came into force on 6 April 2007. This requires all public bodies, including schools, to eliminate unlawful discrimination and harassment on grounds of sex and to promote equality of opportunity between men and women. This will have far reaching implications on school governors, head teachers, school staff and local authorities, particularly those working in governor support services. It will also apply to anyone affected by the Gender Recognition Act 2004 which covers those individuals who have undergone sex change surgery, those in the process of living as their acquired gender prior to surgery and those who intend living their acquired gender for the rest of their lives.

In time, it is to be hoped that there will be statutory duties on public bodies to eliminate discrimination in relation to sexual orientation, religious belief and age. This would entail, among other things, having 'Equality duties' for sexuality, belief and age. This is a challenging prospect for the future; however, it is one which the teaching profession, and society generally, needs to embrace in order to further genuine equality of opportunity for everyone.

Conclusion

Becoming professional is one thing; remaining professional is another. The days when the acquiring of a certificate to teach for life (or up to 40 years) are gone. The rate of change is so rapid and dramatic that the beginning teachers educated in the early part of the twenty-first century may not be equipped to function effectively well into the new millennium unless, and this is the important part for government to understand, time is made available and built into the system for serving teachers to be given the opportunity for extensive professional development, education and training. Examples of good practice are already up and running with courses like the 'Keeping In Touch with Teaching' schemes. These are normally run by LAs and are open to any teacher who wishes to return to the profession after a break in service, usually following absence for family reasons. There are also many successful returnees' courses that LAs and teacher education institutions organise.

There are also examples of the unions offering members not only training in matters that relate to union work but, increasingly, courses that assist in the continuing professional development of members. The NUT is at the forefront of this development, and the TUC is keen to encourage union members to become 'Union Learning Representatives' (ULRs), and to work alongside and within Learning and Skills Councils (LSCs); the role of the ULRs in the forum of LSCs will be to encourage union members to become more involved with life-long learning, taking control of their own educational needs and professional development. This is an area experienced teachers need to develop anyway because of the provisions of moving onto the Upper Pay Spine (UPS) and progression along it.

Perhaps, in the education service, in order to prepare adequately for the future, we might look back to the recommendations of the James Report, written almost 37 years ago (James of Rusholme 1970). This important analysis of teacher education and the needs of the profession suggested a regular system of sabbatical terms or years dependent upon length of service. For example, a teacher with seven years' experience could look forward to a year's sabbatical that could provide valuable time for retraining and battery recharging. Money spent on that rather than on the introduction of the 'advanced skills teacher' would target resources in a more constructive and supportive way for the teaching profession and bring to the education service a precise strategy to improve the overall performance of practitioners, ensure there was adequate time for professional thinking and development, and provide a substantial boost to morale, as well as making the teaching profession more attractive to potential recruits. While it may be true that 'everyone remembers a good teacher', a system must be devised whereby good teachers are not burnt out in a short timescale. The implementation of this recommendation of the James Report is long overdue.

Notes

1   At the present time, 'permanent' only becomes significant after an employee has worked for an employer for a continuous period of one year. For this reason, some full-time union officials use the term 'ongoing' rather than 'permanent'.

2   The James Bulger murder case, in which two ten-year-old boys were found guilty of murdering two-year-old James Bulger, opened up a debate that is still continuing into the concept of the age of criminal responsibility. The age of criminal responsibility is currently ten-years-old; however, courts will consider cases on their merits taking account of range of factors including the public interest.

References

Advisory, Conciliation and Arbitration Service (ACAS) (1998) *Code of Practice for Time Off for Trade Union Duties and Activities*. London: HMSO.

Children Act 1989, [http://www.hmso.gov.uk/acts/acts1989/ukpga_19890041_en_1.htm (accessed February 2005)]. London: HMSO.

Cole, M. (2005) 'New Labour, globalisation and social justice: the role of education', in P. McLaren, H. Sunker and G. Fischman (eds) *Critical Theories, Radical Pedagogies, and Global conflicts*. Lanham, Maryland: Rowman and Littlefield.

Cole, M. (2007) 'Neo-liberalism and Education: a Marxist critique of New Labour's Five Year Strategy for Education', in A. Green and G. Rikowski (eds) *Renewing Dialogues in Marxism and Education: Volume 1 – Openings*. Basingstoke: Palgrave Macmillan.

Commission for Racial Equality (2000) *Race Equality Standards (Learning for All)*. London: CRE.

Council of Local Education Authorities/Schoolteacher Committee (CLEA/ST) (1985) *Conditions of Service for Schoolteachers in England and Wales*, 2nd edn. (The 'Burgundy Book'). Revised edition 2000. London: Employers' Organisation for Local Government.

DES (1987) Teachers' Pay and Conditions Act. London: DES.

DfEE (1994) *Education of Children with Emotional and Behavioural Difficulties*, Circular 9/94. London: DfEE.

DfEE (1995) *Protecting Children from Abuse*. Circular 10/95. London: HMSO.

DfEE (1997) *Education Act 1996*. London: HMSO.

DfEE (1998) *Section 550A of the Education Act 1996. The Use of Force to Control or Restrain Pupils*. Circular 10/98. London: HMSO.

DfEE (2000) Sexual Offences (Amendment) Act. London: DfEE.

DfEE (2001a) Special Educational Needs and Disability Act. London: DfEE.

DfES (2001b) *Special Educational Needs Code of Practice*. London: DfES.

DfES (2004a) *Every Child Matters*. London: The Stationery Office.

DfES (2004b) *Schoolteachers' Pay and Conditions Document*. (The 'Blue Book'). London: HMSO.

DfES (2006) *Schoolteachers' Pay and Conditions Document* (The 'Blue Book'). London: HMSO.

Hatcher, R. (2005) 'The 14 Plus Youth Training Scheme', *Socialist Teacher* 72, Spring.

Hatcher, R. (2006a) 'Privatisation and Sponsorship: the re-agenting of the school system in England, *Journal of Educational Policy*, 21(5): 599–619.

Hatcher, R. (2006b) Academies, Building Schools for the Future and the 14–19 vocational agenda. Talk given at Anti-Academies Alliance conference, London, 25 November. Available at www.socialist-teacher.org.

HM Government (1944) Disabled Persons (Employment) Act. London: HMSO.

HM Government (1974) Health and Safety at Work Act. London: HMSO.

HM Government (1975) Sex Discrimination Act. London: HMSO.

HM Government (1976) Race Relations Act. London: HMSO.

HM Government (1987) *Statutory Instrument (schoolteachers pay and conditions)*. London: HMSO.

HM Government (1988) Education Reform Act. London: HMSO.

HM Government (1995) Disability Discrimination Act. London: HMSO.

HM Government (1998) Human Rights Act. London: HMSO.

HM Government (1998) Schools Standards and Framework Act. London: HMSO.

HM Government (2002) *A Time for Standards*. London: HMSO.

HM Government (2006) Equality Act. London: HMSO.

Home Office (2000) Race Relations (Amendment) Act. London: HMSO.

James of Rusholme, Lord (1970) *Report of a Committee of Enquiry into Teacher Education and Training*. (The James Report). London: HMSO.

Local Government Review (1963) *Lyes v Middlesex County Council* (1962) London: HMSO.

National Employers' Organisation for School Teachers (NEOST) (2004) Bulletin No 493 October.

National Union of Teachers (NUT) (1988) *Towards Equality for Boys and Girls: guidelines on countering sexism in schools*. London: NUT.

New Brunswick Teacher's Association (1995) 'Teacher's Contract 1923: Women in Education' in *New Brunswick Teacher's Association Newsletter*, March 1995.

NUT (1989a) *Job Sharing for Teachers: NUT guidelines*. London: NUT.

NUT (1989b) *Anti-racism in Education: guidelines towards a whole school policy*. London: NUT.

NUT (1989c) *Opening Doors: encouraging returners into teaching as a career*. London: NUT.

NUT (1991a) *Fair and Equal – Union Guidelines for Promoting Equal Opportunities in the Appointment and Promotion of Teachers*, 2nd Report. London: NUT.

NUT (1991b) *Lesbians and Gays in Schools: an issue for every teacher*. London: NUT.

NUT (1992) *Anti-racist Curriculum Guidelines*. London: NUT.

NUT (1995) *Research into the Issuing of Fixed-term and Temporary Contracts on a Full- or Part-time Basis with Particular Reference to Women*. London: NUT.

NUT (2002) *Relearning to Learn. Advice to teachers new to teaching children from refugee and asylum seeking families*. London: National Union of Teachers.

NUT (2004) *Education, the Law and You: the main points*. London: NUT.

Rikowski, G. (2005) *Silence of the Wolves*. Education Research Centre, University of Brighton Occasional Paper (Brighton: University of Brighton).

Training and Development Agency (TDA) (2002) *Handbook on Guidance on QTS Standards and ITT Requirements*. London: DfES.

Training and Development Agency (TDA) (2006) *Qualifying to Teach: professional standards for qualified teacher status and requirements for initial teacher training*. London: TDA. Available at http://www.tda.gov.uk/upload/resources/pdf/q/qualifying_to_teach.pdf (accessed 2 April 2007).

Trades Union Congress (TUC) (1996) *The Disability Discrimination Act, A TUC Guide*. London: TUC.

Communicating effectively

Richard Woolley

Q4 Communicate effectively with children, young people, colleagues, parents and carers.

Learning objectives

To encourage teachers to:

- include all children, carers and parents in the education process;
- reflect on their own values and attitudes and how these impact on effective communication;
- value diversity amongst children, young people, carers, parents and colleagues;
- develop sensitive and professional working relationships;
- consider how schools communicate messages in overt and other ways.

Introduction

TEACHERS RELATE TO a broad spectrum of people within their work. The range of people with a stake in a school is diverse and each has different interests, outlooks, backgrounds and concerns. Effective communication requires that teachers are aware of the individual needs and attitudes of different stakeholders and take these into account when fostering relationships.

This chapter explores communication with three broad groupings: children and young people; colleagues; and parents and carers. Whilst this list is by no means exhaustive, it encompasses a very wide spectrum of people with an interest in the running of a school and in its educational provision at a range of levels. It focuses on what is communicated, how this happens and the ways in which teachers need to be aware of the messages passed on by their communication, both explicitly and implicitly. It is important to note here that the chapter is particularly concerned with implicit communication: with how messages are conveyed through values and attitudes on a macro level. In this sense, it is concerned with the 'big picture' as well as with some practical aspects for work in the classroom.

In the education system there is a constant focus on standards that are measured by the achievement of attainment targets and results in national tests. Schools have been driven by the curriculum, rather than driving forward a curriculum that is relevant to the needs and context of the learners. The key question here is what this communicates to children, young people and those who care for them. This chapter explores how teachers can communicate the message that learning and individual progress are valuable in their own right to create classroom environments where the individuality of each learner is valued.

Children and young people

It may seem obvious that a school exists for its children and young people. Surely the primary purpose of the education system, and its constituent parts, is to nurture these people and to help to develop their learning and interests to the maximum?

A primary aim of the National Curriculum for England (DfEE/QCA 1999a, 1999b) is that all pupils should be enabled to learn and achieve. However, this is underpinned by the intention that all children should be prepared for their role in the workplace. This intention belies the hope that all will grow up to contribute to the economic well-being of the nation and thus contribute to its economic systems and prosperity. This raises important questions about why we educate: is it to promote economic productivity, or because learning is worthwhile in its own right? This idea will be explored in more detail in Chapter 5. However, it is important to note here, as Mike Cole did in the introductory chapter, that the education system does not promote equality for all, but rather claims to promote equality of opportunity: in this sense it claims to be meritocratic.

Meritocracy

As I have argued elsewhere (Woolley 2007) there are three main reasons for the rejection of meritocracy by those seeking to develop a fair and just society. First, without any redistribution of wealth, poverty will remain. Second, without an increase in the higher rates of taxation, the rich will not effectively help the poor; and in any case this fails to question why a system that makes some excessively rich and leaves some in poverty is allowed to continue. Third, the belief that a general increase in wealth will produce a trickle-down effect to benefit the poor does not work, and lacks moral integrity. There is an assumption that if each is rewarded according to the degree of function and service they offer to society, then those who work hardest and make a positive contribution to society will prosper. This is a fallacy, for some people work exceptionally hard for little reward. The same can be true in our classrooms. Some children work consistently hard and yet fail to meet the standards laid down by the Government. It is essential that teachers communicate the value of a learner's efforts and their value as people in order to foster self-esteem and a positive self-image. Teachers need to consider how children are put in positions where they have to compete with others, and where they are compared with others, and to consider the impact this has on their learning and motivation. A competitive learning environment is nothing less than capitalism in the classroom, and it ranks children with diverse backgrounds, interests, motivations and life chances – reinforcing a hierarchy that only exists because the teacher, the school and the education system choose to maintain it. This can communicate messages of failure that destroy learning opportunities and deny children and young people further access to the educational opportunities that they are entitled to enjoy because they become demoralised.

There is a further difficulty with the notion of meritocracy: the idea that social mobility is freely available to all does not take into account the different life chances experienced by each person. In addition, the benefits of a middle-class upbringing afford some individuals opportunities and resources denied to those living in relative poverty. To talk of escape routes from deprivation, and of working hard to rise above poverty, as some politicians do, is an anathema. Rather, the aim should be to eliminate poverty and deprivation. Meritocracy only offers shifting areas of inequality, underpinned by competition. However, freedom and equality imply each other, and are inextricably linked. Freedom cannot be for the few: for the rich and powerful to have choices and opportunities at the expense of others is not true freedom; it is oppression by one social class or grouping over another. Freedom can only come into being when it is equally available for all; one person cannot be free until all are free. Thus, equality is essential for freedom, and freedom for equality.

This argument may seem remote from the education system. However, it is at the very core of what education is all about. If we ask questions about why we educate and what education is for, we may consider that it is about developing people and supporting their learning to the maximum. We educate people because they have an innate potential to learn, experiment, discover and empathise. The reason why I am an educator is that I believe that we can educate so that our children and young people have the skills necessary to face life in this challenging and constantly changing world: they need to be literate (in many senses of the word) and numerate, but they also they need to be able to look at the world with a critical eye and to make sense of what they see around them in an informed, confident and empathetic way. This is not about pitting children against one another in a competitive system; it is about valuing diversity in a wide range of senses.

One reason why we educate is to help one another to develop our world views so that we can contribute positively to the world on a range of levels, so that we appreciate the myriad differences and similarities we see amongst those around us, and so that we can show respect for this world and its people in confident and informed ways. Our education system is based on two main principles: that all should be enabled to learn and to achieve, and that we should enable individuals to develop spiritually, morally, culturally and socially (DfEE/QCA 1999a, 1999b). I think that these two aims of the National Curriculum for England are laudable, but yet the National Curriculum makes it clear that a further purpose of education is to enable people to contribute productively to the economic well-being of society. There is a sub-text here: we educate you so that you can work and thus pay taxes; we educate you so that you can find your place in the workforce, and find your niche; we educate you so that you can make huge profits for capitalist big business.

My grandmother, who was privileged to access an elementary school education in the early part of the twentieth century, used to speak of 'knowing your place'. This is not a sentiment that I want our children to understand in the twenty-first century. I want a prior aim for the education system: to educate people because they are people, able to think and feel and sense and appreciate and celebrate. I want the teachers to communicate this message to their children and young people. I think that good quality education is worthwhile in its own right, it is about developing the individual person and about developing communities, it is not about economic productivity or competition. This is fundamental to what we communicate to our children and young people. We do not educate them to become a part of the economic process; we educate them because they are human beings with potential, sensibilities and emotions. We want them to feel this world, to appreciate its beauty and its pains, to see it with a critical eye and to work for the common good. I am not involved in education to equip some people to achieve at the expense of others in a competitive 'dog eat dog' environment; I am in education to value individuals as unique persons and to extend their learning to the maximum.

Valuing individuals

The Plowden Report (Central Advisory Council for Education 1967) emphasised the need to see children as individuals: 'Individual differences between children of the same age are so great that any class, however homogeneous it seems, must always be treated as a body of children needing individual and different attention'. This view necessitates that each child is seen as an individual with personal strengths, needs and interests. The system in place in the UK at the present time suggests that each person will find their niche or personal role within a system that is competitive. Within a meritocracy, acquisitiveness may remain the driving force behind ambition and even service to others. For example, if a company advertises that its policies and practices are ethical, it is seeking to attract customers sympathetic with its aims. In effect, it may prosper because of the values it espouses. The motive may be to promote ethical business practices, or it may be to attract custom by appealing to the altruistic tendencies of potential clients. Profit will thus be made either as a result of the degree of service offered to like-minded people, or by taking advantage of a niche in the market in which people are prepared to pay higher prices in order to remain true to their principles. I will choose a brand of chocolate because it is 'fairly traded' but what I do not do is to question whether the fair trade label has come as a result of a passion for valuing other human persons or the desire to attract me to spend my money. The same idea may be applied to cosmetic products developed without tests being carried out on animals, or to the current enthusiasm for organic foodstuffs. Similarly, we need to consider why we educate and what we value in education. I may claim to value all people equally, but my practice may suggest that I am really striving to achieve the expected results with my class. This is a difficult area when school managers are setting a results-focused agenda.

In the classroom, we need to consider how we create opportunities for *all* to learn and achieve according to their 'abilities', talents and interests. In an education system where testing and target-setting have a high importance it is possible for teachers to communicate messages about a child's achievement and attainment that demotivate and demoralise the child, albeit unintentionally. Key to successfully avoiding this scenario is the idea that the classroom should not be a competitive environment, but rather a place where each person develops knowledge, skills and understanding at a different pace with each achieving in different ways in different aspects of the curriculum. Our system should not be meritocratic, rewarding individuals on the basis of competitive achievement, it should value every person as just that: a person.

In my career as a primary school teacher, and a member of a senior management team, I have been involved in setting priorities and identifying children to 'boost' in order to meet the targets set by the local authority and the school. Ideologically this was impossible for me, as the suggestion was that the children with the 'potential' to achieve the required results in the end of Key Stage tests should receive additional teaching input, whilst those who were predicted not to achieve received no additional support. My own belief is that all children should receive the support that they need in order to learn and to achieve. This is a significant tension in the classroom, and it is important that teachers think through such issues so that they can maximise the learning of all pupils, no matter what the policy makers and statistics seem to demand.

This discussion of meritocracy raises the question of why we educate our children and young people, and how we communicate the role of education to them. Is the purpose of education to help them to find their place in the existing social order, or to enable them to question the social order, its presumptions, assumptions and limitations? If the first professional attribute is that we should have high expectations for those we seek to educate, working to help them learn to the maximum and establishing fair, trustful and supportive relationships with them (as was discussed in Chapter 1), we need to be aware of the messages that our educational establishments convey and of the ways in which education can control and subdue or give hope concerning what is reasonably attainable and desirable. The first professional attribute relates to all learners; it does not only refer to those with the perceived potential to meet national norms, and nor should it.

It is essential, therefore, to consider the nature of our schools:

- How are schools meritocratic?
- Do they reward the 'most able' (overtly or subtly) and, if so, how is ability identified and who sets the values by which to measure it?
- How are schools competitive and what is the impact of this on learning?
- Can it be just to reward some 'abilities', whilst others may be considered less valuable or go un-noticed?
- How do our schools infer to some children that they are not able to achieve or have less ability than others?

Common curriculum

The notion of a common curriculum and the introduction of a National Curriculum for England brought a stronger political influence on the content of schools' educational provision. Whilst there are compelling arguments for a common curriculum in all schools, particularly the ease of mobility between schools and equality of provision for all children, behind its introduction was the idea that all children should be prepared to fulfil their allotted role in society:

> School education prepares the child for adult life, the way in which the school helps him [sic] to develop his potential must also be related to his [sic] subsequent needs and responsibilities as an active member of our society.
>
> (DES 1981)

Whilst those subsequent needs and responsibilities are important, the inference is that the focus is on the needs of the capitalist society, rather than the potential and interests of the learner. The Plowden Report's focus on the needs of the child was replaced by a system with the curriculum at its heart. Child-centred education was replaced by curriculum-centred education (DES 1981). However, not everyone agreed: 'Education is about nurturing the moral, aesthetic and creative aspects in children's development, not about "getting the country somewhere" ' (Sylva 1987).

In fact, in the 20 years following publication of the Plowden Report, almost every document on the primary curriculum contained echoes of Plowden to a greater or lesser extent. *A Framework for the School Curriculum* (DES 1980a), for example, stressed the need 'to help pupils to develop lively, enquiring minds, the ability to question and argue rationally'. *A View of the Curriculum* (DES 1980b) talked of 'individual differences and common needs' and The Swann Report (DES 1985) asked for 'a powerful commitment to see children as individuals'. These reports and consultations in the 1980s signalled a resurgence of the values espoused by Plowden, yet they also fought against the dominant culture within the political establishment of the time.

In the present day, I suggest that more pressing questions come to the fore in terms of valuing children and young people, their views and their capabilities. Are schools democratic? And to what extent are the voices of stakeholders heard and valued? Who speaks most in lessons: the learners or the teacher? Are opportunities for children to be involved open and transparent or stage-managed so that an 'appropriate' and intended outcome is achieved? What are the values embedded in the hidden curriculum and how are these questioned or challenged? What does all this communicate to the learners?

The rejection of the Plowden values started under the Labour government of James Callaghan in the mid-1970s. It accelerated under the government of Margaret Thatcher from 1979 onwards. She transformed the education system and introduced market forces, significantly through the Education Reform Act of 1988. This legislation effectively established a marketplace in which schools had to compete for pupils; the introduction of testing and league tables meant that teachers came under pressure to achieve results that ensured that their school was attractive to parents and carers; and head teachers started on the road to becoming business managers with a budget devolved under the Local Management of Schools.

Regrettably, Blair's New Labour continued to embrace this approach to education with even more tests, targets and divisive elitism. It also sought to control not just what teachers taught but how they taught it. The Literacy Hour and Numeracy Lesson in primary schools spelled out in detail exactly how children were to be taught literacy and numeracy. Such initiatives increased direct political influence on the school curriculum. The introduction of the National Literacy Strategy placed thousands of primary-aged children on the carpet for half an hour each morning for text, word and sentence level activities, moving on according to rigid timings. As a class teacher at the time of its introduction I do have a sense that my own classroom practice was challenged and developed; I certainly began to teach more specific skills and subject content in a more highly structured manner. I think that I taught in a more focused way and was more aware of the objectives for each lesson. At the same time, opportunities for flexibility and creative learning tailored to the specific needs and interests of the children were stifled. Thankfully, more recent moves have been towards greater participation in lessons with the increasing use of individual wipe boards and the use of discussion partners so that each child is encouraged to contribute as often as possible. Literacy and numeracy are developing in more flexible and creative ways in schools, and this is to be welcomed. The publication of *Excellence and Enjoyment: a strategy for primary schools* (2003) has given teachers powerful messages about reclaiming the curriculum and redeveloping creative and imaginative approaches to its delivery. In addition, discussions about dialogic teaching have moved the focus further away from teacher-direction towards extended questioning both of and by the children (Alexander 2006). Such moves have encouraged participation and child-centred activities. Furthermore, the review of the curriculum for secondary schools by the Qualifications and Curriculum Authority (QCA) aims to create a more flexible curriculum which can be designed at a local level within a national framework from September 2008. The intention is to develop the motivation and interest of learners at Key Stages 3 and 4 through a thematic approach, promoting independent learning and research, with learning blended to include class-based and out-of-school opportunities (Nightingale 2007, Lepkowska 2007, Dunford 2007). All this suggests that the influence and principles of Plowden are still alive and well, and would appear to be on the ascendant across the education system.

Rewarding learning

A key question that challenges us as educators is: do children and young people experience the classroom as a giant Skinner box (1968) where they learn to make the required responses in order to gain rewards and what does this communicate to them as learners? Whether the teacher offers house points, stars, extra privileges, certificates or some other extrinsic (external) motivator, the messages communicated can be that providing the expected response results in a reward. This undermines the message that learning is intrinsically worthwhile. Whilst pupils do enjoy receiving external rewards, they do not tend to lead to a learning culture (Lepper and Hodell 1989). Do the messages communicated by teacher responses lead to children understanding that learning is about gaining a reward, or do they communicate the message that learning is an end and a worthwhile achievement in itself? In our current imperfect education system I do not wish to argue against reward systems *per se* (Woolley and Johnston 2007), as they have a place in encouraging learning and promoting positive behaviour. However, teachers need to question whether their approach to them results in an environment in which the teacher exercises firm control, dictates the content and pace of learning, and allows little opportunity for the children's interests and knowledge to be shared. A fundamental question is: do we reward learning, or is learning rewarding? Do rewards stifle creativity by communicating to children that there is a 'right' answer that gains the reward? Such an approach can be demoralising or demotivating for learners as they come to understand the limiting expectations being communicated by the teacher. It is also meritocratic.

The role of schools

The Plowden Report was clear on the role of the school:

> One of the main educational tasks of the primary school, [and I would argue schools in general], is to build on and strengthen children's intrinsic interest in learning and lead them to learn for themselves rather than from fear of disapproval or desire for praise.
>
> (Central Advisory Council for Education 1967)

The report's recurring themes are individual learning, flexibility in the curriculum, the importance of play in children's learning, the use of the environment, learning by discovery and the importance of the evaluation of children's progress. This means that teachers should not assume that only what is measurable is valuable. Whilst this has not been the assumption of teachers over many years, the education system has tried to propagate this message.

The National Curriculum has taken many schools away from this vision for the past two decades. There is a constant focus on standards that are measured by the achievement of attainment targets and results in national tests. Schools have been driven by the curriculum, rather than driving forward a curriculum that is relevant to the needs and contexts of the learners. The key question here is what this communicates to children, young people and those who care for them. Having experienced the disappointment of children who achieved levels 3 or 4 in the end of Key Stage 2 tests in English (when they were hoping to achieve levels 4 or 5) the great strides made in their learning were undermined by a result arising from a test on one day, undertaken in examination conditions, and which involved producing a piece of work unrelated to their interests or experiences. This does not communicate the message that learning and individual progress are valuable in their own right, but rather that hard work results in failure: to experience this at the ages of ten or eleven years is crushing and communicates messages that stifle creativity and motivation. Such issues apply across the education system. The test result diminishes any sense of achievement that has been provided by careful and accurate teacher assessments, developed over time with a detailed knowledge of the learner's real capabilities.

Colleagues

Teachers are a diverse group. We vary in gender, ethnicity and socio-economic background, we have had different life chances and came into the profession for a range of reasons. We have different philosophies of education; we come from different cultural and family backgrounds; we are straight, gay, lesbian, bisexual, transgender and curious; many of us have impairments and disabilities. We are as diverse as any profession (although such differences are not always apparent).

Working with specific colleagues from within and outside the school is discussed later in detail by Malini Mistry and Krishnan Sood in Chapter 6. What is important here is to consider general issues that support effective communication between colleagues.

Communicating with colleagues

The first issue that we need to address is that of being open to the ideas of others. Teachers tend to be a group of individuals with specific values, attitudes and beliefs. We each have a developing philosophy of education that underpins our professional practice.

My own early professional practice was shaped significantly by several key people over a period of time: my parents, whose involvement in issues of social care was highly significant; my Year 6 teacher, who was a remarkably charismatic, caring and inspirational person; my Year 7 teacher, who was an engaging, encouraging and humorous person; two tutors at college (whose practice still informs my own educational methods); and my final school practice teacher, who helped me to put my values into context and helped me to develop my career path. We all have people, positive and less positive, who have shaped our views of the education system and its importance. This is an important part of our formation as teachers, and we need to acknowledge their impact upon our work.

Within this outlook, we need to develop respect for the social, cultural and economic backgrounds of colleagues. Unless we model the values that we espouse in the classroom in all our professional relationships, we will fail to provide an effective education for our children and young people that maintains a sense of integrity. My own personal approach to colleagues is not to make assumptions about who they are, what they believe, what they value or how they live. Such concerns are often beyond the boundaries of our professional relationships. In my work in school I knew that Mark lived with his boyfriend in the local town, that Helen had issues with gambling, that Cathy's marriage was faltering and that Stevie was finding it hard to make ends meet and felt pressured by the 'middle class' culture in school. Jake was always 'forgetful' about contributing to the tea fund, yet I knew it was because he was struggling to pay his mortgage. However, such knowledge is a privilege and not a right, and did not make any difference to my judgement of their capabilities as colleagues.

How we communicate with colleagues is important. We need to respect the tried and tested experience of some colleagues, whilst also appreciating the new and innovative ideas brought by others. We should not perpetuate heterosexist attitudes by assuming that everyone is straight or married; and we should not ask awkward questions about these areas. There are plenty of reasons for being single, unmarried or celibate in the present day. What we require are positive relationships based on professional values.

Valuing teamwork and working collaboratively

In the current school climate there are many opportunities to work with colleagues. A significant and important opportunity is working with teaching assistants, who have a wealth of knowledge about specific children and an understanding of a wide range of strategies to support their learning. I find that I hear them referred to as 'classroom helpers' less frequently in recent years, which I find hugely encouraging. In many instances they are exceptionally capable colleagues with a wide range of skills, talents and interests to offer to a school; they are fellow professionals and play an essential part in the learning process.

Key to developing effective relationships with teaching assistants (TAs) is the need to develop effective lines of communication. It is essential to share planning and to do this in sufficient time to ensure that they can adapt it to fit the needs of their groups and to allow them to identify or prepare resources. There is also the need for them to communicate to you the children's achievements. I have seen some very effective assessment formats, with sections for comments by TAs. I have also used notebooks, where comments about the particular needs and achievements of children with specific needs could be recorded on an ongoing basis. These were particularly useful in review meetings with parents and carers and when reviewing individual education plans (IEPs). There can be an element of dialogue in such books – with the TA recording their observations and the teacher also contributing, so that a dialogue is developed.

Further reading and examples of effective practice of work with teaching assistants can be found in Chapter 6 of this book and in Balshaw and Farrell (2002), Kay (2002), Kerry, (2001) and Lee (2002). An effective guide for teaching assistants which also raises pertinent issues for teachers and those in teacher education is Watkinson (2002). The role of teaching assistants is crucial and must not be underestimated.

Asking for help and valuing others' experience

Valuing the experience of colleagues is a very important part of developing effective communication. In your school there will be colleagues who have faced what you are experiencing at the present time. If you approach your challenges in a professional manner they will be willing to share their experience and to support you. All of us have been newly qualified at some point, have faced challenging classes, and some colleagues may have worked with the children that are currently in your care. All these factors are important.

In addition, we have a range of Subject Leaders or Heads of Department to consult, who have particular interests or responsibilities in specific areas of the curriculum. Whilst circumstances do not always allow us to lead the subject that we are most passionate about (I have taken on responsibility for PE with more enthusiasm than competence), these colleagues are able to help you to identify where support is available and are frequently able to find things out. Being able to discuss curriculum and learning issues is a valuable opportunity in itself, and in my experience, colleagues are pleased that you are showing an interest in their subject area. In addition, the *Leading from the Middle* training that is available at the present time means that more teachers are becoming middle managers with an interest in leading and developing the curriculum. This training from the *National College for School Leadership* provides the opportunity for groups of staff to work with a learning coach in their school in order to develop the skills necessary to manage change. It promotes teamwork and the development of self-confidence and helps teachers to understand their role in leading teaching and learning.

A further opportunity for collaboration comes through team teaching and planning with colleagues. This provides an excellent opportunity to share ideas and practice, to engage in dialogue about effective methods and approaches and also provides a chance to interact with a peer rather than teaching in isolation. The opportunity to discuss the effectiveness of a lesson without being in a formal appraisal situation, to play to each other's strengths and to bounce ideas off one another (whether in the planning situation or during a lesson itself) can help to bring support and encouragement, so long as it is approached in a positive manner within the context of a willingness to learn (Asprey *et al.* 2002, Montgomery 2002).

There are others with expertise on which you can draw in school. Some parents and carers will have significant skills, often drawn from their working lives and other interests, that will be of help if you feel able to make contact. Whilst you will remain the education professional, with legal responsibility for the safety of the children and young people, you can draw upon significant expertise and enhance the learning opportunities available for the pupils. Similarly, there will be people in your local community who have interests, expertise and skills that are of significant value to your children and young people. Representatives from sporting clubs, religious leaders, trade unionists, community and local government representatives and members of the business community are just some of the people who may be interested in engaging with the learning that you are seeking to promote. Initiatives such as the Community Service Volunteer programme to encourage retired members of the community to become reading partners with children in school (Docking 1990) provide highly valuable support. The key is to find people who are enthusiastic and passionate about what they do – and then to give them the opportunity to work with your classes; your classes also need the opportunity to question and learn from these people in a supportive and caring environment, so that all involved can develop their learning.

Carers and parents

Successful and effective home–school relationships are essential to the learning process: 'A successful home–school relationship can be a key element in making a school stronger and more effective. In particular, it can make a real difference for groups of underachieving pupils and their families' (Teachernet).

However, it is important to remember that such relationships are based on trust, mutual respect and a value for the diverse society in which we live, for: 'Parents/carers are often seen as a homogenous group, devoid of class, culture, sexuality and diversity' (Hurley 2005: 78).

Effective communication

Effective communication ensures that parents and carers are fully informed about the progress that their children are making:

> Parents [and carers] deserve and need to know about how well their children are doing in school and they need to be informed about any learning difficulties their child may have. They are entitled, also, to learn if their children have strengths and exceptional talents.
>
> (Jacques 2003: 195)

There is a need to feedback honestly and it is not always easy to share difficult messages. However, all parents and carers have a right to know how their children are progressing in school, and of any specific needs and provision. It is important to be sympathetic and empathetic when relating to carers and parents:

> You need to recognise that the school is a world in which some parents (and carers) have failed and they fear that their children may fail also. School is a world where some parents (and carers) have not felt welcome in the past. It is a world where some parents (and carers) do not have the self-esteem to feel able to talk to teachers.
>
> (Jacques 2003: 195–6)

In past decades the school was a place where carers and parents did not go unless invited. Today, many schools have an open door policy and welcome visits by carers and parents. This is a positive move, but on occasion there will be difficult personalities with which to deal.

I remember working with Jayne's mother who always came into school with 'all guns blazing' telling me that we were failing to cater for her daughter's needs. Gradually I began to realise that her accusations were not levelled at the school, but were the result of feeling isolated and frustrated as the sole carer for her child. She had no one else with whom to share her frustrations. At the other extreme, Samuel's father would come into school and threaten legal proceedings, but once he had calmed down and 'taken stock' he was very happy to discuss the behaviour policy and the strategies we used to support his son. He was very frustrated by his family situation, and extremely pressured at work. The teachers in school were the only people open and available to listen, and so they often 'took the flack'. I cannot say that any of this was easy, but once we understood the family situations, and the ways in which the parents/carers reacted, it became more possible to deal with some situations.

Effective communication can often take a great deal of hard work and patience; relationships are nurtured over time, they do not exist as of right:

> It is essential that the diversity of desires and interests among parents be recognised, as such recognition provides the basis for the dialogue which can then lead to consensus. In such a manner, it is possible to develop an integrated and systematic approach to parental involvement at the level of the school. And from such a perspective, a clear shift can be elicited from a request situation – in which parents are occasionally called upon to lend a helping hand and schools occasionally help parents at home – to an interaction situation – in which teachers, parents, (carers) and schools exchange ideas as equals with regard to the education and development of children and pupils.
>
> (Dreissen et al. 2005: 239)

It is important to note that these ideas relate equally to parents *and* carers, and to ensure that carers are not neglected or omitted when considering such issues.

Reports and reviews

Teachers communicate with parents/carers formally through reports and reviews. It is important to remember that a review meeting can be a stressful, even threatening, experience for parents/carers. Often a group of professionals is present including the class teacher, teaching assistant(s), SENCo and the educational psychologist. This can be a daunting prospect for parents/carers (and their children), and teachers need to help to alleviate anxiety by making sure that the environment and the processes are as comfortable and clear as possible. Parents and carers are able to access support from Parent Partnerships organisations, which can offer advice and support and can even provide colleagues to accompany them at reviews in order to provide support and a 'critical friend' to help to make the process less daunting and more accessible.

School reports can be too general and ambiguous. They need to include specific detail about a learner's attainment, expressing what has been achieved and not only the curriculum that has been covered.

One parent told me:

> I already know what he has *done* at school, he tells me when he gets home each day. I need the report to tell me what he has *learned*.
>
> Sammy (parent)

It is important to avoid the use of educational jargon and to ensure that the language used is appropriate for the audience: this does not only relate to the use of appropriate vocabulary but also to the need to provide translations of communications for some parents and carers.

Home circumstances

'Family' can be a difficult and sensitive topic for three main reasons. The first is the increasing diversity in family life in contemporary Britain; although the teachers did not refer to sociological trends within family life over the last 30 years, the rising numbers of single and divorced parents, cohabiting couples, extramarital births and reconstituted families suggest that the traditional nuclear family is only one option among several in which to raise children. In addition, although adoption and fostering have always challenged the idea of biological parenthood as 'best', cases of surrogacy together with technological changes that allow sperm and egg donation bring further confusion to the issue of what family might 'be'. These factors may be added to the increased post-war immigration that has brought different family-related cultures, beliefs and lifestyles into mainstream British society. Within the classroom, the practical effect of these developments is that teachers may be faced by a group of children who have a variety of different family forms, different interpretations of how family life is lived and different ideas on the values that they believe should underpin family relationships.

(Passy 2005: 725–6)

Learners may be intensely loyal to their families and any specific critique – implied or overt – may therefore be taken personally. Teachers need to be accepting of a child's home circumstances; it is not their role to pass judgement on the particular model of family experienced by the child, whatever their personal views. Any indication of discomfort or disapproval will send messages to both the parent/carer and the child which suggest that their pattern of life is somehow less acceptable than that of others. This difference may be something over which the child has little or no control, and they may themselves have strong feelings about their own family. The teacher's views may drive a wedge between child and parent/carer, may influence the views of other children in the class, or may affect the teacher–child relationship:

Briefly put, it could open up a whole range of emotions that may be very difficult to deal with in the context of the classroom, that may cause the child personal anguish and that may erode his or her confidence in the teacher as a person who can be trusted.

(Passy 2005: 726)

The teacher needs to be adept at welcoming carers from all backgrounds into their classroom. These may be people with whom the teacher has little or nothing in common in terms of life experience; however, what they do have in common is an interest in the learner's well-being and development. It is important to focus on this shared interest as central, rather than to be distracted by other, more peripheral, issues:

It has been shown to be important for teachers to have a number of strategies for dealing with a heterogeneous socio-cultural population before they enter into cooperative relations with parents (and carers). For this purpose, continuing education and support are absolutely necessary. More than is now the case, teacher training should also include attention to the knowledge, insight and skills needed to successfully cooperate with groups of parents from very different sociocultural backgrounds.

(Dreissen *et al.* 2005: 239)

Specific types of parental and carer involvement are explored in Chapter 5 as a part of considering how carers and parents can contribute to raising the levels of attainment of their children and young people. What is important here is the sense that communication with parents and carers needs to be clear, detailed and offered in a non-judgemental manner:

Remember always that parents (and carers) are, in a sense, your professional clients. You are accountable to them for the performance of their child and they are entitled to know what you are doing to support their child's learning.

(Jacques 2003: 197)

Conclusion

This chapter has explored communication on a range of levels. Teachers communicate with children and young people, colleagues, parents and carers through a variety of means. The ways in which they present their classrooms, the resources and displays available, and their values and attitudes all send out messages which will be interpreted by different people in different ways. Many of the ways in which we communicate are indirect, yet they still send out powerful messages about what we value.

A focus that concentrates on the attainment of targets or the performance in tests communicates messages about what is seen as important. Similarly, the content and scope of the curriculum suggests what is valued and valuable. There is a danger that a meritocratic approach to the education system is accepted unquestioningly by teachers, reinforcing the idea that people succeed or fail within a competitive system. This need not be the case: teachers and schools need to consider how their values and ethos communicate the intrinsic value of each person and make clear that each has potential to maximise.

Effective communication with colleagues is key to developing a shared ethos in school. Colleagues are a valuable source of support and ideas and work in a range of teaching and support roles in the school. Each person makes a significant and unique contribution to the whole. Professional relationships require a great deal of hard work, but this is very worthwhile. The school community includes a wide variety of people from different backgrounds and circumstances and with different beliefs and values. It is important to avoid making assumptions about colleagues and to make sure that our own attitudes show that we value and respect diversity within the workplace.

Communication with carers and parents is essential in order to share in the role of educating their children and young people. Teachers need to develop open relationships that promote dialogue. Listening to parents and carers is very important and we need to show that we appreciate their knowledge of their own children and young people. As teachers we need to value life experiences and backgrounds very different to our own and to work towards a set of shared values, rather than letting our own world views undermine relationships. We have to work hard to earn the respect of parents and carers and, in turn, need to show that we respect them and their role. Again, this is about diversity and inclusion.

Finally, we need to reflect carefully on our own values. Each of us has been formed by a range of experiences, influences, beliefs and attitudes. We need to be clear about how these affect our classroom practice and to be open to learn from the many people with whom we work in our schools. Our philosophies of education are not set in stone, and continue to develop over time. How we communicate with children and young people, colleagues, carers and parents needs to be reflected on in the light of this, so that we respect diversity and promote inclusion.

References

Alexander, R. (2006) *Towards Dialogic Teaching: Rethinking Classroom Talk*, 3rd edn. Cambridge: Dialogos.

Asprey, E., Hamilton, C. and Haywood, S. (2002) *Professional Issues in Primary Practice*. Exeter: Learning Matters.

Balshaw, M. and Farrell, P. (2002) *Teaching Assistants: Practical Strategies for Effective Classroom Support*. London: David Fulton.

Central Advisory Council for Education (1967) *Children and their Primary Schools* ('The Plowden Report'). London: HMSO.

Department for Education and Employment & Qualifications and Curriculum Authority (1999a) *The National Curriculum: Handbook for Primary Teachers in England (Key Stages 1 and 2)*. London: DfEE & QCA.

Department for Education and Employment & Qualifications and Curriculum Authority (1999b) *The National Curriculum: Handbook for Secondary Teachers in England (Key Stages 3 and 4)*. London: DfEE & QCA.

DfES (1980a) *A Framework for the School Curriculum*. London: DfES.

DfES (1980b) *A View of the Curriculum*. London: DfES.

DfES (1981) *The School Curriculum*. London: DfES.

DfES (1985) *The Swann Report*. London: DfES.

DES (2003) *Excellence and Enjoyment: a Strategy for Primary Schools*. Nottingham: DES.

Docking, J. (1990) *Primary Schools and Parents: Rights, Responsibilities and Relationships*. London: Hodder & Stoughton.

Dreissen, G., Smit, F. and Sleegers, P. (2005) 'Parental Involvement and Educational Achievement', *British Educational Research Journal*, 31(4): 509–32.

Dunford, J. (2007) 'Scrap Key Stage 3 Tests to Give Teachers Free Reign', *Guardian* Online at http://education.guardian.co.uk/curriculumreform/story/0,,2048426,00.html (accessed 17 April 2007).

Hurley, L. (2005) 'Communication with Parents and Carers' in M. Cole (ed.) *Professional Values and Practice: Meeting the Standards*, 3rd edn. David Fulton: London.

Jacques, K. (2003) 'Emerging as a Professional' in K. Jacques and R. Hyland (eds) 2nd edn. *Professional Studies: Primary Phase*. Exeter: Learning Matters.

Kay, J. (2002) *Teaching Assistants Handbook*. London: Continuum.

Kerry, T. (2001) *Working with Support Staff: their Roles and Effective Management in Schools*. Harlow: Pearson Education.

Lee, B. (2002) *Teaching Assistants in Schools: the Current State of Play*. Slough: National Foundation for Educational Research.

Lepkowska, D. (2007) 'Teachers Promised Freedom', *Guardian* Online at http://education.guardian.co.uk/curriculumreform/story/0,,2048219,00.html (accessed 17 April 2007).

Lepper, M.R. and Hodell, M. (1989) 'Intrinsic motivation in the classroom' in C. Ames and R. Ames (eds) *Research and Motivation in the Classroom*. Vol 3: 73–105. San Diego: Academic Press.

McNamara, O., Hustler, D., Stronach, I., Rodrigo, M., Beresford, E. and Botcherby, S. (2000) 'Room to Manoeuvre: mobilising the "active partner" in home–school relations', *British Educational Research Journal*, 26(4): 473–89.

Montgomery, D. (2002) *Helping Teachers Develop Through Classroom Observation*. London: David Fulton.

Nightingale, J. (2007) 'Think Outside the Timetable', *Guardian* Online at http://education.guardian.co.uk/curriculumreform/story/0,,2048356,00.html (accessed 17 April 2007).

Passy, R. (2005) 'Family values and primary schools: an investigation into family-related education', *British Education Research Journal*, 31(6): 723–36.

Skinner, B.F. (1968) *The Technology of Teaching*. New York: Appleton.

Sylva, K. (1987) 'Plowden: history and prospect', *Oxford Review of Education*, 13(1).

TeacherNet (undated) http://www.teachernet.gov.uk/wholeschool/familyandcommunity/ (accessed 23 December 2006).

Watkinson, A. (2002) *Assisting Learning and Supporting Teaching: a Practical Guide for the Teaching Assistant in the Classroom*. London: David Fulton.

Woolley, R. (2007) *The Ethical Foundations of Socialism: The Influence of William Temple and R.H. Tawney on New Labour*. Lampeter: Mellen Press.

Woolley, R. and Johnston, J. (2007) 'Target Setting' in J. Johnston, J. Halocha and M. Chater (eds) *Developing Teaching Skills in the Primary School*. Maidenhead: Open University Press.

Development, well-being and attainment

Richard Woolley

Q5 Recognise and respect the contribution that colleagues, parents and carers can make to the development and well-being of children and young people, and to raising their levels of attainment.

Learning objectives

To encourage teachers to:

- recognise and appreciate the contribution that colleagues, carers and parents can make to the development and well-being of children and young people;
- consider the influences on the levels of attainment of children and young people;
- develop professional, supportive and empathetic relationships;
- work in cooperation with those who have direct contact with children and young people on a regular basis.

Introduction

EDUCATION SHOULD EXIST to help learners understand the value of learning in its own right and for its own sake, developing the critical skills to engage with the world around them at a range of levels and to question the values, standards and assumptions of that world. In order to support the development, well-being and attainment of children and young people it is important for all those involved to be aware of the aims and purposes of education as set out in National Curriculum documents, to consider these critically and to develop personal and collective philosophies of education, and for teachers to work with colleagues, parents and carers towards common goals.

The focus of a significant part of this chapter is on the development and well-being of children and young people. It is my contention that without this focus we cannot begin to consider their attainment. Fundamental to this is the provision of safe and supportive learning environments where all people are valued and where there is a clear vision for the role of education. In schools we need to ensure that the importance of well-being is not overshadowed by a standards-driven agenda.

Why do we educate?

In order to consider the development of children and young people it is essential first to consider the purpose of the education system itself and the reasons why we educate. This is fundamental in ensuring their well-being.

I argued in the previous chapter that we educate so that our children and young people have the skills necessary to face life in this challenging and constantly changing world: they need to be literate and numerate, they need to be able to look at the world with a critical eye and to make sense of what they see around them in an informed, confident and empathetic way. One reason why we educate is to help one another to develop our world views so that we can contribute positively to the world on a range of levels, so that we appreciate the myriad differences and similarities we see amongst those around us, and so that we can show respect for this world and its people in confident and informed ways.

The education system in England is based on two main principles: that all should be enabled to learn and to achieve, and that schools should enable individuals to develop spiritually, morally, socially and culturally (DfEE/QCA 1999a, 1999b). Some of the values that we promote in schools are to do with living a good life, free from discrimination, injustice and insecurity. Explicitly and implicitly we also educate our children and young people in the norms of society as a whole: what is acceptable and unacceptable behaviour, what is tolerated and what is unacceptable. We impart the moral values built up in society over hundreds if not thousands of years. We see this as a part of helping our children and young people to develop so that they can take their place in society: how we do this is fundamental to their development and well-being.

Influences

At a straightforward level, moral values are the beliefs of what we feel is right and wrong or good and bad. We all know that they come from a range of sources:

- our upbringing;
- political views;
- religious and philosophical outlooks;
- personal experience;
- peer pressure;

- the 'norms' of society;
- our education;
- personal reflection;
- people who inspire us.

Of course some of these sources stem from the others, and the whole is intertwined in quite a complex way. Each one of us can consider what has influenced our own personal development, and can prioritise those that have had the most significant impact on our lives.

The cumulative effects of such influences help to shape the way in which we see the world and inform our world views. To talk of morality can sound quite narrow or polarised, and so I propose to use the term *world views* in order to embrace the range of influences and outlooks that make up how we respond to the world around us. Perhaps we might equate our world view with our philosophy of education, for, from a personal point of view, I cannot separate my views about education (why we educate, how we educate etc) from the way in which I see the world and regard the value of all people. The two are certainly linked, possibly to the point of being inseparable.

There are some aspects of morality on which we might all agree. I think we would all agree that it is wrong to murder. However, we might disagree on what constitutes murder and whether it is ever permissible to end a human life. Some people would equate euthanasia or abortion with murder, while others would say that there are circumstances where they are permissible; some would argue that capital punishment is effectively legalised murder, whilst others would see it as an appropriate response to the most heinous crimes. Our interpretation of certain moral attitudes is shaped by our world view. This chapter is not concerned with such emotive issues, about which many of us care passionately. However, they provide stark examples of how a shared morality might be interpreted differently by various people. As we begin to develop our moral values into an ethical system we face the practicalities of how we express those values. Here, then, is a further reason why we educate: we educate to give our children and young people the reflective skills necessary to be able to consider values and principles for life – and to be able to interpret, question and develop them. This is an important part of ensuring their well-being.

Critical skills

It is important to note at this point that teachers work with a range of colleagues, parents and carers who bring a wide range of views, values and attitudes to the school community. I touched on these issues in Chapter 4, and note here the impact of such diversity on the establishment of effective working relationships. Education must enable children and young people to deconstruct what they see around them and to evaluate what they are told. This will help them to develop the critical skills that will enable them to interpret the ideas presented by the media, the education system, political and religious groups, campaigning and pressure groups, and by capitalists and their representatives. These skills will empower children and young people to serve their communities, both now and in the future, so that they are able to get involved and help to shape the world in which they live. Teachers and other adults can help to develop an atmosphere in school which allows children to question and to debate so that they can develop their own world views and develop a sense of who they are and what they believe. Respect for differences is key to the success of this approach, and is an attitude that we need to model ourselves and to encourage amongst all stakeholders in the school.

Education should exist to foster equality, building a society in which the innate potential of all is acknowledged. It should foster imaginative, creative and independent thinkers able to interpret the world around them and to hold well thought-out and sensitively developed views, capable of dealing with controversy and contrast. Education should seek to educate the whole person, considering spiritual, social, moral, cultural and academic development and the interrelationship of these facets of a person. It must maintain a balance between these elements and ensure that systems do not neglect any aspect. Because of this a school needs to have a clear ethos and to make plain that intolerance, bullying and stereotyping are not tolerated within its confines. This applies equally to children, young people, members of staff and parents and carers. It is fundamental to the development and well-being of all members of the school community and essential if all people are to learn and achieve.

Developing values

I believe that the core values that should be upheld and advanced in the education system include:

- equality – establishing a setting in which all can learn and achieve;
- respect for differences;
- empowerment and the ability to explore and voice one's values;
- the development of a mutual understanding and appreciation of other people.

Formal education should prepare children to engage critically with others in society and to question their roles, power and authority. It should provide the skills to build strong communities in which optimism is able to flourish, relationships are strengthened and regeneration can take place. It should help children and young people to learn about the needs and aspirations of others in society and to deal with conflict in a positive and productive way. It should help learners to believe that things can be better and that their choices and actions can make a difference for good.

The education system should prepare children and young people for life in a diverse world, and help them to develop the positive self-image, confidence and sense of identity essential for this. It should support the educational role of the home and nurture positive relationships with carers and parents as partners in the education process. Finally, core values should be the notions that education is enjoyable and never ending. These are the values that need to be explored with colleagues so that the school develops a vision shared by all members of staff that enables pupils to flourish.

Education should enable learners to understand what is meant by democracy, including differing interpretations (e.g. democracy in the UK, in Cuba, Kerala in southern India and in Venezuela), and to appraise the effectiveness and implementation of such systems. It should involve children and young people in establishing what the aims and purposes of education are, so that they appreciate the process in which they are engaged. It should help children and young people to evaluate alternatives and ways forward, helping them to think for themselves and to engage in critical reflection. In this sense, children and young people should be viewed as partners in the education process, as opposed to recipients. This partnership should continue into adult life. A significant part of helping to develop well-being is empowering children and young people to realise that their voice is important and that they have a role to play in shaping the world around them. It is not only parents, carers and colleagues that need to think about the development of children and young people, but also the children and young people themselves.

Curriculum issues

Our education system needs to have a structure at a national level that allows for the provision of a curriculum tailored to the individual needs and interests of children and young people and which is able to take into account the local setting where learning takes place. It should make links to local, national and global issues, using partnerships with schools in other contexts to help children to hear different views and challenge stereotypes. It needs to consider issues of environmental destruction and to help children to understand the role of campaigning and how collective voices can be effective (Oxfam 2006). It should nurture a sense of responsibility for the environment and for the fair and equitable use of the world's resources. It should include the discussion of capitalism and socialism as different world systems. Education should help children and young people to understand that people can make a difference – and should encourage active involvement in working to build a more inclusive and coherent society in which all are valued. It should foster a sense of personal indignation, a willingness to speak up for others and a sense of justice and fair play. There needs to be a sense of common humanity, that all are different yet all

are human, underpinned by a sense of empathy. I highlight all these areas as important parts of enabling children and young people to develop positive and confident
outlooks that contribute to their own well-being and the well-being of others.

During a visit to the Richmond area of Kwa-Zulu Natal in South Africa I visited a
primary school that had an aspirational set of aims:

> We educators are committed to do the following in a successful way:
>
> - 100% pass rate and attendance of learners.
> - Competent learners.
> - Involving parents in the education of their children.
> - To provide empowerment to enable learners to have good adaptation to a continually
>   changing society.
> - To promote analytical, critical and creative thinking in our learners.
> - To encourage cooperation and self-esteem.
> - To encourage competition, challenge and research among learners.
> - To develop disciplined learners.
> - We hope to achieve the above by cooperation amongst educators and communication
>   between educators and learners and to be a self-reliant school.

I found these aims inspiring and challenging, although I find a tension between the
notions of cooperation and competition. They reflect the thinking within a school
that is seeking to implement the overarching aims of the education system in South
Africa:

> The Preamble to the South African Schools Act [1996] states that the education system
> should 'redress past injustices in educational provision . . . contribute to the eradication of
> poverty . . . and advance the democratic transformation of society, combat racism and sex-
> ism and all other forms of unfair discrimination and intolerance, [and] protect and advance
> our diverse cultures and languages'.
>
> (West Midlands Commission on Global Citizenship, 2002: 26)

I was impressed by how aware the teachers I met were of these aims for education.
Whilst the aims are ambitious and complex to implement, the teachers had a clear
sense of what they were working together to achieve. It made me question how often
we discuss the aims and purposes of education in the English education system, and
how knowledgeable teachers are of the overarching aims of the National Curriculum for England. If we do not share a sense of what the system is seeking to achieve
and why it exists, it is difficult to communicate effective messages about the overall
purpose of education except from our own practice and experience in our local setting; it is also difficult to critique and challenge the system and to question whether
its aims are appropriate.

An emerging system

The education system is constantly changing and evolving, like the world in general. I do not believe that there will never be a point when the system is judged to have 'arrived'. There needs to be a cycle of constant review and re-evaluation within a continuum of seeking to achieve core values. In envisaging the future shape of education, it is not possible to set targets and dates for achievement: what is required is the establishment of a clear set of values underpinned by a vision for the transformative nature of education. Teachers, and those in teacher education, need to be supported to continually revise and develop their personal and collective philosophies of education so that the education that is delivered goes beyond the practicalities of technical method and is supported by passion, enthusiasm, commitment and vision. Similarly, children can be supported in developing the values and vision to underpin their own emerging philosophy of education: its role, purpose and potential for change. In the present climate the focus on short-termism in the education system ensures that such values and vision are impeded and, at worst, crushed.

Every Child Matters?

Whatever the motivation for the development of the *Every Child Matters* (ECM) agenda (DfES 2004), we now have a system that seeks to promote joined-up thinking between the various agencies that seek to care for children and young people from birth to 19 years. Some teachers will argue that we have been working in these ways for years; however, this does not keep us from celebrating the possibilities provided by ECM. However, how we work with children, young people and their families will be affected by our own values and attitudes, and it is important to reflect on how these impact on our practice. One teacher recounted an incident which illustrates how our own values can affect relationships within a school:

> Ben's mum was delighted to bring her wedding photographs into school to share with the staff. She loved the attention that she gained from the staff and was always pleased to talk and to share her stories. When Ben was a page-boy at the wedding she brought cake for all the staff and even left the wedding album so that people could see the occasion and the honeymoon. Ben had significant behavioural problems and very low self-esteem; it was important to build relationships with his parents. However, the judgements of the staff, reflected by the conversations and comments in the staffroom, revealed that Ben's mum was a figure of fun rather than a valued friend, colleague or partner in the education process. The staff tolerated her, rather than sharing her delight in making a significant step forward in her life. She had made a huge stride forward in her own life, marrying the man who had been her partner for many years, and yet the staff in school found the whole thing amusing. One colleague commented that: 'She looks like a huge meringue in that dress.'
>
> Shirley (secondary teacher)

There can be a tension between our personal values, beliefs and attitudes as teachers and the client group with which we work. This raises questions of personal attitudes versus professional values. One relates to the ways in which we choose to live ourselves, and the other to the ways in which we operate within the work environment. For some of us this will create a tension, especially if we hold passionate or very specific views on the ways in which the world should operate.

When Celina and Shaun speak of all living together with their two mums, how can I support their experience of family life? One way is by providing positive images and stories that show that their family is valued, another is by making sure that their family is welcomed and by making sure that my language in the classroom includes the variety of home situations that the children come from. In my own classroom I talked of the children's 'adult at home' and of 'your family' rather than 'mum and dad' to ensure that all the children were included. I believe that we need to take an approach that appreciates the diversity of the experience of our learners and includes them all.

A former colleague recounted to me the story of a child in Year 1 who drew his family during a lesson focusing on 'Our Homes'. He drew his mum, who he lived with, and his two dads; mum and dad had separated not long after he was born, and dad now lived with his male partner. His teacher asked who the second man was, and when told responded: 'We don't want to see that here.' She told the child to rub out his father's partner. The devastating affects of such a situation must not be underestimated. Whatever the personal views of the teacher, their professional role is to support and nurture the child. They are not in a position to judge the child's home circumstances and should not reject or devalue the child's experience of family life. I find this story heart-breaking.

Whatever one's own personal thoughts about the validity of such a moral view, and however we feel that families should be constructed in an ideal (or other) world, it is inappropriate for us to use our own world view to undermine the experience of the children and young people in our care. Perhaps the value here is the belief that children should be brought up in safe, secure and loving environments. I suspect that none of us would reject such a view; it may be a value to which we can all subscribe. The ways of working this out may be interpreted differently by each one of us, and by those we work with in school: colleagues and carers/parents, children and young people. However, the overarching principle provides common ground that goes beyond our personal values and provides a basis for the professional views which underpin our classroom practice. Such professional views must also extend to the staffroom, where we need to remember that education workers also reflect the diversity of society whether or not they choose to share this with us.

I heard the story recently of a child that had been taught by their mum how to draw a house whenever the topic of 'homes' came up at school. The child learned to draw a square house with a pitched roof, four windows and a door (Tierney 2007, speaking at a conference to launch the North Lincolnshire Inclusion Strategy). The parent felt that there would be a stigma attached to the fact that they lived in a trailer as a part of a traveller community.

These accounts present a challenge for us to develop inclusive schools and inclusive classrooms. A great deal has been achieved in recent years in terms of developing inclusion for children and young people with special educational needs and in terms of addressing 'race'. This process of inclusion needs to continue in order to ensure that we support the development and well-being of all learners and also that of carers, parents and colleagues.

Inclusive practice

Let us now apply these views to the stories, illustrations and displays available in our own workplaces. In our own work settings, how do we ensure that we do not perpetuate world views or misconceptions about the ways in which people live – even the ways in which those within our schools live? Key questions to consider include:

- How do we enable children to speak about their families in an atmosphere that is safe and accepting of diversity?

- Do we discuss what constitutes a family, including the ideas that not all families live together, some people come from foster and adoptive families, and some families may include more than two parents/carers including those of the same sex?

- How does our school environment show that these positive attitudes are fully embedded within the ethos of the whole school?

- Is it possible to maintain a professional welcome to diverse family groups, even if members of staff hold strong beliefs on the moral standing of those relationships?

- How do we make sure that all parents/carers feel welcome at a parents' evening (and why continue to use this term rather than 'open evening' given the diverse patterns of family life experienced by our children and young people?) and other events?

How do we ensure children's well-being if we perpetuate the myth that families are made up of two parents, one male and one female, with 2.4 children? Such a stereotype has always been ridiculous. This idea is not only outdated and outmoded but also provides the ammunition used by bullies in the playground or school yard. If we perpetuate such attitudes in our schools, then we are complicit with the bullies and fail to show our children that their backgrounds are valued whether they come from one- or two-parent households, families with several parents, adoptive or foster families, traveller or extended families, or families which include same-sex parents/carers. We need to challenge stereotypes from the earliest years of education.

Valuing backgrounds

Recently, I have had the opportunity to discuss texts (mainly from the United States) showing different models of family with teachers and teaching assistants from several different Local Authorities and with teachers in training. Although they have raised issues and concerns about some of the Americanisms and some of the illustrations (some of which I must admit that I share), they have all been very interested in the ways in which different families are included in the texts. A useful list of texts for use in primary and secondary schools has been developed by the Brighton and Hove Library Service and can be accessed via the teaching resources section of the *No Outsiders Project* website (http://www.nooutsiders.sunderland.ac.uk). One useful book for use with primary aged children is *Who's in a Family?* (Skutch 1998) which shows how different families live together, or apart, both multicultural human families and different animal families. The final section provides a place for a child to draw her or his family. This presents a very inclusive view of the various and varied family backgrounds that exist.

Key to *Every Child Matters* (DfES 2004) is the idea that we should foster children's physical and mental health. If we do not organise our classrooms in ways that show that we value the diverse life experiences of the children, we are creating tensions that fail to promote mental health and will cause children to feel, at best, uncomfortable and undervalued.

One teacher admitted that he had never considered how families are shown in his Year 1 classroom. I asked how many children were from single parent homes, and how many were from traveller or black and minority ethnic backgrounds or living with same-sex parents or carers. I also asked whether these children had access to any age-appropriate literature that showed that their family and background were valued by the school. It was an interesting conversation and he was surprised that he had not considered the issues before. It is important that schools consider such issues, and essential that those involved in initial teacher education explore with their students how to create inclusive classrooms.

In contrast, I am sure that we would wish to consider how children and young people access positive images of different types of family that are not represented within their classes, but which are still significant within the society in which they live. Sometimes we show our views and what we value by omission – what is missing can be as powerful as what is represented.

A colleague reflected on her experience of telling her son that his uncle was gay:

My [seven year old] son thinks that there is nothing strange about his uncle being gay and living with his male partner (indeed they are both regarded as his uncles). They all get on well and he loves to visit them. In fact, he was surprisingly accepting and didn't raise any of the issues that I was expecting when I decided to explain the situation to him. He has told a couple of his school friends, and their reactions have been quite matter of fact. My nervousness about the whole issue has proved to be unfounded. At this point in time we have not discussed sex education and I know that it has not been covered at school. He knows that his sister developed in 'Mummy's tummy', but he has never asked how she got there or how she was born. At the right time I think that he will ask such questions, and as and when he is interested I will talk this through with him. We are very close and I know he can ask me questions; I trust that he will ask about sex as and when he is interested, and it may be that at some point I will broach the subject with him if I think it is important. In the meantime, he seems very accepting of different relationships and sexualities without needing to be aware of the actual sexual acts themselves.

Zoe (parent)

I am not arguing here for us to share the detail of sexual acts with children at an age when it is not appropriate: there is a significant difference between sex and relationships education and the issues of how we ensure that children feel included and valued no matter what model of family they come from or what relationships they come across. A range of resources relating to Lesbian, Gay, Bisexual and Trans families, which may be useful in this regard, can be accessed from *Schools Out* (www.schools-out.org.uk) and through the *No Outsiders Project* (www.nooutsiders.sunderland.ac.uk). Detailed guidance on addressing issues about sexuality in the secondary school with a range of colleagues and young people can be found in Forrest, Biddle and Clift (2006) and Forrest (2006). In addition, there is an interesting programme on Teachers' TV developed by staff and students at the Turton High School Media Arts College in Bolton (Year 9) and my own students at Bishop Grosseteste University College Lincoln, which addresses some of the complexities relating to issues in primary and secondary education (http://www.teachers.tv/video/44).

Bastiani (1989: 105) considers the ways in which different models or patterns of family life may impact on the classroom; for example, the variety of parenting and caring arrangement and styles, particular needs arising from family breakdown (including communicating with parents/carers and issues raised by re-marriage), the problems raised by long-term unemployment, issues raised by different patterns of family life resulting from religion and culture. It is important that teachers appreciate the diverse experiences of the children in their classes and take these into account; it is also important that they understand that there will be many issues in the children's homes of which they are not aware.

Home–school partnership

Having considered the ways in which different patterns of family may impact on children and young people, and indeed on relationships with parents and carers, this section will explore the importance of links between home and school in terms of developing opportunities for learning:

> Within the schools themselves, the different desires and interests of parents should also be taken more into consideration. The school itself should work more actively on the attainment of greater insight into parental desires and interests which may or may not be raised explicitly by the parents themselves. The extent to which such efforts successfully activate the more reticent (or less involved) parents strongly depends on the extent to which these same groups of parents are approached and treated as serious educational partners.
>
> (Dreissen *et al.* 2005: 239)

This view raises some interesting issues, not least the repeated reference to parents within documents and texts without a corresponding reference to carers. This suggests that there is still a long way to go in creating an inclusive ethos within education settings that values all kinds of families.

The relationship between home and school is important for several reasons. First, it can help to ensure continuity and consistency in a child's learning; second, schools and teachers are accountable to parents and carers for the educational provision being made; third, carers and parents have many skills and interests that can contribute to a child's learning and to the school community. Vincent (2000: 2) identifies three roles for parents and carers:

- Partner.
- Consumer.
- Citizen.

The first expresses the role of the parent/carer as a learner alongside the child and the teacher and acknowledges the importance of the support that they provide. The second denotes the parent/carer's role in funding the education system via taxes, in choosing which school should provide an education for their child (although such choice is often limited) and in seeking value for money and effective results (this area is also problematic and will be discussed in the next section). The third highlights the role of the parent/carer as a participant in the local and school community with views and values to help to inform the process. I would add that parents and carers also participate in national and international communities and bring views and values which relate to their own global citizenship and which will impact on the school community. At times these will be positive (reflecting the need to value difference and to respect diversity) and at others they may be negative (promoting intolerance, for example non-inclusive views about immigration or 'race'). Munn (1993) offers a similar model which involves accountability, client-centred orientation or 'parent-teacher' cooperation.

Part of the relationship between home and school is to require the school to be accountable for its strategies, policies and methods. Teachers give account for a child's progress through verbal and written reports, through informal and formal meetings, and through the sharing of targets. The consumer model suggests that parents and carers have the opportunity to move their child to another school if they are dissatisfied, effectively moving the spending power that comes as a result of funding based on pupil enrolment. However, such choice is often either limited or not available. In addition, it suggests a system in which the 'best' schools in terms of results and league tables become popular and over-subscribed, whilst other schools are viewed as 'failing'. This is inequitable and is one indicator of why market forces are inappropriate within the education system. The whole notion of 'value for money' (already identified as problematic) raises questions about the aims and purposes of education and of why we educate. The measures identified by national government lack the subtlety to demonstrate how children have developed in social, moral, spiritual and cultural terms. In addition, they have skewed the curriculum so that some skills are valued disproportionately to others. For example, the tests for 11 year olds in Literacy are focused on reading and writing. This has effectively marginalised speaking and listening for several years and devalued this very important aspect of the curriculum. The focus on results and value for money has led to many other parts of the curriculum being undervalued, including the arts and humanities, yet surely these are essential parts of human development.

The introduction of market forces and measures has effectively limited the curriculum and led to the dominance of Literacy and Numeracy in primary schools; it has led to greater selection of pupils in the secondary sector as schools seek out the 'most able' students in order to meet performance indicators. What is of far greater value than the operations of the market is the opportunity to share in dialogue about a child's progress, needs, development and well-being: schools need to develop priorities, in consultation with carers and parents, to identify what is important for their learners and to identify what is important in the education process: 'Parental voice (sic) opens up . . . greater possibilities for school improvement than parental choice' (Munn 1993: 173). This notion of *parental voice*, to which I would add the allied notion of *carers' voice*, needs to be supported by effective communication from the school so that parents and carers are aware of what the school is trying to achieve and how it is going about this. Rather than moving their child from a school, surely it should be far more productive for carers and parents to work with the school in order to address a learner's needs? This reinforces the importance of developing clear and informed values, as discussed in the earlier parts of this chapter. It also raises questions of what is meant by the term *school improvement*, for this may be measured using a limited set of data which reflect little of a school's values and ethos. Whilst this is not easy, it should be a goal that we seek to work towards: communication is key because it minimises the opportunity for misunderstanding, misinformation and misconception; it also opens up opportunities for partnership and collaboration.

Parents and carers are the primary educators of their children; they also know their children and young people better than anyone else. Teachers need to appreciate the role that parents and carers play in nurturing and teaching their children, and to show that they welcome a partnership with parents and carers as an essential part of a young person's learning journey:

> Many parents [and carers] made it clear that being a consumer is not just about choice: it is also about the continuing relationship between parents [and carers] and schools once the initial choice has been made. Specific elements in the relationship which parents indicated as being important included the knowledge of what is going on in the school, their ability to keep a watching brief over the quality of their child's education, their feeling of being listened to by schools, and their capacity to have a say in the school's decision-making process.
>
> (Hughes, Wikeley and Nash 1994: 76)

Whilst I dislike the use of the term *consumer* and all its connotations of the market, the focus on developing relationships and partnerships is important. Parents, carers and education professionals should be enabled to develop a curriculum and a school ethos that consider the nurturing of the whole child, rather than their attainment in limited areas of a curriculum driven by tests and examinations.

Involving parents and carers

Carers and parents can be involved in schools in a variety of ways. They have an interest in their child's learning and progress and will hear accounts of the school day, its highs and lows, in conversation with their child. They may be involved in parent/carer-teacher organisations, fund raising activities or extra-curricular activities. They may be members of the school's governing body, representing the whole body of parents and carers. They may give time as a volunteer, helping with classroom and other activities. They may be education or health professionals involved in school directly or indirectly as a result of their working lives. Whatever their role or involvement, Hurley (2005) makes the important point that:

> Research has shown conclusively that *all* parents are interested in their child's education (Tizard *et al.* 1981; Lareau 1989; Reay 1999). However, some schools have their own ideas about what makes a 'good' parent.

It is important to remember that a parent or carer's lack of involvement in the school does not necessarily reflect their interest in their child's learning. Teachers need to avoid making judgements about parenting and caring which may not be based in reality:

Just which forms of parental [and carer] involvement are particularly effective and which aspects of the development of children are specifically affected remains unclear. Research on the differential effects of parental involvement on pupil-related outcomes is scarce.

(Dreissen *et al.* 2005: 510)

A project undertaken by *Human Scale Education* (an education reform movement committed to small-scale learning communities based on the values of democracy, fairness and respect), in conjunction with the Department for Education and Skills, has explored how schools can develop the use of 'Parent Councils' in order to increase participation and 'parent' voice. Again, carers remain largely unacknowledged. It has found that:

Parents have to get used to the idea that their views are genuinely being sought and also that the school is looking to establish a real partnership with them. School staff need to be prepared to work in different ways and to be convinced of the benefits of working more closely with parents. Some staff are unprepared for this, feeling that they were trained to work with children, not with adults.

(Carnie 2006)

The schools involved in the project are still in the process of developing parental/ carer involvement:

However each school now has a mechanism in place through which any parent or carer can make his or her voice heard, whether it is a parents' council, a parents' forum or a representative parent teachers' association.

(Carnie 2006)

The whole notion of 'partnership' with parents and carers is highly ideological and politically weighted. It can be interpreted as suggesting the transfer of power from one group to another: of teachers passing responsibility to parents and carers, or of teachers losing power and influence and having to respond to the demands of parents and carers. However, this is not an issue of 'winners' and 'losers'. Developing partnerships is never easy. It can only be undertaken where there is a genuine willingness for the enterprise to succeed and openness on each side to listen and to learn. Partnership is not about losing power, but about sharing responsibility.

Additional issues for home–school relationships and further disussion can be found in Hallgarten (2000) and Hurley (2005). Further reading on involving parents and carers includes: Berk (2001), Hornby (2000), and Whalley (2001). Merttens and Vass (1990) provide useful insights into how children and parents/carers can learn together.

Homework

The place of homework has become the focus of particular debate in recent times. Parents and carers can find it difficult to support their children with homework, particularly as approaches to learning have changed since they were at school them-selves. One carer illustrated this when he explained to me how he had explained long multiplication to his child:

> I couldn't understand the way she was trying to work out the problem. But once I showed her the *proper* method that I was taught at school she managed it without any difficulty. Why didn't her teacher show her *the proper way* in the first place?
>
> (Darren, carer)

Learning a method that works, without understanding why it works and what the process involves, may have its place but is not the ideal. Parents and carers may feel inadequate because of their own level of curricular knowledge, but the school expects that they will support their child's learning:

> It's changed a lot since I went to school. It's like with maths – times and long division, no worries. But then you go on to areas. I never really understood that myself. I say 'Tell your teacher your mum can't even do this.'
>
> Chelsea, parent (cited in Hurley 2005: 87)

Hurley's research showed that homework was one of the areas that caused parents and carers most concern:

> Those who are least equipped to deal with homework are those from cultures where their school experience has been very different, and those whose own school experiences and at-tendance were poor.
>
> (Hurley 2005: 87)

Homework can also cause additional stress for single parents and carers or those managing the home alone whilst a partner works away; there may not be other adults around who can share the role of interpreting the tasks and solving the prob-lems. Carers and parents who find it difficult to interpret homework tasks or to support their children can feel guilty about this. Sometimes this is compounded by a sense that their child is underachieving or failing to achieve in school. Staff need to be aware that it is possible to infer that such difficulties are the fault of the parent or carer, and this needs to be avoided if an effective partnership is to be developed (Amatea and Sherrard in Ryan *et al.* (eds) 1995: 68).

Additional stresses can be experienced by those without access to a computer. However, teachers can design homework tasks in such a way as to ensure that chil-dren and young people are enabled to access the resources necessary. One teacher explained to me:

> We planned homework tasks so that once each week the children needed to use a computer. We allowed plenty of time for this task to be completed so that the children could book com-puter time in the local village library. This made sure that every child could complete the

tasks, and also increased the usage of the library. It was important to make sure that every child could access the facilities.

(Ben, Year 6 teacher)

It is important that schools inform parents and carers about the nature and content of the curriculum, so that a better understanding can be gained of what the school is trying to achieve. Homework tasks can be set with clear instructions or guidelines, so that adults in the home are able to gain a sense of what the teacher is seeking to achieve. Schools need to make sure that any homework that is set is purposeful, providing an extension of the learning that is taking place in the classroom, rather than being set for its own sake. One view that a parent expressed to me was:

I can't see the point in the endless round of worksheets that are sent home week after week. How is this meant to excite my child about learning?

(Sunita, parent)

Sunita's point is pertinent, and could be addressed by using homework as a vehicle to provide a stimulus for learning in real life settings:

- investigating number in the home and applying the skills learned at school;
- gathering information by interviewing family members and other adults, using speaking and listening skills, developing questioning, note taking and recording;
- identifying scientific processes in the home and gathering ideas/reflections.

Furthermore:

Homework activities do not have to be set, written or recorded but can be based on a tea-time discussion or a game. Homework can also be activity-based, and linking school work to real life.

(Hurley 2005: 88)

In addition, schools can recognise that learning already takes place in the home through many activities that occur naturally as a part of everyday life; carers and parents can be encouraged to value their important role in capitalising on such opportunities through: 'encouraging, listening, reacting, praising, guiding, monitoring, and discussing' (Epstein 1995). Indeed, homework may well get in the way of such opportunities for learning as it takes up part of a child's time in the home and may well cause pressures on the carer/parent-child relationship which are counterproductive and fail to create positive learning opportunities. Key questions that I feel it is important to consider include:

- How does the homework activity build on what has been learned in school?
- Is it explained clearly so that parents and carers can understand what is intended?

- Does the activity link to what will come next in class?
- How is the task differentiated to take into account the child's current academic level, needs and interests?
- What level of recording is necessary, and does this have to be in written form?
- How will feedback be give to the child and parent/carer?
- How will learning be affected if the task is not completed?

Homework can place stresses on family life, and can be an additional strain that leads to feelings of guilt amongst carers and parents. It needs to be planned and presented in a careful way in order to make sure that it helps parents and carers to contribute to their child's learning and attainment.

Conclusion

Valuing the contribution that parents, carers and colleagues can make to the development and well-being of children and young people requires a clear sense of the purpose of education. If we educate to nurture free-thinking, empathetic and reflective learners we must also model these attributes through our words and actions and through the policies and practices of our schools. We must value the contribution that all people can make, and appreciate how diverse these contributions will be. In this context, we will create an atmosphere in which all can learn and achieve.

Central to this is an understanding that the education system should exist to nurture and support individuals and communities. Teachers need to question whether a primary aim or purpose of education is that it should prepare people to contribute to the economic well-being of the nation, whether it should be the purpose of education at all, and how this relates to the more significant and far reaching aim to nurture all people and value their circumstances, interests and needs. Schools need to consider how the curriculum can be tailored to such individual needs and made interesting, exciting and accessible. This is essential to promote attainment. As teachers we need to consider how our practice and attitudes communicate messages about the nature of success and how we inspire and support our children and young people in their learning. Key to this is an understanding that learning is valuable in its own right.

Teachers need to value not only the backgrounds and circumstances of their children and young people but also of carers and parents. On occasion, we may need to challenge views and attitudes which do not reflect the key value of respect for diversity. In addition, colleagues also come from a range of backgrounds and have a wide range of experiences of life. All those involved in a school contribute to its diversity and it is important to consider all people and to value their positive contributions. Schools also need to consider whether their staff team reflects the diversity of society as a whole. Exclusion can be either overt or unthinking, it can exist in subtle forms that devalue or undermine certain persons associated with the school community. This requires careful reflection on the language, activities, resources and images that we use in schools. In positive settings, that are thoughtful about such issues, all those with a role in promoting and valuing learning will be able to contribute to the attainment of learners.

Acknowledgements

I am extremely grateful to the carers, parents and teachers who have shared their stories and views with me; the contributions have been appropriately anonymised.

References

Amatea, E. and Sherrard, P. (1995) 'Inquiring Into Children's Social Worlds: A Choice of Lenses' in B. Ryan, G. Adams, T. Gullotta, R. Weissberg, and R. Hampton (eds) *The Family-School Connection*. London: Sage.

Bastiani, J. (1989) *Working with Parents: a Whole School Approach*. London: NFER-Routledge.

Berk, L. (2001) *Awakening Children's Minds: How Parents and Teachers can Make a Difference*. Oxford: OUP.

Boethe, M. (2003) 'Diversity: school, family and community connections.' Annual Synthesis 2003 (Austin, TX, Southwest Educational Development Laboratory).

Carnie, F. (2006) *Setting Up Parent Councils: Case Studies*. Human Scale Education and DfES.

Department for Education and Employment and Qualifications and Curriculum Authority (1999a) *The National Curriculum: Handbook for Primary Teachers in England (Key Stages 1 and 2)*. London: DfEE and QCA.

Department for Education and Employment and Qualifications and Curriculum Authority (1999b) *The National Curriculum: Handbook for Secondary Teachers in England (Key Stages 3 and 4)*. London: DfEE and QCA.

DfES (2004) *Every Child Matters – Change for Children*. London: DfES.

Dreissen, G., Smit, F. and Sleegers, P. (2005) 'Parental Involvement and Educational Achievement', *British Educational Research Journal*, 31(4): 509–32.

Epstein, J. (1995) 'School/family/community partnerships', *Phi Delta Kappan*, 76(9): May, 701–11.

Forrest, S., Biddle, G. and Clift, S. (2006) Talking About Homosexuality in the Secondary School. 3rd edn www.avert.org/media/pdfs/homosexualityinschool.pdf Horsham: Avert. Accessed 25 March 2007.

Forrest, S. (2006) 'Straight Talking: Challenges in Teaching and Learning About Sexuality and Homophobia in Schools' in M. Cole (ed.) *Education, Equality and Human Rights: Issues of Gender, 'Race', Sexuality, Disability and Social Class*. London: Routledge.

Hallgarten, J. (2000) *Parents Exist, OK!?: Issues and Visions for Parent-school Relationships*. London: Institute for Public Policy Research.

Hornby, G. (2000) *Improving Parental Involvement*. London: Cassell Educational.

Hughes, M., Wikeley, F. and Nash, T. (1994) *Parents and Their Children's Schools*. Oxford: Blackwell.

Hurley, L. (2005) 'Communication with Parents and Carers' in M. Cole (ed.) *Professional Values and Practice: Meeting the Standards* (3rd edn). David Fulton: London.

Lareau, A. (1989) *Home Advantage: Social Class and Parental Intervention in Elementary Education*. London: Falmer Press.

Merttens, R. and Vass, J. (1990) *Bringing School Home: Children and Parents Learning Together*. London: Hodder & Stoughton.

Munn, P. (1993) *Parents and Schools: Customers, Managers or Partners?* London: Routledge.

No Outsiders Project (2007) www.nooutsiders.sunderland.ac.uk (accessed 20 March 2007).

Oxfam (2006) *Education for Global Citizenship: A Guide for Schools*. Oxford: Oxfam GB.

Reay, D. (1999) *Class Work: Mothers' Involvement in Their Children's Primary Schooling*. London: University College Press.

Ryan, B., Adams, G., Gullotta, T., Weissberg, R. and Hampton, R. (eds) (1995) *The Family-School Connection*. London: Sage.

Schools Out (undated) www.schools-out.org.uk (accessed 25 March 2007).

Skutch, R. (1998) *Who's in a Family?* Berkeley, CA: Tricycle Press.

Tierney, A. (2007) *Travellers and Gypsies*. Presentation at a conference to launch the Local Authority Inclusion Strategy: 'Turning the Tables: Perception and Realities.' North Lincolnshire Council, 2 March 2007.

Tizard, B., Mortimore, J. and Burchell, B. (1981) *Involving Parents in Nursery and Infant Schools*. London: High Scope Press.

Vincent, C. (2000) *Including Parents? Education, Citizenship and Parental Agency*. Buckingham: Open University Press.

West Midlands Commission on Global Citizenship (2002) *Whose Citizenship? Exploring Identity, Democracy and Participation in a Global Context*. Birmingham, Development Education Centre.

Whalley, M. (2001) *Involving Parents in their Children's Learning*. London: Paul Chapman Publishing.

6

Working with paraprofessionals: challenges and opportunities

Malini Mistry and Krishan Sood

Q6 Have a commitment to collaboration and co-operative working.

Learning objectives:

By the end of this chapter beginning teachers should:

- have a clear understanding as to who support staff and other professionals are;
- understand the contribution made by support staff and other professionals;
- develop an ability to work cooperatively with a range of people to support them and the learners;
- understand the limits of their own expertise and authority, and know how to seek help from others.

Introduction

UNDER THE PROFESSIONAL STANDARDS for the Award of Qualified Teacher Status document (Training and Development Agency (TDA) 2006), those awarded qualified teacher status (QTS) (section 1.6) must understand and uphold the professional code of the General Teaching Council for England by demonstrating that they understand the contribution that support staff make, and have a commitment to collaboration and cooperative working (TDA 2006). This chapter will highlight some of the issues involved in forming effective collaborations with different people and organisations under the umbrella of *Every Child Matters* (DfES 2004).

With the ever-changing educational landscape, the need to understand the contribution made by the wider workforce, called the paraprofessionals in this chapter, will be explored through examples drawn from the primary and secondary school contexts. The key agendas in the UK educational settings of: *Every Child Matters* (DfES 2004), Workforce Reform (Cheminais 2006), and the New Standards (TDA 2007), has required all professionals to adopt new ways of working and re-organisation in order to maximise the learning support offered to all children and young people. Such huge changes are likely to impact all teachers' and paraprofessionals' work as their roles provide different challenges and opportunities. From synthesising this debate, a working model of how fostering better closer partnerships with different stakeholders (social and health services) will be posed.

Over the last few years, the emphasis in schools has moved away from teachers and teaching and towards learners and learning. This is an inevitable outcome of the drive towards the measurement of quality, and towards achieving higher standards and levels of attainment. But we suggest that the relentless pace of change needs to be better managed and based on current thinking about distributed leadership for supporting change.

There has been an increase in both the number and type of paraprofessionals working in schools over the last few years. The *Every Child Matters* agenda sets out the Government's intention to extend school paraprofessional roles in order to support personalised learning, and also, to support the expansion of out of hours opportunities for learning. This is illustrated by Watson who suggests that 'extra support staff inside and outside the classroom will help teachers focus on their teaching role and provide more support for pupils learning so that higher standards can be achieved in the future' (2005: 1).

Schools are highly complex places where people have to 'deal continually with an array of changes' (Cockburn and Handscombe 2006: 12). Hence, effective teamwork is of paramount importance. As a beginning teacher, the practical implications of this new cultural shift of collaboration with different partners in your own practice will be developed to help support your work.

Impact of *Every Child Matters*

The *Every Child Matters* (ECM) legislation was the recognition for change following the Victoria Climbié case (Cheminais 2006). It took forward the Government's vision of radical reform for children, young people and families, and perceivably to close the gap in outcomes between the disadvantaged and their peers. Therefore, it strove for improved integration and accountability across all children's and young peoples services. We believe that *Every Child Matters* highlights better outcomes for all children and young people through its stated aims of:

- Being healthy.
- Staying safe.
- Enjoying and achieving through learning.
- Making a positive contribution to society.
- Achieving economic well-being.

However, outcomes alone will not improve the quality of educational experiences. We need a climate of expertise, enthusiasm, and a mix of experienced and early para-professionals to work closely with teachers to deliver high quality teaching and learning. How learners learn, how they cultivate respect, and how schools work with parents/carers and the wider community is more likely to deliver the Government's vision of an educated workforce. The Green Paper (DfES 2005) mentions a number of related areas to ECM to improve the life chances of children at risk including parenting/caring, fostering, young people's activities and youth justice. It proposes to build on what has already been achieved, including Sure Start, raising school standards and steps to help eradicate child poverty in the most deprived neighbourhoods. Many schools are exploring innovative ways to reach out to the wider community through Sure Start Children's Centres, full service extended schools and holding more activities for children out of school. Therefore the main impact of ECM is the creative ways in which effective partnerships are forged in strategic ways with different agencies.

New TDA Standards

The important issue is to ensure that the school development plan and daily practice shows strategic alignment to the Standards and the ECM agenda. Equally important will be to map the delivery against practice through appropriate monitoring and evaluation tools set in place. This may include self-assessment and using appropriate research tools to be used with the community to check where the school stands on ECM. For example, by carrying out parents/carers surveys, or having a suggestion box in school, or an open meeting to gain the views of the parents/carers regarding the effective coordination of services. This is a new territory for all who are involved in the delivery of high quality education to children and young people. It is therefore imperative that the voices of children and young people, professionals in the school and stakeholders outside the school are captured. This requires strategic drive, systems and structures to be set up, and appropriate monitoring undertaken to take account of practice. It is equally important that such accountability is kept simple, otherwise, alienation may hinder overall progress. There are no formal route maps for moving forward the ECM agenda. What we hope in this chapter is to offer you ideas for discussion, debate and dialogue, in an inclusive way. The following section looks at the workforce reform agenda and tries to identify the implications for practitioners in driving change.

Workforce reform: the changing role of the teacher

Remodelling was being seen by governors and teachers as a way of using and celebrating community spirit, to bring the needs of the school back to the forefront of their and their community's thinking. The way our schools are deploying their workforce from teachers to paraprofessionals is changing. Schools are encouraging teachers to use their time for what they are qualified to do, and focus on teaching and learning of the learners, whilst allowing other members of paraprofessional staff to take on more roles and responsibilities to free up teachers hence, the introduction of the Planning, Preparation and Assessment (PPA) time.

As a result of ECM, radical changes are now in place for all professionals. The autonomy that teachers have been accustomed to has increased, but with this, so has accountability in terms of practice and outcomes. More emphasis is now placed on the personalised learning of children, which is an approach to teaching and learning that 'concentrates on an individual's potential and learning skills' (Cockburn and Handscombe 2006: 23). A key factor of this personalised learning is the teacher's role in organising appropriate, effective, and stimulating learning experiences that extend beyond the school context and into the local and wider community.

In terms of the five outcomes of ECM, the greatest change for teachers regardless of their experience is how effectively to collaborate with a variety of colleagues both within and beyond the school contexts, as illustrated in Figure 6.1.

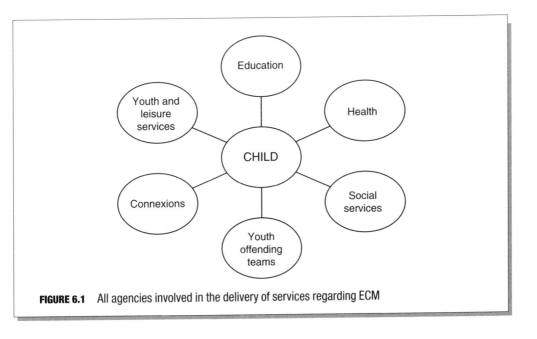

FIGURE 6.1 All agencies involved in the delivery of services regarding ECM

The above services will need to be coordinated effectively so that all children, young people and parents/carers have access to them. Most importantly, there needs to be a clear line of accountability for addressing issues that might need to be improved. A brief review of the roles of paraprofessionals is considered next.

Who are the paraprofessionals?

In each external agency there are those people who are deemed as being a professional as they have the relevant qualifications in their chosen area of expertise such as teachers, doctors, school nurses and educational welfare officers. The paraprofessionals are those people who support the professionals in their role, for example teaching assistants (TAs) supporting teachers. However, it is important to remember that paraprofessionals are professionals in their own right. Although the DfES (2005) acknowledges the contribution of other support staff, they fall short of explaining exactly what their role is, nor is there any analysis of the effectiveness of it. Therefore, we have attempted to clarify the main paraprofessionals in relation to *Every Child Matters*, but it is important to note that there are many others in addition to those mentioned below in Figure 6.2. The challenge for all collaborators is to understand better the language each uses in the delivery of services, and to coordinate effective, joined-up communication between all.

Challenges faced by paraprofessionals

This section focuses on the challenges faced by paraprofessionals in the education sector. However, many of these challenges are not unique to education alone, as they can also be applied to paraprofessionals in other sectors associated with ECM.

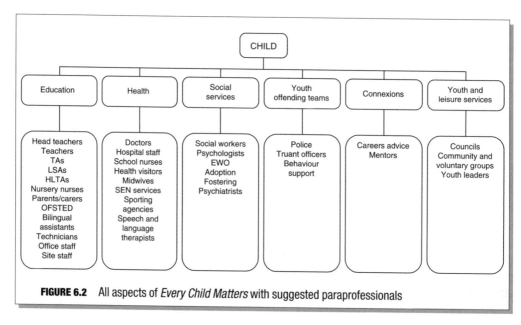

FIGURE 6.2 All aspects of *Every Child Matters* with suggested paraprofessionals

Overlapping of roles

It is vital for beginning teachers to remember that at times there will be an overlapping of roles between teachers and paraprofessionals, and even between the paraprofessionals, whereby staff are not clear where each other's responsibility lies. For example, with regard to curriculum issues there could be an overlap in terms of whose responsibility would it be to change aspects of assessment, would it be the curriculum coordinator?, the class teacher?, or the assessment coordinator? Another example could be an overlap of roles regarding administration tasks; for example, whose role would it be to gather and input SATs data for local authorities? A clear job description will help but more importantly it is essential to have clear lines of communication.

Power relationships

Beginning teachers will have to learn to establish effective collaborative working relationships with experienced teachers and all paraprofessionals. It is crucial to understand each others' roles and responsibilities so that there is a shared agenda for supporting young people's learning. Furthermore, effective relationships in schools are fostered where there is a conducive learning environment and where all people feel that they are listened to, are valued and regarded as worthwhile individuals by learners, parents/carers, governors and all staff. Mortimore *et al.* (1994), however, found that the voices of associate staff (the term they used for paraprofessionals in schools) were seldom heard, an image which tends to distort the balance of relationships that exist in schools. Even though the culture of collaboration is evident in many schools today, it is important to remember that this situation could occur at anytime. It is therefore crucial for beginning teachers to understand how the structures, systems and interpersonal relationships operate in schools and work within these parameters. For example, if line management structures are made clear to all staff in a school then it would mean that different team leaders are responsible for dealing with issues on a daily basis rather than the head teacher.

Key Stage expertise

Some TAs may have only worked in one Key Stage within a school and are therefore very experienced with this age group. Although some TAs would relish the challenge to work in a new Key Stage, it is important to remember that they may also feel anxious about any new situation. Some paraprofessionals (those who are employed to work with a specific child) may lack confidence in certain areas of the curriculum as the child progresses through primary school, especially if the adult moves up each year group with the child. In such situations, it is important to realise the importance of appropriate training and where to go for help and support.

Job specifications

Job specifications for all paraprofessionals need to be explicitly clear in both their wording and their understanding. Many paraprofessionals will undertake tasks in addition to what is indicated on their job description; however, as beginning teachers there needs to be some awareness as to the strengths, skills, and areas for development regarding the paraprofessionals that we work with on a daily basis. This is so that a mismatch of delegated tasks to given abilities does not occur.

Contractual restrictions

As beginning teachers, it is important to remember that many of the paraprofessional staff have contractual restrictions such as starting at 8.50am (as the children arrive to school), due to child care and other responsibilities. Therefore, they are not available at 8.30 in the morning to discuss the format for the day. Equally, their working day could end at 3pm, before the children have actually gone home, so they are not available to have discussions after school. It is important for beginning teachers to remember that in these type of situations, many schools tend to release paraprofessional staff from assemblies and other tasks to liaise with teachers. Many paraprofessionals also give up part of their lunch time to also liaise with teachers. With regard to ECM, it can be very frustrating for beginning teachers to try to liaise with outside agencies early in the mornings as many professionals may not start work until 9am, a time when teachers are in full flow of classroom teaching. With regard to ECM implications, it may mean that contracts need to be constructed in a more flexible manner to ensure that staff get paid for any additional agreed communications undertaken outside the set contractual hours.

Budget restrictions

It is important to remember that not all schools have the same budgets, and that a number of factors are responsible for this. As a result, some schools may not be able to afford the internal paraprofessionals needed to support teachers. For example, a special needs child who has severe needs may have to go through the process of being statemented, but even then there is always the issue of 'time lag' as to when the appropriate person can be hired to support the needs of the child effectively. With regard to ECM implications, it may mean that aspects of budgets in each sector of ECM could be combined for the same purpose; that is, the sooner an assessment of a child that may require a statement can be undertaken, the better it is for all.

Opportunities faced by paraprofessionals

There are many opportunities open to teachers where they can better foster partnerships with different stakeholders internally and externally through collaboration with paraprofessionals. They may well be the eyes and ears of teachers. Time constraint is acknowledged as the biggest drawback but creative ways are already employed in schools to make things happen for the interests of children and young people. There are many professionals and volunteers who help and support in schools. In one secondary school, effective collaboration between an NQT and a mentor is established where both have ensured that their working relationship operates smoothly. In a primary school, a school policy to work with social workers, educational psychologists, education welfare officers, youth justice and health professionals and others, is written and used by all, rather than each member of staff having to devise their own ways to manage their working relationship.

Schools operate as 'open' organisations, subject to pressures and influences from the wider environment (Coleman *et al.* 1994). They are becoming more proactive in making links with other agencies, like education welfare officers and health professionals, and this is indeed a good opportunity. The links between schools and external advisors and support personnel is improving through careful management. In turbulent times for example, a school needs to be 'flexible and adaptive' (Hoyle 1986: 98), whereas in a stable environment, a more formal 'mechanistic' model may be most effective. Additionally, with schools forming a range of relationships with people, they are increasingly required to be accountable. The notion of accountability is explored next as this is an important function of celebrating and further nurturing partnerships with paraprofessionals.

Accountability may be considered by some critics as a 'nanny state' or a 'big brother watching' idea but it is an essential tool for developing better leadership and management of the wider workforce and as such, an ideal opportunity to engage with different sectors of the public. Accountability, as discussed by Scott (1989), is a multi-faceted concept which includes public accountability, professional accountability or consumerist accountability. Teachers should be able to identify examples of all three types of accountability in their establishments, and also as good practice train the paraprofessionals within their team to recognise aspects of accountability such as target setting. Within the normative concept of professional accountability for example, is importance placed upon the accountability of teachers to their profession. It is linked with self-reporting or self-evaluation, but may involve some level of dialogue with interested parties. In planning a collaborative partnership with other professionals, the notion of accountability to parents/carers, learners and other stakeholders is crucial.

So the need to understand each other's role and differing responsibilities is a vital opportunity for teachers. In analysing the needs of an SEN child through observations and notes made, for example, inexperienced teachers could refer to an experienced staff member first, and then, with their help and guidance, the SEN coordinator needs to be involved. For anything more serious, for example in cases of suspected abuse, they need to consult an identified person, usually the head teacher or other senior leadership team member who is the named person for driving and monitoring the Child Protection policy.

An understanding of the roles and responsibilities of different professionals in meeting the needs of learners is an important element of teaching. Not only do you have to know who to call on (e.g. social workers, educational psychologists, education welfare officers, youth justice and health professionals), you also need to be aware of the systems which exist to support you. You may also find that the school has a range of communication networks with voluntary agencies as well. It is therefore essential to be proactive and strategic in collaborating with a range of professionals as this will reduce the likelihood of duplication (Sweeney 1999).

Examples of working with other paraprofessionals are considered here. The school needs to have a clear job description for each type of teaching assistant as their duties will differ from one area to another, from one Key Stage to another. For example, teaching assistants in the foundation stage may have a different job description to teaching assistants involved in literacy or numeracy in Key Stage 2. In secondary schools where learning mentors are employed, a range of roles and tasks are undertaken both within and outside a classroom. For example, a learning mentor may be working outside a classroom to produce resources and materials to support learning, or in another role, they may be physically escorting learners to school. TAs' job descriptions need to be available to the teachers with whom they work so that they can give them appropriate tasks. Indeed, Ofsted look for the effective deployment of TAs in lesson planning.

As teachers you need to ensure that all adults in the classroom are clear about their respective roles in the lesson. For example, extra adults in the classroom could have photocopies of your planning with their activity highlighted so that they know exactly what they are doing and why (something stressed by Ofsted inspections as good practice). You can make the learning support staff aware of any difficulties before the lesson starts so that they can contribute to the positive management of learners' behaviour or they can let you know of any problems. The TAs also need to be familiar with the teacher's procedures regarding discipline. In this case, it will be easier if there is a whole school policy regarding discipline, so that all staff are clear. In one school, a method called assertive discipline is used and in the main this works well for most learners, with the exception being where extreme forms of negative behaviour are exhibited by learners. Assertive discipline means that learners are very clear of what is expected of them as regarding exhibiting good behaviour and conduct. Equally important is to reward good behaviour by encouraging, praising and rewarding with special activities. In another secondary school, proactive leadership of the student learning mentors has improved good discipline around the corridors and reduced the detention numbers drastically.

Shaw's (2001) work on learning supporters show that this group carry out a range of activities under the management of the teacher. They perform tasks like, 'spotting early signs of bullying and disruptive behaviour and implementing behaviour management policies' (p. 5). So it is essential for all teachers to work closely with such colleagues so as to draw on their considerable knowledge, understanding, skills and abilities.

The great untapped energy and abilities of other visiting professionals from the community can enhance a school's curriculum and go some way to revitalise staff enthusiasm. The important message is that these visitors should be made to feel valued by the whole school community. There are many good examples like suspending the school's timetable for a week to permeate intercultural activities across the curriculum. So trips to a Gurdwara or a Synagogue (Sikh and Jewish places of worship respectively) can be made educationally exciting by inviting people from such faiths to raise initial awareness. In three primary schools, for example, rituals and celebrations formed a project where multicultural dance focused on Chinese New Year celebrations. A visiting musician, dancer and cultural artist from China enchanted teachers and others alike with the sounds of her Ku-Cheng (Chinese harp). In one county, several secondary schools had planned the entire term's curriculum around an arts project. In another two secondary schools, there was collaboration of Year 8 classes focusing on a language week.

On a practical basis, in every curriculum subject there are opportunities to engage learners by showing respect for learners' cultural and personal identities. Here, issues of inequality and injustice can be explored using role play, developing knowledge and understanding of the history and development of one's own cultural traditions and of the ways in which these both foster and constrain one's own personal identity. There has been much borrowing, mingling and mutual influence over the centuries between different countries and cultural traditions (Richardson 1990). This gives teachers an opportunity to develop in their learners an ability to learn from different cultural experiences, norms and perspectives, and to empathise with people with different traditions. Equally important is the development in learners of the willingness to challenge instances of isms/phobia of any kind (see the introductory chapter to this book).

Deployment of bilingual and multilingual adult support for bilingual and multilingual learners requires the same sensitivity and tact by teachers as shown to any other adult. Indeed, bilingual and multilingual staff should be enabled to work in all areas of a school's programme. Bilingual and multilingual staff play a vital role in promoting learning and need to be supported in the work they do with learners and families. Bilingualism and multilingualism is a positive benefit to all for educational, social, economic and family reasons. Indeed, the TDA and other agencies in consultation with teachers and various community groups need urgently to consider the role of Asian languages and the way the National Curriculum renders them less important than European ones.

Some practical strategies of working with bilingual and multilingual staff offered by Siraj-Blatchford and Clarke (2000) include: encourage bilingual and multilingual staff to add to all school resources as well as bilingual and multilingual resources; encourage bilingual and multilingual staff to plan group times in both or various languages every day. Other examples include having bilingual and multilingual signs in and around the school, translating various notices around the school and have these next to the English ones, and making sure the physical environment reflects the home languages and cultures of the learners. Using photographs in the classroom can be a challenging and exciting activity, full of potential for language work. Involving learners in the experience of preparing for and meeting a visitor can be a rich source of pleasure and interest and give many opportunities for language work. There should be many chances to develop skills across different language levels like casual talk, response to visual and aural stimuli, listening to and telling unscripted stories and letter writing.

Diverse teams

In the 21st century, we can envision future scenarios in which both the education workforce and a range of partners including, critically, learners, become increasingly diverse. Managing a diverse group of people has its own challenges and opportunities. Forming diverse partnerships involving a variety of people to deliver the ECM and Workforce Reform agendas thus becomes a conundrum, namely the paucity of engagement with what diversity and diversity management means both, in theory and in practice.

Effective teams do not happen by chance, they have to be created deliberately and managed and nurtured systematically. As a member of a team, you need to be concerned with feelings and consciousness as well as with structures. Effective team building is facilitated by getting to know individuals, to know their strengths and to know how you can work together. It also means that we make a determined effort to understand the background of the diverse people with whom we work and with whom we are likely to form partnerships. So what does diversity mean in this context?

Diversity is defined and understood in multiple ways. Some definitions are broad and some narrow (Wentling *et al.* 2000: 36). Broad definitions draw on a wider range of diversity criteria, including age, disability, religion, sexual orientation, values, ethnic culture, national origin, education, lifestyle, beliefs, physical appearance, social class and economic status (Norton and Fox 1997). Narrow definitions of diversity, focusing on 'race', gender and disability may be inadequate for dealing with the variety of context, experience and perceptions within the education sector. Diversity is also defined in terms of the range of attributes, skills and experiences that individuals bring to the organisation. This means that we have to recognise that diverse strengths may need to be nurtured differently. If there are different kinds of diversity, this suggests a range of strategies may be needed to embed diversity into school planning, processes, and intended outcomes.

However, leading diverse people is challenging and can lead to positive as well as negative outcomes (DiTomaso and Hooijberg 1996). Some of the negative outcomes may result from a perceived lack of awareness of the needs and cultures of a varied workforce, which can easily be overcome through appropriate education and training. There is also evidence to indicate that diverse groups outperform homogeneous groups in creativity and problem solving (Mayo et al. 1996; Dreachslin et al. 2000). It is therefore crucial to develop leadership skills and management interventions that emphasise the positive aspects of team diversity whilst minimising its likely negative effects. Working with different cultures and backgrounds sometimes inadvertently throws up misunderstandings that need to be addressed quickly.

A study by Morrison et al. (2004) on diversity management in the learning and skills sector shows that practice is quite varied. First, the issue of diversity in some cases was seen as hostility and also diversity was understood in multiple ways. This suggests that a school's policy and values need closer alignment where the values of all staff are considered both in 'all white' and 'multicultural' schools. To be inclusive means to celebrate diversity and to use each others' skills, abilities and experiences as resources with potential to improve school practice.

Second, much of the leadership theory continues to mirror and reinforce indifference and confusion about diversity. As a starting point, where collaborations and team work are to work effectively, more conceptual clarity is needed. Cross-cultural studies are welcomed, but are not a substitute for in-depth engagement with diversity and diversity management (see Osler and Morrison 2000; Walker and Dimmock 2004). What then of the future? Recent ideas draw on ideas of a capabilities approach. This approach uses ethical theory to assist understandings of workplace equality and diversity and provides a set of conceptual building blocks (Gagnon and Cornelius 2000; Singh 2002). What remains crucial for teachers is that they continue to voice their opinions to leaders in schools, in committees and in the political arena, to make people listen, as repetition of old ideas will no longer suffice.

Schools operate partly on the basis of teams. Examples include working alongside other colleagues in a cooperative team teaching situation. We have noted good examples where English as an additional language specialists, bilingual and multilingual teachers and instructors and special educational needs specialists have planned and taught some sessions together. Teachers and other adults who belong to these groups are expected to act collaboratively with each other in order to meet school or team objectives. Collegiality places emphasis on teamwork where the talents of all team members can be harnessed.

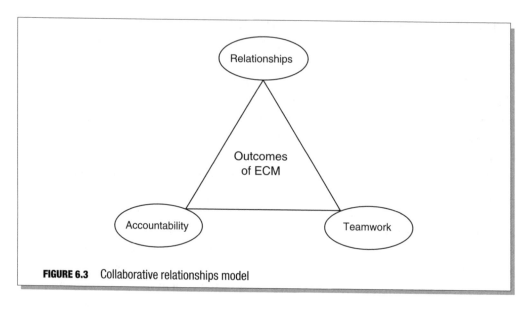

FIGURE 6.3   Collaborative relationships model

Different stakeholders are currently working in creative ways to deliver an integrated service which incorporates the values of ECM, the principles of Workforce Reform modelling, and the outcomes mapped against the TDA Standards. No 'one size fits all' model is likely to work, thus requiring a local model for local issues. Such a model of 'collaborative relationships' is proposed above, see Figure 6.3.

The thrust of the ECM principles is indicated within the large triangle in the model shown. All organisations are required to reflect on and develop their own practice to meet the outcomes of ECM. The monitoring and evaluation of such practice, as indicated before, is more likely to move the institution forward. At the edge of the triangle are three key terms: relationships, accountability and teamwork. We believe that by working in strategic and cohesive ways through effective communication, schools can develop good practice in embedding ECM. This is a dynamic model where an input from different stakeholders at different times of the school year is going to shift the balance of priorities. Therefore, this simple model offers one way which allows leadership of an institution to take a more flexible approach in developing innovative ways of embedding ECM and the Standards. The balance and relationships between stakeholders and schools is crucial to develop and beginning teachers have a vital role to play.

Conclusion

In a fast-changing educational landscape, the urgency to provide the highest standard of education and care to all children and young people remains paramount. The Government's mindset to impose ever demanding new challenges to schools without giving adequate resources or time to embed any practice continues unabatedly. Schools are drawn to their knees in order to deliver, allegedly, increasingly demanding 'targets' for the sake of improving standards. The evidence of targets and delivery remains to be researched and proven one way or the other.

In this chapter some notion and rationale for developing a clearer understanding of the role of paraprofessionals, or support staff, has been advanced. Their enormous contribution as unsung heroes is celebrated through brief examples, with many still to be accounted for. The thrust of our argument is that fostering relationships with a diverse group of people supporting and nurturing learners is the first essential step in successful delivery of high quality education. Also, developing an understanding of what diversity management means is the second step in this strategy for improving the life chances of children, young people and adults.

References

Cheminais, R. (2006) *Every Child Matters: A practical guide for teachers*. London: David Fulton Publishers.

Cockburn, A. and Handscombe, G. (eds) (2006) *Teaching Children 3–11: A Students Guide*. Paul Chapman: London.

Coleman, M., Bush, T. and Glover, D. (1994) *Managing finance and external relations*. Harlow: Longman.

DfES (2004) *Every Child Matters: Change for Children in Schools*. London: DfES.

DfES (2005) *The Green Paper*. London: DfES.

DfES (2006) *Qualifying to Teach*. Training and Development Agency: London.

Dreachslin, J.L., Hunt, P.L. and Sprainer, E. (2000) 'Workforce diversity: implications for the effectiveness of health care delivery teams', *Social Science and Medicine*, 50: 1403–14.

DiTomaso, N. and Hooijberg, R. (1996) 'Diversity and the Demands of Leadership', *The Leadership Quarterly*, 7(2): 163–87.

Gagnon, S. and Cornelius, N. (2000) 'Re-examining workplace equality. The capabilities approach', *Human Resource Management Journal*, 10(4): 68–87.

Hoyle, E. (1986) *The Politics of School Management*. London: Hodder and Stoughton.

Morrison, M., Lumby, J. M. and Sood, K. (2004) 'Unpacking a Conundrum: Leadership, Diversity and Diversity Management', paper submitted at BELMAS 2004 Annual Conference, Stone, Staffs.

Mayo, M., Pastor, J.C. and Meindl, J.R. (1996) 'The Effects of Group Heterogeneity on the Self-Perceived Efficacy of Group Leaders', *The Leadership Quarterly*, 7(2): 265–84.

Mortimore, P., Mortimore, J. with Thomas, H. (1994) *Managing Associate Staff: Innovation in Primary and Secondary Schools*. Paul Chapman: London.

Norton, J.R. and Fox, R.E. (1997) *The Change Equation: Capitalising on diversity for effective organisational change*. Washington DC: American Psychological Association.

Osler, A. and Morrison, M. (2000) *Inspecting Schools for Racial Equality. Ofsted's Strengths and Weaknesses*. Stoke-on-Trent: Trentham Books for the Commission for Racial Equality.

Richardson, R. (1990) *Daring to be a Teacher*. Stoke-on-Trent: Trentham Books.

Scott, P. (1989) 'Accountability, responsiveness and responsibility' in R. Glatter (ed.) *Educational Institutions and their Environments: Managing the Boundaries*. Milton Keynes: Open University Press.

Shaw, L. (2001) *Learning supporters and inclusion*. Bristol: CSIE.

Singh, V. (2002) *Managing Diversity for Strategic Advantage*. London: Council for Excellence in Management and Leadership.

Siraj-Blatchford, I. and Clarke, P. (2000) *Supporting Identity, Diversity and Language in the Early Years*. Buckingham: Open University Press.

Sweeney, D. (1999) 'Liaising with parents, carers and agencies', in M. Cole (ed.) *Professional Issues for Teachers and Student Teachers*. London: David Fulton.

TDA (2007) www.fda.gov.uk.

The Runnymede Trust (1993) *Equality Assurance in Schools: quality, identity, society – a handbook for action planning and school effectiveness*. Stoke-on-Trent: Trentham Books.

Walker, A. and Dimmock, C. (2004) 'The International Role of the NCSL: Tourist, Colporteur, or Confrere?', *Educational Management Administration and Leadership*, 32(3): 269–88.

Watson, A. (2005) *Professional Values and Practice*. David Fulton: London.

Wentling, R.M. and Palma-Rivas, N. (2000) 'Current Status of Diversity Initiatives in Selected Multinational Corporations', *Human Resource Development Quarterly*, 11(1): 35–60.

Useful websites

http://www.everychildmatters.gov.uk/

http://www.tda.gov.uk/

http://www.skills4schools.org.uk/

Reflection and professional development: becoming a creative teacher

Valerie Coultas

Q7 (a) Reflect on and improve their practice, and take responsibility for identifying and meeting their developing professional needs.

(b) Identify priorities for their early professional development in the context of induction.

Learning objectives

To promote understanding of:

- how to become a self-critical, reflective practitioner;
- the importance of collaborative planning and teamwork;
- how to develop classroom management skills and subject knowledge;
- how to use professional development to improve teaching and become a creative teacher.

Introduction

AN EFFECTIVE TEACHER is someone who sees herself or himself as a learner. Teachers who evaluate and change their own practice to benefit their pupils are rewarding colleagues to work with. They make teaching a highly creative experience. Often the most useful lesson observations can be those carried out by a teacher who is a peer, someone who has to battle with similar problems. By planning lessons collaboratively, focusing on the same topic /text or the same type of pedagogy, and then evaluating these lessons together, teachers can improve classroom practice. It is through close collaboration, shared evaluation and team teaching that teachers can make breakthroughs and deliver the most successful lessons. A colleague can often notice a detail in the instructions that has been missed out in a lesson that is team-taught because they are paying close attention to pupil responses. Even the most experienced teachers can benefit from this process of collaboration.

It is far more positive to have these discussions with colleagues than to wait for an inspector to point out your errors. If teachers start teaching with this view of classroom practice, they will automatically evaluate lessons. An energetic professional teacher is self-critical, collaborative and creative. Once a teacher adopts this approach to teaching they will never lose it. This view of teachers values the voice of the teacher and sees the teacher as an agent of change within the school.

Teamwork

Many schools encourage this kind of collaboration through teamwork in departments and joint planning between teachers in different phases. Teamwork takes place formally and informally in schools and the degree to which a teacher feels supported by other colleagues is of great importance in developing teaching repertoires and dealing with the challenges of teaching. Good teachers can act autonomously but they also benefit from working collaboratively. The best schemes of work/ medium-term plans are often produced and evaluated collectively. Team teaching and peer reviews also promote reflective practice. This formal teamwork is excellent practice. Sometimes it is through a one-to-one discussion with a line manager during, for example, a feedback from a lesson observation that useful advice will be offered. Sometimes useful advice can be offered to a line manager in a support and supervision interview. Often it is the informal discussion with a colleague at break or after school that can also lead to a new approach in teaching.

However, the attempt to impose quantitative targets on those discussions by the Government through performance-related pay fails to comprehend the essence of good teaching, which involves being responsive to children's needs and evaluating teaching through teamwork and intellectual collaboration. A department or a school's results are not good because of isolated, inspired individuals but because good practice is shared, knowledge and expertise are recognised and valued, and colleagues and managers give positive support and advice to staff when required. Teachers are not working on production lines in industry. They are nurturing, training, educating and developing young people. Their intellectual energy is encouraged by good advice, good leadership and shared values – not through the imposition of individual targets linked to pay. Support and supervision that discusses training needs is often more effective in encouraging teachers to evaluate their strengths and weaknesses than systems that discourage honest self-assessment because they are linked to pay rises. The teacher is a creative professional educating children and their accountability should be to the community. They do not have to view themselves as managers or skilled technicians implementing the advice of government departments. The new pay schemes that are lowering or abolishing responsibility points for pastoral heads and the attempts to classify teachers into Post Threshold/Excellent and Advanced skills teachers threatens the collective identity of teachers and may serve to weaken teamwork in schools.

The Government's search for quantitative, measurable data to prove success can often dismiss qualitative improvements in schools. Education cannot be reduced to the acquiring of skills; the 'ticking boxes' agenda is reductionist. As Caroline Benn (2001) suggested, the 'limited target culture' can have the effect of losing sight of the broader aims of education and the emotional and moral aspects of learning. Fortunately, many practitioners and head teachers are more aware of the different ways good practice can be developed in a school and have attempted to set individual targets that are more holistic and relate to broader educational and training needs but there is renewed pressure on school leaders to impose harsher forms of performance management.

Targets for improvement

It is suggested that teachers should identify areas for their own development and set targets for improvement. Schools are encouraged to base this on evidence from results. It may be that this will involve closely analysing exam results at the end of a Key Stage of a group that you have taught in order to evaluate your success. Sometimes your school will ask the subject coordinators or heads of subject to produce yearly comparisons of results. This overall comparison can help you make a real evaluation of your results, taking into account the actual ability of your pupils; for example, by comparing predicted levels or grades with final results. Looking closely at how individual pupils perform, linked to discussions with other teachers, will give you a range of ideas about how to improve your teaching. The figures must be analysed and discussed to give this process real meaning. The new professional standards put more emphasis on coaching and mentoring and if this is interpreted as allowing staff time for non-judgemental peer reviews, this could also assist creativity and reflective practice.

But qualitative evaluations with pupils can be just as important for reflection on your teaching. Such pupil evaluations are sometimes less valued by the male managerial 'quantitative analysis is best' culture that has been fostered by recent governments. These could involve an evaluation with the all the pupils at the end of a unit or course using their individual self-assessments, or it could involve a more in-depth discussion with a particular group to get feedback. You need to carry this out orally on some occasions and in writing on others. The response of the pupils themselves to a unit of work or a course is often a key indicator of successful teaching and it can help you to make adjustments to improve the content or the pedagogy, or focus more closely on particular skills the pupils need. Such an assessment, a qualitative judgement or piece of research, is of particular value to the teacher. It shows the pupils that you value their opinions and it is useful for setting really useful subject targets (Coultas 2006). Sharing your findings with other staff can promote a much deeper discussion about how pupils are learning. If whole departments engage in this process it means that the course will continually improve. The process of identifying areas for development individually can therefore be assisted by an INSET session, a departmental or phase discussion led by a team leader, or a line management review. But as a learning teacher you will come to those discussions with an awareness of where you have done well and how you can improve. You will even suggest themes for INSET and training to ensure that staff development serves your needs.

Teachers should also seek to improve their subject knowledge and build on areas of specialism. It is vital that teachers not only have secure knowledge of the subjects they teach but that they are aware of the new developments in those subjects, for example the National Frameworks for teaching literacy and numeracy (DfEE 1998) and the Primary and Secondary Strategies (DfES 2006a) and the debates these have generated. There are also areas of specialism within a subject that teachers may wish to become more familiar with. For example, in a core subject, such as English, there are many possible subdivisions – oracy, ICT, media studies, poetry, drama, non-fiction writing and research. To gain greater expertise in one of these areas could be a goal that strengthens your teaching.

Equality and equal opportunity

In primary and secondary schools it may be a Key Stage or pastoral issue where you wish to specialise. An important area of knowledge the new teacher will have to develop relates to equality and equal opportunity issues. The new legislation *Every Child Matters* (2006) outlines some very high ideals in five key areas for teachers and other professionals. The shift from a focus on learners' achievements to the 'cultivation of learners' achievements and *wellbeing*' (Broadhead and Gordon 2006) will be welcomed by many and schools will be looking at how the ECM approach can enhance equal opportunities, inclusion and working with professionals outside schools. Equal opportunity is relevant to how you teach and how you build relationships with pupils, colleagues and parents/carers. A teacher must ensure they can identify and address all the different needs in the classroom. Lesson planning needs to address pupils with special needs, with English as an additional language and high attainers. Even though setting is more common in secondary schools, the teacher cannot assume the same achievement level in each class. Enjoying and achieving means planning lessons that cater for the different levels of achievement through some form of differentiation and pupil involvement (Coultas 2007). The teacher must also be aware of how to involve boys and girls in the lesson. A teacher can ensure that boys do not dominate oral work by preparing pupils to answer questions and asking particular pupils to answer on some occasions. They can use drama to engage all pupils and writing frames/planning activities and clear time limits to ensure that everyone is able to complete a piece of extended writing.

It is important that teachers have a sophisticated understanding of equal opportunity issues as they are constantly alive within the classroom and they have to be aware of all the different social divisions to mediate effectively between them. This includes all forms of sexism, towards boys and girls, and the need to combat racism and homophobic bullying. You must also recognise the divisive effects of social class, and the way in which the formal middle-class values of schools often undervalue the skills of working-class pupils, and counter any discrimination based on disability. You must also show, by the way you use praise and how you choose pupils to help you, that you value all pupils equally, regardless of 'race', gender, social class, sexual orientation or disability. You must be alert to children's social and emotional development and be prepared to seek advice where it is necessary. You are a role model for the pupils and they will watch what you do and compare it with what you say.

As Cole (2006: 4) has argued, these social divisions 'are not inevitable features of any society' but specific to given societies. Children can respond in contradictory ways to these issues. Often they will challenge these divisions quite spontaneously because their socialisation is incomplete. On other occasions, they will also reproduce these social divisions very crudely. Teachers can intervene in this process to educate children very effectively if they understand equality and equal opportunity issues. For a wider discussion of the breadth of these professional issues related to equality, see Cole *et al.* (eds) 1997; Cole 1999; Hill and Cole (eds) 1999; Cole (ed.) 2006; and Hill and Cole (eds) 2001.

Classroom management

For many teachers new to the classroom a key area will be the issue of classroom management. This is often the primary concern of a new teacher and it is an area where they feel they have the least training. A teacher will gain a lot of good ideas by observing good practice in their own school but two useful guides with particularly practical advice on classroom management and good advice on handling challenging pupils have been written: these are Marland (1991) and Blum (1998). The latter text is useful for understanding how positive behaviour policies and praise can be used very effectively in turbulent classrooms. The new teacher would benefit from learning more about the idea of positive or assertive discipline, as it is one of the most important and practical theories that teachers have developed to handle disruptive behaviour. While many formally subscribe to it, the importance of rewarding good behaviour is often underestimated in practice, particularly in secondary schools.

As a teacher in charge of PHSE, at an inner London school, I was involved in developing a Year 9 careers and sex education course that taught staff and pupils the ideas behind assertive behaviour. In a series of drama lessons, in separate all-boy and all-girl groups led by male and female members of staff, pupils learnt about aggressive, assertive, manipulative and passive forms of behaviour and how we had a choice about how we behaved: how we could learn to say no, distinguish between flattery and compliments and give and receive criticism. These lessons led on to a discussion of sexual/racial harassment and bullying and then into the sex education unit and anti-sexist careers guidance part of the course. These lessons were carefully designed to tap into the psychological, physical and social stage of development of the 13–14-year-olds. I used these assertiveness training sessions in several other school contexts and they were always extremely successful. All teachers and pupils should be taught about assertiveness to improve techniques in behaviour management and relationships in schools.

Since the Thatcher era there has been an increase in selection in secondary schools. The decision to develop Specialist, Faith, Trust schools and City Academies will not only continue but as Hattersley (2002) argues will actually extend this process and dismantle the comprehensive system. There has been recent research by educational charities, such as the Sutton Trust cited in *Casenotes* (Birket 2005), highlighting the lower numbers of pupils on free school meals in, for example, Church schools that control their admissions policies, a process that is likely to deepen as more schools control their own admissions. This has meant that many teachers working in schools that have a more socially disadvantaged intake now face challenging behaviour in all their classrooms. Such schools are also under constant pressure to raise standards and compete with schools that have creamed off the less disadvantaged pupils where the behaviour is, in general, less challenging. Thrupp (2000), in an article reviewing the school improvement agenda, has listed some of the possible negative effects of this kind of pressure on such schools. In this article he argues that this 'over-optimistic view of schools improving against the odds' could mean that the school improvers fail to question the 'further polarisation of school intakes by educational quasi-markets' (p. 2). Thrupp's points are also relevant to the new ECM agenda. Large numbers of children in urban areas still live in poverty and schools, even working with others, cannot overcome this problem. Tackling child poverty and really ensuring that every child matters requires the Government to take a more radical stance on income redistribution. Despite promising to eradicate child poverty, the Blair/Brown Government has failed to do this. Thrupp also suggests that school improvement theories 'downplay the importance of state support for disadvantaged schools by putting too much emphasis on their ability to be self-managing' (p. 2).

For the new teacher strategies to improve their classroom management skills will be a top priority, particularly in these challenging environments. All schools should have induction programmes to assist new staff and allow them time to observe other colleagues to gain knowledge of the range of strategies that can be used to address the needs of these pupils. Team teaching is also a valuable way to mentor and build confidence among new staff. I would argue that in challenging schools new staff and beginning teachers need more time to observe and teacher tutors should be given time to really tutor. Teachers need to be particularly resilient in these settings and they need extra support to teach successfully.

Pedagogy

The methods that you use in the classroom are very important if you wish pupils to really learn something new each lesson. Didactic teaching methods are still relied on by large numbers of teachers, particularly in secondary schools, but there are a lot of young learners who find this a difficult way to remember what they are told. Many teachers fear losing control or lack the preparation time that is required to plan the more interactive lessons. But all pupils need to be actively involved in the learning process to really make academic progress, particularly the pupils who are less motivated. Collaborative talk before writing is essential for bilingual and SEN pupils but it also improves the writing of all pupils. Lessons need to be planned that have an interactive element at their core (Coultas 2001, 2003, 2006, 2007). Primary school teachers can ensure this through joint planning for group work, but in secondary schools, where teachers may teach 150 children a day and follow a broad scheme of work, staff can often avoid planning interactive lessons and rely on teacher talk or ask children to copy large chunks of text from the OHP or the blackboard. Even the 'interactive' whiteboard can be used in a highly didactic way where, for example, a text is deconstructed by the teacher and the pupils have little input.

There are many strategies that can stimulate pupils' interest and engagement in lessons. The key element of a successful lesson is that the pupils really engage with the learning and this usually takes place when they collaborate on a short or longer task, when their imaginations are sparked. One example that comes to mind is a class discussion about flying after reading the first few chapters of *Harry Potter and the Philosopher's Stone*. The question on the board was: What if we could all fly? The pupils had to discuss using three columns, the plus points, the minus points and the interesting points. I expected a 10–15-minute discussion at the most. But the pupils would not let the discussion go. Hands kept on going up to give more ideas – traffic jams in the sky, new kinds of maps, how exactly we would be able to fly – the speculations were endless and the discussion went on for nearly 45 minutes.

Widening styles of teaching and addressing the multicultural identity of the pupil population was an area of expertise that really flourished during the lifespan of, for example, the Inner London Education Authority. A London-wide authority with large numbers of advisory teachers was able to assist teachers in experimenting with collaborative and pupil-centred materials and to produce literature based on the pupils' writing. A whole host of new literature was made available to teachers and much of it is still used in schools. Professional Associations such as the National Association of Teachers of English (NATE), the National Oracy Project (1992) and training centres such as The English and Media Centre have continued to promote styles of teaching that focus on collaborative and child-centred forms of pedagogy.

The child-centred approach to teaching was an important feature of PGCE teacher education courses prior to the Thatcher era. Teacher education for primary and secondary teachers emphasised the importance of real talk in the classroom and the links between talking with confidence and writing with confidence. This approach recognised the alienating features of teacher talk for working-class pupils and suggested ways of establishing real dialogues between teacher and pupil – through anecdote, group work, visiting speakers, investigation, research and discovery. The National Curriculum, informed by the Cox Report (1989), gave equal status to speaking and listening alongside reading and writing.

The National Literacy Strategy had some good advice about the modelling of oral work, reading and writing. It also usefully developed the idea that every lesson needs to be literacy-aware. But there was a danger in aspects of the strategy that it could reinforce old-fashioned, didactic methods of teaching English. If teachers are forced to study short, separate texts and decontextualised grammar exercises, this could become a new version of the comprehension textbooks that made some English lessons so tedious in the early 1960s. Wyse and Jones (2001) point out that in primary schools the literacy and numeracy strategies leave little opportunity for 'creative and unpredictable aspects of development such as talk' (p. 193). They are concerned that talk takes on 'a functional quality; a means by which the skills of reading and writing may be enhanced' (p. 193). They recommend that teachers of all subjects allow talk to become 'open, exploratory, tentative, questioning, insightful and collaborative' (p. 195). The new QCA documentation (2003) on Speaking and Listening, Excellence and Enjoyment (QCA 2003) and the new Primary Strategy (2006a) have gone some way to address the imbalances in the National Literacy Strategy and give primary schools more flexibility in curriculum planning. An approach that encourages pupil-led talk has long been the hallmark of good teaching and learning and will continue to be a goal for the most creative teachers. To explore and experiment with different forms of pedagogy will be a vital goal for any learning teacher.

There are also some interesting new developments in this area of pedagogy in the debate surrounding able and gifted pupils and the present discourse on thinking skills, accelerated learning and the different types of learner – kinaesthetic, auditory and visual learners (Smith 1996; Eyre 1997). Kinaesthetic learners are people who learn best through movement or touch. Auditory learners learn best through sound, and visual learners store images in their brain. Some researchers such as Noble *et al.* (2001) have suggested that boys 'form a preponderance of kinaesthetic learners' (p. 100), that they are 'active and athletic', they 'learn best through doing what is being taught' (p. 100) and that 'if there is a dearth of kinaesthetic techniques', boys will fall behind 'into a vicious circle of under-achievement' (p. 101). These theories underline the importance of teachers using multi-sensory learning styles but they must not be used to place children in rigid categories that could lead to a new form of streaming where the 'learners by doing' are separated from other children.

It is important also to think carefully about how adults can acquire new knowledge. It cannot be assumed that all teachers learn in the same way or wish to be trained in the same way. It is up to each individual to define their own needs and learning styles as graduate teachers. Some teachers, as graduates with high levels of concentration, like to be lectured and told clearly what is expected of them at a training session. Others prefer to be involved in a much more active way in new proposals and initiatives. Some staff prefer to be given documentation before a session begins. Yet others gain knowledge and expertise from colleagues in similar roles in other schools. Another way of acquiring knowledge within school is through action research projects. I have initiated several of these projects – on gender and literacy, on oracy and teaching styles – and carried out literacy audits/work sampling in different schools. I have used samples of pupil evaluations of oral work to demonstrate how the pupils gain in enjoyment and enthusiasm for learning through collaborative-based talk and how this increases their self-awareness (Coultas 2006). I recognise this as a valuable way of teachers acquiring expertise, learning more about the institution they teach in and the needs/interests of the pupils. This is an approach which operates on a grass roots, cooperative model of teaching and on a belief that schools work best when teachers are allowed to have free souls to enquire and develop good practice.

Professional development

A learning teacher must have initiative, seek out and make use of sources of professional development. As an INSET coordinator, I assisted my colleagues by passing on the relevant training information. But individual teachers can also access the National Grid for Learning, join subject associations and attend network meetings to find the relevant forms of training to address their individual needs.

It is not only participation in training that defines the self-motivated teacher. It is also the ability to evaluate and use professional development opportunities appropriately that is vitally important. In work, as in schools, it is how we apply knowledge that marks us out. The teacher who tries out new techniques quickly after the training will incorporate that knowledge and adapt it to suit their situation. Some schools encourage each individual member of staff to evaluate their training through the provision of some kind of structure – a discussion with your line manager or an evaluation form. If not, the individual should develop his or her own records and process of evaluation to ensure that training is used constructively. Staff who keep a professional development portfolio will find this useful when applying for promotion.

It is often surprising how much expertise exists among staff in any one school. Schools sometimes seek advice from consultants and experts from outside the school on the assumption that there is not a lot of knowledge on that subject within the school. Yet knowing your staff and where real knowledge and expertise lies and how to use it is a feature of good management and good teachers. I have often been surprised how willing overworked and stressed staff are to share expertise and assist other colleagues with formal and informal training. As with pupils, teachers should approach other staff carefully with specific requests for assistance and always give staff a lot of notice of extra demands. This applies to assistance with all routine duties as well as INSET. It can refer to making requests of your line manager to assist you or even your head teacher. Using the expertise of those around you is therefore a key indicator of the teacher who is a learner.

Being able to respond positively to praise, advice and criticism is also a crucial feature of a good practitioner. Having taught in two very tough London boys' schools and other challenging schools, I can attest that it is hard to accept some of the abuse that can come from pupils, nor should a teacher tolerate any disrespectful remarks, for example racist or sexist abuse. But when a colleague or pupil makes a thoughtful criticism it is worthwhile stepping back and deciding whether the criticism has any truth in it. Is there anything I can improve on here is a question the beginning teacher can ask her/himself. Perhaps part of the criticism can be acknowledged while part of it maybe unfair. Likewise with praise – too often we are too stressed or embarrassed and fail to acknowledge praise with a confident and positive response. Yet a motivated teacher knows that we can only survive in schools with the trust, help, support, advice and criticism of our colleagues/pupils and that it is this collective spirit and sense of purpose that makes teaching a worthwhile profession.

The teacher's role is a nurturing one towards the young. The best teachers ensure that they build good relationships with the pupils they teach in many subtle and important ways. Although a teacher has to deal with a class as a group, a successful teacher is also able to communicate with pupils as individuals. A teacher not only has to be available for one-to-one discussion with pupils but also has to interact with colleagues. To be available for and willing to assist your colleagues is an intrinsic skill required of all teachers regardless of their status or position within a school. In my experience, the more challenging the behaviour of the pupils, the greater the need for teachers to share their expertise and be available for each other. Knowledge of the individual child's background can be vital to understanding behaviour and academic progress and schools need to plan for staff to share this information in an appropriate context. Having led several academic and pastoral teams in different schools I know how important it is that staff understand school procedures if they are to follow them accurately. Staff who ask detailed questions about how exactly a section of a scheme of work breaks down in practice or who are able to admit that they do not fully understand what their role as tutor involves, assist all new staff. This is the same with whole school issues in staff meetings. Teachers who fail to articulate their difficulties and concerns are far less likely to be following the school and department policies as consistently as those who acknowledge their need for help.

One of the negative features of re-structuring 'failing' schools in the 1990s was that staff were prevented from asking questions and reflecting on new policies because of the pressure of continuous inspection and the fear of being labelled troublesome. This led to many good teachers, particularly some of the most altruistic ones, changing schools, careers or even opting for early retirement and voluntary redundancy, which added to the crisis of teacher supply, a particularly severe problem now in challenging inner-city schools. Tony Blair's brave new managerial world has made it unfashionable for teachers to talk of the realities of social deprivation and its effects in schools because this is ridiculed as an apology for 'low expectations'. But social class continues to influence academic achievement and it is the poor that experience the most disruption in their education today. Mackie (2000) has written a very personal account of the effects of continual change and restructuring of schools that serve disadvantaged communities and the negative impact this process has on the lives of pupils and teachers in these schools. The reality is that social class has always played and continues to play a vital role in determining educational achievement (Hill and Cole 2001) and while all teachers must have high expectations for all, they must also have a realistic understanding of how social class affects educational achievement.

An excellent NUT training programme I attended as a young teacher suggested that all teachers should view themselves as 'managers' of the classroom and managers and leaders of others. This view of the classroom teacher is important as it emphasises the variety and breadth of knowledge and skills a teacher possesses. The teacher's role was to empower pupils and manage the classroom. As teachers we could also empower each other by the way we relate to each other in schools, sharing expertise and good practice.

Collaborative teaching

When assistance is offered to the beginning teacher he or she should know how to use it appropriately. Having worked very closely with EAL and SEN colleagues and learning support assistants, I am very interested when they give me examples of staff who do not know how to receive and use support. If lessons have an interactive/pair or group work element, teachers should always provide a role for another adult as they can easily target one group or the teacher can target a group and they can circulate. Reading aloud can always be made more enjoyable for the pupils when different adults participate. If it is planned support, teachers or support staff can read with a group or individuals or prepare a reading for the class with a particular group. Specialist staff are often willing to prepare materials for particular pupils if the classroom teacher makes the task clear. Collaboration with support staff is much easier when the support is a regular feature of a lesson each week and the relationship between the two adults has time to develop. When SEN and EAL staff are allocated to departments or year groups the collaboration is greatly improved as the support staff have a clear overview of the curriculum.

A second adult, who is there to help, is always welcome in my classroom. The very presence of another adult makes me feel more relaxed and able to be more adventurous in my teaching. There are often unusual spin-offs from lessons that are taught by two adults. For example, once I was sent a supply teacher to team-teach my lesson. The teacher enthusiastically joined in the lesson on war poetry where the pupils were asked to draw a collage of pictures to illustrate the poem 'Dulce et Decorum Est' by Wilfred Owen in a unit on war poetry. The teacher not only joined in the reading of the poem aloud but he also drew his own sketches of the poem to the delight of the students around him. They were very good sketches. The next lesson I used those sketches on an OHP to revise the poem and take the pupils into the next exercise.

The pupils and the staff had a good feeling about that lesson. The assistance of another adult can be of great benefit to the pupils and the teacher. There is often a more democratic ethos in a classroom where the teaching is shared on a more long-term basis and more independent learning can take place. Even short-term assistance, to remove a troublesome child or quieten down a noisy group, is also sometimes required and teachers should learn to welcome that assistance and not be fearful that it diminishes their authority.

Conclusion

The teacher who is a learner can always contribute to the development of other colleagues. Your enthusiasm for your subject or favoured forms of pedagogy may motivate both pupils and colleagues. Your belief in the value of teaching and education as a source for the enrichment of society can inspire others. Your belief that education can be a source for change towards building a more egalitarian society will motivate pupils and colleagues alike. Your practical advice and explanations of how to overcome difficulties and persevere will always be of value to your colleagues. Creative teachers can adapt, amend and integrate new ideas about teaching. Beginning teachers, fresh from higher education, as well as learning from others, can enrich schools by looking at them with new eyes, and can contribute new ideas, approaches and insights. As teachers and learners, our minds should never be closed to learning something new.

References

Benn, C. (2001) 'A Credible Alternative: Some Tasks for the Future', *Education and Social Justice*, 3(2), (Autumn).

Blum, P. (1998) *Succeeding and Surviving in Difficult Classrooms*. London: Routledge.

Birket, P. (2005) 'Do faith schools show commitment to the poor?' *Casenotes* Issue 10, August 2005.

Broadhead, P. and Gordon, K. (2006) *ECM and Teacher Education: Towards a UCET Position Paper* (Draft), University Council for the Education of Teachers.

Cole, M. (1999) 'Professional issues and Initial Teacher Education: what can be done and what could be done', *Education and Social Justice*, 2(1): 63–6.

Cole, M. (2006) 'Introduction: Human Rights, Equality and Education', in M. Cole (ed.) *Education, Equality and Human Rights: Issues of Gender, 'Race', Sexuality, Disability and Social Class*. 2nd edn, London: Routledge/Falmer.

Cole, M. (ed.) (2006) *Education, Equality and Human Rights: Issues of Gender, 'Race', Sexuality, Disability and Social Class*. 2nd edn, London: Routledge/Falmer.

Cole, M., Hill, D. and Shan, S. (eds) (1997) *Promoting Equality in Primary Schools*. London: Cassell.

Coultas, V. (2001) Oracy Across the Curriculum: Selhurst High School. Unpublished paper.

Coultas, V. (2003) 'Unwrap the Gift – An element of surprise keeps the able alive', *TES*, April 2003.

Coultas, V. (2006) 'Investigating Talk in Challenging Classrooms – Boys enjoy the power of talk', *English in Education*, 40(2): Summer 2006.

Coultas, V. (2007) *Constructive Talk in Challenging Classrooms*. London: Routledge.

Cox Report (1989) Department of Education and Science and The Welsh Office.

DfES (1998) *The National Literacy Strategy – Framework for Teaching*. London: DfES.

DfES (2003) *Every Child Matters*. London: DfES.

DfES (2005) *Secondary National Strategy for School Improvement 2005–6*. London: DfES.

DfES (2006a) *Primary National Strategy Draft Framework for Teaching Literacy Consultation Document*. London: DfES.

DfES (2006b) *Professional Standards for Teachers*. London: DfES.

DfES *English for Ages 5–16* (The Second Cox Report). York: National Curriculum Council.

Eyre, D. (1997) *Able Children in Ordinary Schools*. London: David Fulton Publishers.

Hattersley, R. (2002) 'Education, Education, Education: A Commitment Reviewed', *Education and Social Justice*, 4(1): 2–6 (Winter).

Hill, D. and Cole, M. (eds) (1999) *Promoting Equality in Secondary Schools*. London: Cassell.

Hill, D. and Cole, M. (2001) 'Social Class', in D. Hill and M. Cole (eds) *Schooling and Equality: Fact, Concept and Policy*. London: Kogan Page.

Mackie, J. (2000) 'The Death of the Inner London Comprehensive', *Education and Social Justice*, 2(3): 2–5 (Summer).

Marland, M. (1991) *The Craft of the Classroom: A Survival Guide*. Oxford: Heinemann Educational.

National Oracy Project (1992) *Thinking Voices: The Work of the National Oracy Project.* London: Hodder and Stoughton.

Noble, C., Brown, J. and Murphy, J. (2001) *How to Raise Boys' Achievement.* London: David Fulton Publishers.

Qualifications and Curriculum Authority (QCA) (2003) *The Primary National Strategy Speaking and Listening for Key Stages One and Two.* London: DfES.

Smith, A. (1996) *Accelerated Learning in the Classroom.* Stafford: Network Educational Press.

Thrupp, M. (2000) 'Compensating for Class: Are School Improvement Researchers Being Realistic?', *Education and Social Justice,* 2(2), (Spring).

Wyse, D. and Jones, R. (2001) *Teaching English, Language and Literacy.* London: Routledge/Falmer.

8

Innovation and improvement

Ian Woodfield

Q8 Have a creative and constructively critical approach towards innovation, being prepared to adapt their practice where benefits and improvements are identified.

Learning objectives

To promote an understanding of:

- the need to recognise the importance of creativity as a fundamental quality of successful classroom practice;
- the need to develop as a reflective practitioner, actively and critically engaged with policy and process;
- the need to contribute to the development of a collegiate culture within a professional learning community.

Introduction

AS A NEWLY QUALIFIED TEACHER in the 1970s I left training college fired with an enthusiasm to teach my subject, history, but with I readily confess only a very limited idea of how to go about it in the classroom. My training college course focused on the nature of the various disciplines that commonly comprised teacher education – psychology, philosophy and sociology – coupled with the academic study of history. However, few if any of my lecturers really addressed the issue of how to link up these areas of study with the classroom experience, that – it was generally felt – was up to me. In the decades that followed that 'sink or swim' approach had some positive outcomes, it made *me* think about how to teach my subject and how to engage my pupils, to reflect on the relationship with my colleagues and to plan for sustained improvement. However, in the first instance my on-the-job experimentation did not meet with unqualified success, but this was a world where provided you could contain your pupils within the classroom, few if any of your colleagues would intervene. In this relatively unstructured and permissive atmosphere, inspection was a distant and unlikely experience and performance review was largely a matter of *not* being brought to the head teacher's attention. My pupils and I survived our shared experience and eventually achieved some success together, an outcome that ultimately left me with the firm conviction that successful teaching is a creative act rather than a repertoire of technical skill sets or custom-made lesson plans. Such materials where they exist may well be a useful starting point, but ultimately the successful practitioner must engage creatively and critically with teaching *and* learning – constantly seeking to adapt to the needs of their pupils. More than this, as a true professional they must seek to contribute to a wider learning community – engaged critically with policy as well as practice.

Teachers in the 21st century are better trained and better resourced than any previous generation. However, what they need to maintain and in some senses to recapture is the freedom to engage creatively with pupils and colleagues in the process of schooling. Neither the National Curriculum, examination specifications nor management regimes can really prevent this process as these constraints can only make it easier to achieve or more difficult to achieve; for the critically engaged professional, the challenge is to work successfully within the macro and micro political environment, to go *beyond* narrow expectations of the nature and purpose of education and to resist any attempt to impose 'one size fits all solutions' to the classroom experience. Successful lessons are those where pupils learn (a simple nostrum but ultimately the foundation upon which the whole edifice of education is built) – the style of teaching should be determined in a dynamic process of adaptive exchange rooted in a shared experience and not by the prescriptive application of a predetermined formula. Our pupils learn from us once we have begun to learn from them; the reflective practitioner is always evaluating the success of particular strategies and they are always seeking new ideas and fresh techniques – it is a process that never stops and never ceases to be rewarding. It is a genuinely professional discipline that can only be developed by a well-qualified workforce secure in their status and appropriately rewarded for their expertise.

Key strategies for innovation and improvement

Watkins (2006) provides a telling summary of research evidence to help teachers of all ages and experience to focus on two key ideas:

- A focus on learning enhances performance.
- A focus on performance can depress performance.

TABLE 8.1   Research summary

Learning orientation	Performance orientation
■ We believe that effort can lead to success.	■ We believe that ability leads to success.
■ We believe in our ability to improve and learn, and not to be fixed or stuck.	■ We are concerned to be seen as able and to perform well in others' eyes.
■ We prefer challenging tasks whose outcome reflects our approach.	■ We seek satisfaction from doing better than others.
■ We gain satisfaction from personally defined success at difficult tasks.	■ We emphasise competition, public evaluation.
■ We talk to ourselves: when engaged in a task we talk ourselves through.	■ When the task is difficult we display helplessness: 'I can't do X.'
A concern to improve performance.	A concern to prove performance.

Source: Adapted from Watkins (2006: 122)

Watkins (ibid.) counsels against any reliance upon a 'mechanistic discourse' of 'better teaching to raise standards', ultimately he believes such pronouncements to be formulated on a culture of performativity where everything is measured except the value of measurement itself, a culture that can lead schools down a narrow and ultimately futile path:

> . . . Putting effort into limited goals, giving up when things get tough, aiming to 'look good' rather than to learn, and to adopt any strategy that might get a better showing in perform-ance measures – cheating in tests, fiddling results, fixing cohorts and so on.
>
> (Watkins 2006: 122)

This is not to deny the importance of accountability, nor to attempt to return to some illusory past 'golden age' of state education. As professionals we must be held to account for the success or failure of our efforts, a return to the isolated classroom of the past is simply not on the agenda. However, if the new teacher is to be successful in the classroom they must be allowed the freedom to engage creatively with their pupils, this involves an element of trust sadly missing from much of the literature on school improvement. However, it is only by working in a climate of mutual trust that teachers can experiment and become liberated from the sterile micro-management of centrally directed policy. Watkins challenges the 'purveyors of compliance, and its associated enemy of learning, *consistency*' (ibid. p. 125). If we consider the nature of the 'good teacher', the memory of those that impacted upon our own lives, they are seldom memories of faceless drones engaged in the technocratic task of delivering informa-tion. Rather, I would suggest that the teachers we remember engaged us intellectually, emotionally and creatively with an infectious enthusiasm for learning – such an approach is certainly *not* mutually exclusive of examination success – after all is said and done teachers have a professional responsibility to their pupils and no teacher 'worth their salt' would be at all interested in directing their pupils to fail. However, it is interesting to note that 'successful' schools are those that *empower staff to contribute* towards a shared vision of further improvement (Briggs, Bush and Middlewood 2006). It is with the classroom teacher that the ultimate success – or failure – of a particular school rests, it is most definitely not the singular preserve of a leadership elite who arrive on a 'white horse' to rescue failing schools. Leadership is important – it sets the climate in which a particular school operates and provides direction and support – what it can never guarantee without the enthusiasm and commitment of the teacher in the classroom, is successful lessons and high-achieving pupils.

Barker (2006) provides a telling account of the limitations of transformational leadership alone to raise the standards of a 'failing' or 'coasting' school:

> By the time [the new head teacher] departed in 1998, his 'resonance' is said to have faded. The 'guy on the white horse' faltered and his 'rollercoaster' threatened to get out of control, whilst his departure threatened the improvement project. [The school] was suffering from 'innovation overload' and the changes needed still to be consolidated . . . as the *examination results were still no better* than under [the previous head teacher], there was little tangible evidence of transformation, despite the legend he left behind.

> (Barker 2006: 285)

Barker calls for a deeper understanding on the part of government agencies, local authorities, governors and school leaders themselves of the limitations of trans-formational leadership. Such an understanding would, he believes, lead to an appreciation of the 'complex lifecycle of relationships, that unfold between leaders, followers and their internal and external contexts' (ibid. p. 290). To this I would add the need to appreciate that if teaching staff are not actively engaged in the process of reform it will inevitably fail to produce sustainable improvement by any measure. What we should be seeking is sustainable change and a definition of 'educational success' above and beyond the expectations of a culture of performativity where only that which can be measured is worthwhile; such an aim cannot be achieved without the creative engagement of highly motivated and well-qualified professionals at all levels of the service.

Loi and Dillon (2006) refer to Sternberg and Lubart's (1999) conception of three intellectual abilities associated with creativity:

- The analytic ability to recognise which of one's ideas are worth pursuing and which are not.

- The synthetic ability to see problems in new ways and escape the bounds of conventional thinking.

■ The practical-contextual ability to realise new ideas and persuade others of their value.

Loi and Dillon (ibid. pp. 363–4) suggest that formal educational environments, such as schools, place great emphasis on analytical ability whilst synthetic ability and mechanisms for transferring ideas are less well served. Analytic ability, they contend, 'results in powerful critical but *not* creative thinking'. They contend that educational environments that 'claim to foster creativity must incorporate potential for analysis and, especially, transference and synthesis between and across disciplines as well as within disciplines'. They suggest a model for educational environments as adaptive, collaborative workplaces, in such an environment teachers and learners engage with resources and relate these to prior experiences, the interaction between learner and context results in a 'mutual transformation'. They represent this relationship between adaptive educational environments and creative spaces diagrammatically:

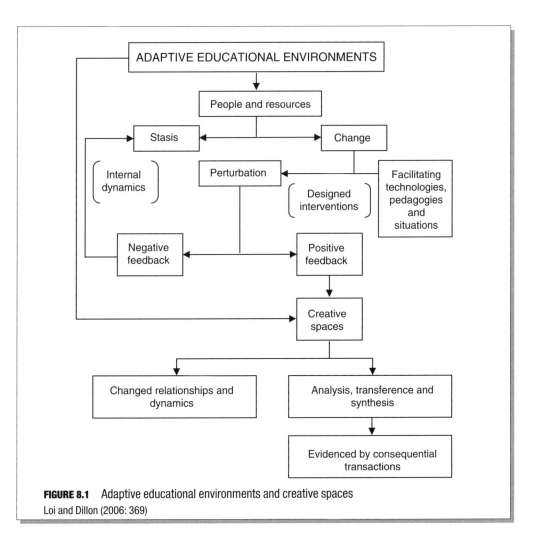

FIGURE 8.1 Adaptive educational environments and creative spaces
Loi and Dillon (2006: 369)

Drawing on the work of Beach (1999) and Stevenson (2004), Loi and Dillon (ibid. p. 375) suggest that the outcomes of such a 'creative space' should be seen 'in terms of the way in which individuals transform their understanding of themselves in relation to the social', involving a developmental change in the relationship between an individual and one or more of their professional activities. Such an environment constitutes a form of 'ecology' of continuous development and improvement – the school as an organic learning system enriching both pupils and teachers.

Case study: collegial and creative working practices

A new head of department takes over the leadership of a subject area with an established teaching staff in a 'satisfactory' comprehensive school, the department's results are not particularly impressive, option numbers have declined and teaching methods are stale and unimaginative. He introduces a collegial approach to the management of change and innovation, replacing a previous 'top-down' management style. Best practice models are examined and discussed by the members of the department, leading to an emergent consensus view of the direction that the department should take to improve the learning experience of students at Key Stages 3 and 4. Performance and predictive data (cognitive ability test scores and SAT scores) are available for staff to refer to and students are encouraged to be aware of their 'target' levels at both Key Stages; however, far less emphasis is placed on this information than is the case with other subject areas within the school. For example, the head of department deliberately decides to adopt a flexible approach to ability grouping in KS3 and to continue with mixed-ability teaching in KS4. In the first years of his leadership budget limitations restrict the purchase of new curriculum materials but members of the department are encouraged to think of new and creative ways to engage with their students using existing curriculum materials. A team-based structure is adopted with different members of the department taking responsibility for particular schemes of work; these documents are regarded as dynamic and open to a constant process of modification and improvement. The documents are available to all teaching staff electronically via the schools intranet on a dedicated departmental area – this use of information technology allows all teaching staff to download and modify documents and to share experience of best practice. The department is identified as performing to a high standard by two subsequent Ofsted inspections, results at both KS3 and KS4 show a sustained improvement, take-up of the subject as a GCSE option dramatically increases.

Worral and Noden (2006) draw upon the work of Desforges (see also Worrall *et al.* 2006) to present a four-stage historical analysis of educational change that can be related to the emergence of a collaborative and creative learning community as the most recent stage of development:

1 Doing work – the 'traditional classroom model' in which the teacher imparts knowledge to largely passive pupils. High pupil test scores and maintenance of 'good order' are the two fundamental goals at this stage.

2   Making sense – at this stage pupils begin to gain a deeper understanding of the curriculum. Classrooms are characterised by being learner centred, knowledge centred, assessment centred and community centred. But experience is still subject dominated, teacher dominated and focused on individual progress.

3   Community of learners – learning *per se* is now on the curriculum, pupils learn how to learn and have some say over how their learning is managed and arranged; there is some voice and choice and there is much evidence of the hallmarks and processes of community as set out by Watkins (2005).

4   Learning community – the learning community is described as the 'state of the art' mode of working towards the objectives of *Every Child Matters* (DfES 2003a) and the personalisation agenda, it is consistent with the most advanced models of human cognition and it therefore reflects the contemporary emphasis on democratic self-expression and self-determination. At this level there is a focus on knowledge generation and the creation of ideas beyond the curriculum; the wider community is used as a resource for learning; and crucially much of the learning experience itself is co-produced by pupils and teachers.

The role of information and communication technology

It may well be that new teachers will find the ideal of the learning community somewhat removed from the hierarchical status and performance driven structures within which many teachers still spend their professional lives – hierarchical structures that current models of workforce reform seem more likely to reinforce rather than to dismantle (DfES 2005). However, that being said the information technology revolution in schools gives teachers both the ability to communicate with their pupils in new and exciting forms and to interact with a wider professional community in ways that even ten years ago would have seemed more like science fiction that practical classroom reality. This is not to overstate the role that information and communication technology can play in the process of schooling – some proponents of such technologies frequently overstate the case for ICT as *the* pedagogy of the future.

In reality we have limited evidence that current forms of information and communication technology (certainly in terms of those that are readily available in schools) actually improve standards at all. Indeed, we have some largely anecdotal evidence to suggest that a generation of 'cut and paste' pupils may well be equating a virtual equivalent of tearing the pages out of library books with the process of creative thought. But on the positive side the ability to exchange ideas and to interact with teaching materials offers an almost limitless view of a *potential* future – no teacher who has actually experienced the way in which pupils can be engaged by these technologies will cease to be encouraged by the way in which they can improve 'time on task' amongst groups of pupils who are frequently disengaged by more conventional, text-based learning materials. Again a word of caution – as those older professionals who remember the introduction of video players into schools should know only too well the medium is *not* the message.[1]

Familiarity breeds contempt and an over-reliance on technology as a substitute for human interaction may well *discourage* rather than encourage pupils who one hopes will go on to develop independence and the ability for creative thought. As with every innovation it is for the skilled professional to strike an appropriate balance between that which is a useful and productive learning experience and that which is not, a dynamic interface between pupil and teacher that should not be seen in terms of a 'gatekeeping' role but rather as part of a conversation about learning.

Case study: the student voice

A new assistant head teacher in a large comprehensive school (well in excess of a thousand pupils) becomes concerned with the level of disengagement from the publicly expressed values of the school amongst a significant number of pupils – 'mission statements' and the head teacher's frequently expressed desire to respond to the needs and concerns of both parents/carers and pupils are often greeted with indifference or cynicism. There is no active school council and an existing Parent/Carer Teacher Association has become moribund. He embarks on a series of meetings with parents/carers and pupils, encouraging a debate about all aspects of school life. Although many of his senior colleagues retain concerns that this process may create 'unrealistic expectations', positive changes result from the process. A school council is established and the Parent/Carer Teacher Associations revived. Changes to the curriculum offer made to pupils are now openly discussed with pupil representatives, pupils are encouraged to take an active part in planning events such as the annual awards ceremony and physical changes to the school environment are made following representations from pupils. Some parents/carers and pupils remain concerned that their particular views are not heard, but in general terms there is evidence of an improvement in pupils' attitude and behaviour and there is a sustained improvement in the reputation of the school in the local community.

Teachers as professionals

Thompson (2006, p. 190) draws upon the work of Freidson (2001) to describe the 'ideal' type of professionalism:

- Specialised work in the officially recognised economy that is believed to be grounded in a body of theoretically based, discretionary knowledge and skill and that is accordingly given special status in the labour force.

- Exclusive jurisdiction in a particular division of labour created and controlled by occupational negotiation.

- A sheltered position in both external and internal labour markets that is based on qualifying credentials created by the occupation.

- A formal training programme lying outside the labour market that produces the qualifying credentials, which is controlled by the occupation and associated with higher education.

- An ideology that asserts greater commitment in doing good work than to economic gain and to the quality rather than the economic efficiency of work.

Thompson (ibid.) goes on to argue that the process of workforce reform (e.g. the introduction of new contracts and conditions of service) under New Labour *is* an unfounded attack on the professional status of teachers:

> My contention is that . . . safeguards are not securely present in the provision of the (Workload) Agreement (DfES 2003b) and that the concept of remodelling the teaching workforce, by Freidson's analysis, is deprofessionalising. So far re-modelling offers no vision for a profession, except in relation to work/life balance and workload. Important though these may be in relation to recruitment, they do very little to offer a respected and professional future for today's teachers.
>
> (Thompson 2006: 192)

Thompson quotes David Miliband, former Minister of State for School Standards, who in 2003 spoke of his commitment to a better-paid and better-supported teaching force, whilst simultaneously championing a further erosion of their status as professionals (Miliband 2003):

> . . . [It] makes no sense for the teaching profession to be untouched by the breakdown in demarcations, and by the development of front-line flexibility, that is the basis of effective service across the public and private sectors . . . The key is to make much more use of a wider range of adult expertise, from the learning mentor to the lab technician to the language specialist. It is said that we should never ask the nurse to do brain surgery. Fair enough. But which surgeon operates without a well-equipped and well-trained nursing team?

Thompson finds the analogy with the specialist nursing team singularly lacking in persuasive power when applied to teaching, she examines the specified activities that teaching assistants are allowed to carry out including (Thompson 2006: 195):

- Planning and preparing lessons and courses for pupils.

- Delivering lessons to pupils, including via distance learning or computer-aided techniques.

- Assessing the development, progress and attainment of pupils.

- Reporting on the development, progress and attainment of pupils.

Given the wide range of this remit her case is that they represent skills that we expect of *specialist teachers*, in this respect the removal of demarcation allows an unqualified paraprofessional to replace a qualified teacher at a lower cost to the school – a reform programme admittedly driven in the first instance by the need to provide teachers with time for planning, preparation and assessment. But also, she contends, by a more radical and potentially damaging hidden agenda to seek a reduction in the total number of qualified teachers in order to pay for a better adult–pupil ratio. She refers to a private DfES paper 'Workforce Reform – Blue Skies Thinking' reported in the *TES* (Stewart 2003); although subsequently disowned by the minister, this internal paper characterised such a radical restructuring as 'essential but presentationally uncomfortable'. Thompson (ibid. p.199) relates this to Freidson's assumption that 'the aim of both state and capital . . . is to reduce the cost and the independence of professional services'.

Hargreaves (2003: 54–6, 127) draws parallels between the failure of Railtrack and the problems facing state education in Britain in the 21st century. In essence, his metaphor concerns the abandonment of an organisational culture rooted in *knowledge and experience* and its replacement with one based on regulation through *contracts of performance*, the substitution of quality assurance based on mutual obligation, trusted relationships and local knowledge with one reliant upon detailed performance targets imposed on a mobile, low cost, flexible workforce of contract labour. For Britain's rail system the consequences of systemic failure were catastrophic with a resultant loss of life. The 'derailing' of our state education system will not involve broken rails and spectacular, fatal train crashes, but the potential consequences for the individual and society are none the less significant. Hargreaves identifies the same fundamental errors of managerialism[2] within education: the imposition of performance standards, an increasingly casualised workforce, the contracting out of support services and the rise of alternative and private options. However, he cautions against a view of the past as a 'golden age' of local democracy; in his view, local education cultures could be 'paternalistic, even feudal, in the ways they cultivate compliant loyalty among their teachers and leaders . . . too often they have camouflaged incompetence, moving problem teachers and leaders (including abusive ones) around the system instead of confronting them and their unions' (ibid. pp. 127–8). It is regrettable that in his overt suspicion of trade unionism, Hargreaves allows himself to fall back on the political rhetoric of the 1980s. Whatever the future direction of education it cannot be built on a foundation of distrust and confrontation. Those who seek to provide leadership at both a local and a national level may well be frustrated by the need to negotiate in pursuit of a workable consensus. But the alternative – the centralised imposition of unpopular policy – is ultimately a sterile dead-end incapable of producing the ideal outcome that Hargreaves champions.

For Hargreaves the solution to the mistakes of the past lies in the evolution of the *professional learning communities*. He believes that these communities would represent an educational take on the values of the knowledge economy and the learning organisation as expressed through the work of management theorists, for example the influential writings of Etienne Wenger (1998, 2002).[3] Hargreaves represents the variety of organisational cultures and contract regimes in tabular form as shown in Table 8.2.

Combinations in the left-hand column assume weak contractual systems, with performance data in short supply and accountability reliant on personal judgement rather than formal procedures. This model can be placed in an historical context and may usefully be compared with that predicated by Desforges (Worrall *et al.* 2006). Hargreaves dates the period of permissive individualism to an era (the 1980s and before) when teachers taught alone, isolated and insulated, their formal qualifications a protection from outside interference. During this period attempts to *reculture*[4] schools were made, with the best collaborative efforts focused on the improvement of teaching and learning but with few if any external or independent reference points and the consequent inconsistent application of standards with ineffective practice perpetuated alongside effective innovation. The imposition of contrived collegiality, collaboration that is forced and artificially imposed from above, is equally ineffective 'a prison of micro-management' (ibid. p. 130); for example, the imposition of the Literacy and Numeracy Strategy and the Foundation Strategy can be seen as an attempt to impose centrally determined models of 'best practice' upon the classroom experience. Those teachers who have worked through these government initiatives will be familiar with a process that begins with fairly rigid 'one size fits all' solutions monitored by unsympathetic external inspection in an attempt to 'drive up' standards. However, as time passes these models tend to break down with teachers adapting rigid centralised formats to more flexible models that work with their pupils. Ironically, we can see in current practice central government acquiescing in this process of adaptation as the evidence builds that rigid, centrally determined models do not significantly improve outcomes. Hargreaves dates this era of reform from the 1990s with the introduction of contracts and competitive individualism, an innovation that created a 'new educational

TABLE 8.2   Organisational cultures and contract regimes

Permissive individualism	Corrosive individualism
Collaborative cultures	Professional learning communities
Contrived collegiality	Performance training sects

Source: Adapted from Hargreaves (2003: 128)

orthodoxy ... a paradoxical combination of choice that is supposed to promote diversity, with standards that impose uniformity' (ibid. p. 131). For Hargreaves the future lies in the formation of professional learning communities that combine contracts with culture, such communities would, in his view, 'put a premium on teachers working together but also insist that this joint work consistently focus on improving teaching and learning (using) evidence and data as a basis for building classroom improvement efforts and solving whole school problems' (ibid. pp. 133–4). Such a vision is inclusive and implies an element of trust between teachers and their employers that does not currently exist, such professional learning communities cannot flourish in a political climate where teachers and their trade union representatives feel ignored and at times besieged by a managerialist culture that seeks a compliant workforce rather than partnership in a common enterprise. Hargreaves also cautions against imposed regimes of intensive performance training, 'training sects', on the basis that whilst they may improve performance in basic skills in the short term, in the longer term they 'imperil more complex learning society objectives' (ibid. p. 141).

A real danger for schools operating under the framework of new legislation is that once left to their own devices in a market-led vacuum, lacking the values of any cohesive social movement, they will readily confuse learning communities with contrived collegiality. I see little indication in the pronouncements of central government to be optimistic that fundamental lessons have been learned. In the search for solutions both schools and central government may well be reaching for the chimera of 'what works' (in reality solutions that seem to reflect the latest fashion or dominant local circumstances) rather than 'what *should* we be doing' (a perspective rooted in a more considered view of the nature and purpose of education). Moreover, I am increasingly aware – perhaps unsurprisingly given my background and experience – of the primacy of economic imperatives that seem to offer little in terms of the enrichment of individual lives over and above the material values of the moment. Indeed, this process seems to mirror the ways in which the language of educational reform on the national stage has become corrupted by a version of 'newspeak' and 'doublethink' (Orwell 1949): a language that allows for 'collegiality' in a managerialist culture; where top-down decisions can be presented for 'consultation' and where 'consensus' can readily be achieved despite the existence of significant dissent; where the values of the global marketplace can be presented as 'social democracy' in action.

The future of education

Cole (2004) postulates an alternative vision of the future direction of education rooted in the radical traditions of the 19th century. Drawing upon the work of Johnson (1979) Cole identifies four aspects of popular 'radical education' that he believes to have 'considerable relevance to today' and that could ultimately serve to 'inform a radical education for the twenty-first century' (Cole 2004: 155–6):

1   A running critique of all forms of 'provided' education, involving a political grasp and a theoretical understanding of cultural and ideological struggles.

2   The development of alternative educational goals, including the notion of 'educational utopias' and 'really useful knowledge'.

3   A debate about education as a political strategy or as a means of changing the world.

4   A vigorous and varied educational practice concerned with informing mature understanding and with the education of all citizens as members of a more just social order.

Cole rejects the notion that education can ever be apolitical, in the contemporary world he believes that teachers need to look beyond the core and undoubted importance of literacy and numeracy to include critical debate. He suggests that historical and cultural issues, such as the legacy of imperialism, should be coupled with a consideration of 21st century manifestations of British and American global imperialism. Such an approach, Cole believes, will serve to promote 'a democratically controlled and accountable education service at all levels and should apply the principles of equality and non-discrimination to all parts of the service', to move education away 'from the current destructive preoccupation with institutions as competitive private businesses divorced from localities' (ibid. p. 161) towards a more positive role as 'agents of development' within wider national and global communities. He believes that in the modern world information technology presents choices that democratise relations between pupils and teachers by undermining the role of teachers as gatekeepers of knowledge; furthermore, he believes that pupil rights should be increased as part of the process of effective citizenship education. In his view, a 'learning society' opens up all aspects of social, business and industrial life to educational enquiry – a counterpoint to the involvement of business and industry in schools as potential markets. He raises the central concern of education for equality – social class, 'race', gender, sexuality and disability – underlying themes that should, in his view, appear in all areas of the National Curriculum (see Cole *et al.* (eds) 1997; Hill and Cole (eds) 1999; Cole (ed.) 2006). Ultimately, he counsels 'children have a right to know what is going on in the world' (ibid. p. 158). Such a vision is at some remove from a target-driven competitive culture – wherein a school's success is measured in terms of a total points score. An educational environment where historical and cultural concerns have validity only in as much as they present opportunities for examination, where 'appropriate pathways' can be interpreted as presenting pupils with 'easier options' that generate more points but little understanding. Without such a critical and radical perspective schools become cost-monitored service providers to an economic system that requires an unquestioning workforce, learning to labour and not learning for life.

Goodson (2005) reminds us of the need to contextualise experience within the larger framework of historical time. It is his contention that many studies of school change operate within an a-historical perspective that serves to present the rhetoric of change as somehow 'uniquely powerful at this time of global restructuring' (ibid. p.157). He draws upon the *annaliste* perspective (Febvre 1925, Burke 1993) and that of economic historians such as Kondratiev (1923) to locate change in historical periods. For the annaliste school of historians change operates at three levels of time – long, medium and short term. In Goodson's view, much of contemporary educational innovation operates on the surface of society in the short term, thus its 'legacy is unlikely to be enduring' (Goodson 2005: 159). In terms of economic history, he discerns a link between the medium-term change patterns described by the annaliste school and the life cycle of technology systems (ibid. p.161, Freeman and Louca 2001):

1   Laboratory invention – early applications.

2   Decisive demonstrations – widespread potential applications.

3   Explosive take-off and growth – structural and political crisis whilst the economy adapts and new regimes of regulation are established.

4   Continued high growth with the system now accepted as 'common sense' and the 'dominant technological regime'.

5   Slow down and erosion of profitability as the system is challenged by newer technologies.

6   Maturity, with some 'renaissance' effects possible through co-existence with newer technologies.

Goodson suggests that with regard to educational systems, there is a process of adjustment to new technological and economic regimes analogous with this model. He believes that the 1960s and 1970s represented a period of rapid acceleration – 'explosive take-off and growth'. In his study of the Canadian school system he finds that the 1990s represent, in some schools at least, an age of 'retrenchment and intransigence' comparable to the later stages of the technology model. He cautions that 'cohorts of teachers who are disenfranchised politically, alienated intellectually, depressed emotionally and drained physically' mark this period (ibid. p. 185). However, it is his belief that this process of medium-term change is 'running towards the end of its provenance and that new conceptions of improvement will begin to work their way to centre stage in our classrooms and schools' (ibid.). Beneath the surface of society, marked by the noise and confusion of the moment, beneath even the medium-term trends towards greater accountability, over-prescribed targets and market fundamentalism; Goodson discerns the movement of history in the long term, the 'broad epochal shifts' (ibid. p. 159) that move slowly in the depths and whose significance is not of the moment but inevitably far more enduring.

Conclusion

The neo-liberal public sector educational reforms (see the introductory chapter of this book) championed by New Labour can be interpreted as superficial and transient. Lacking as they do any sense of a deep and lasting commitment to social democracy, let alone socialism, or a realistic attempt to address the fundamental concerns of social justice, they seem unlikely to endure. However, for the engaged professional this does not imply that these policies should be ignored in the futile hope that they will simply disappear – the development of a 'bunker mentality' of the type described by Goodson (2003: 81) is ultimately a surrender of professional responsibility – the 'political battlefield' of education is not a formal 19th-century set piece but a messy 21st-century, morally ambiguous series of skirmishes argued over in schools across the country. The lack of a unifying social movement creates both problems *and* opportunities. Our educational Jerusalem is apparently to be demolished and rebuilt by each generation and it is for a new generation of teachers to engage with this process as they struggle to meet the needs of their pupils. However, it is clear that if we are truly to meet those future needs with a creative and dynamic workforce of engaged and socially aware professional educators, then teaching can never be seen as 'just a job'. For those who champion the technocratic interpretation of teaching as a series of skill sets that can be learned by paraprofessionals, to be delivered in a context-free, cost-effective social vacuum, there are lessons to be learned from the mistakes of the past and from other areas of social life. Ultimately, the sticking plaster solutions of 'what works' can be seen as a form of crisis management, underlying concerns are hidden by the noise and confusion of the moment, lost in a plethora of tests and inspections, policy initiatives and 'blue skies thinking' that in reality can see little beyond the next media moment. Once this rhetoric is set aside what we are left with is a managerialist culture that neither empowers nor engages creative professionals – a culture that is ultimately lacking in any real understanding of the fundamental challenges that face our unequal society. Whatever the future shape of public education in the 21st century and beyond, it cannot be dependent on policies and processes that lack a genuine sense of social purpose – a real and lasting commitment to social justice.

Author's note

Parts of this chapter are drawn from an unpublished thesis submitted to the University of Brighton.

Notes

1   'In a culture like ours, long accustomed to splitting and dividing all things as a means of control, it is sometimes a bit of a shock to be reminded that, in operational and practical fact, the medium is the message. This is merely to say that the personal and social consequences of any medium – that is, of any extension of ourselves – result from the new scale that is introduced into our affairs by each extension of ourselves, or by any new technology' (McLuhan 1964: 7).

2   Managerialism is a global phenomenon that reflects a market-led ideology – public servants have their roles transformed to managers and the public to customers. In schools this trend is reflected in the growing divide between school leadership teams and teachers; the leadership team have different contracts (indeed they may not even be qualified teachers), enhanced salaries and, for those who are qualified teachers, dramatically reduced or non-existent teaching commitments. This trend can be contrasted with the more traditional model of the 'leading professional'.

3   For Wenger a learning community is one where colleagues learn from each other in the sustained pursuit of a common enterprise. It is his belief that such communities of practice can provide resolutions to organisational conflicts; support a communal memory – not everyone needs to know everything; help new staff to integrate; enable the organisation to achieve what needs to be done and make the job habitable – people become involved members of the community with an investment in communal life.

4   In this sense culture is used to represent the value systems and working practices of schools – the intention to *reculture* reflects a desire on the part of government to change schools to fit new models of best practice.

References

Barker, B. (2006) 'Rethinking leadership and change: a case study in leadership succession and impact on school transformation', *Cambridge Journal of Education*, 36(2): 227–93.

Beach, K. (1999) 'Consequential transitions. A sociocultural expedition beyond transfer in education', *Review of Research in Education*, 24: 101–39.

Briggs, A. R. J., Bush, T. and Middlewood, D. (2006) 'From immersion to establishment. The challenges facing new school heads and the role of "New Visions" in resolving them', *Cambridge Journal of Education*, 36(2): 257–76.

Burke, P. (1993) *History and Social Theory*. New York: Cornell University Press.

Cole, M. (2004) 'Rethinking the Future: the Commodification of Knowledge and the Grammar of Resistance', in *A Tribute to Caroline Benn: Education and Democracy*, M. Benn, and C. Chitty, (eds). London: Continuum, pp. 150–63.

Cole, M., Hill, D. and Shan, S. (1997) *Promoting Equality in Primary Schools*. London: Cassell.

Cole, M. (ed.) (2006) *Education, Equality and Human Rights: Issues of Gender, 'Race', Sexuality, Disability and Social Class*, 2nd edn. London: Routledge/Falmer.

DfES (2003a) *Every Child Matters*. London: HMSO.

DfES (2003b) *Raising Standards and Tackling Workload: a national agreement*. London: HMSO.

DfES (2005) *School Teachers Pay and Conditions* (and associated guidance on restructuring) www.teachernet.gov.uk/pay/2005.

Febvre, L. (1925) *A Geographical Introduction to History*. New York: Alfred Knopf.

Freeman, C. and Louca, F. (2001) *As Time Goes By: From the Industrial Revolutions to the Information Revolution*. Oxford: Oxford University Press.

Freidson, E. (2001) *Professionalism: the third logic*. Cambridge: Polity Press.

Goodson, I. (2003) *Professional Knowledge, Professional Lives*. Maidenhead: Open University Press.

Goodson, I. (2005) *Learning, Curriculum and Life History*. London: Routledge/Falmer.

Hargreaves, A. (2003) *Teaching in the Knowledge Society: Education in the age of insecurity*. Maidenhead: Open University Press.

Hill, D. and Cole, M. (1999) *Promoting Equality in Secondary Schools*. London: Cassell.

Johnson, R. (1979) 'Really useful knowledge: radical education and working class culture, 1790–1848', in J. C. Critcher and R. Johnson (eds), *Working Class Culture: Studies in Education History and Theory*. London: Hutchinson, pp. 75–102.

Kondratiev, N. (1923) 'Some controversial questions concerning the world economy and crisis (answer to our critics)' in Fontvielle's (1992) edition of *Kondratiev's works*. Paris: Economica, pp. 493–543.

Loi, D. and Dillon, P. (2006) 'Adaptive educational environments as creative spaces', *Cambridge Journal of Education*, September: 363–81.

Miliband, D. (2003) *The Radical Reform of the Teaching Workforce*, North of England Conference, 8 January.

McLuhan, M. (1964) *Understanding Media: The Extensions of Man*. New York: McGraw Hill.

Orwell, G. (1949) *1984*. London: Secker and Warburg.

Stevenson, L. (2004) 'Developing technological knowledge', *International Journal of Technology and Design Education*, 14: 5–19.

Sternberg, R. J. and Lubart, T. I. (1999) 'The concept of creativity: prospects and paradigms' in R. J. Sternberg (ed.) *Handbook of creativity*. Cambridge: Cambridge University Press, pp. 3–15.

Stewart, W. (2003) 'Schools without teachers', *Times Educational Supplement*, 5 December, p. 6.

Thompson, M. (2006) 'Re-modelling as de-professionalisation', *Forum*, 48(2): 189–200.

Watkins, C. (2005) *Classrooms as Learning Communities: what's in it for schools?* London: Routledge.

Watkins, C. (2006) 'When Teachers Reclaim Learning', *Forum*, 48(2): 121–9.

Wenger, E. (1998) *Communities of Practice: Learning, Meaning and Identity*. Cambridge: Cambridge University Press.

Wenger, E., McDermott, R. and Snyder, M. (2002) *A Guide to Managing Knowledge: Cultivating Communities of Practice*. Boston: Harvard Business School Press.

Worral, N. and Noden, C. (2006) 'Working with Children, Working for Children: a review of Networked Learning Communities', *Forum*, 48(2): 171–9.

Worrall, N. and Noden, C. with Desforges, C. (2006) *Pupils' Experience of Learning in Networked Learning Communities*. Nottingham: NCSL.

Coaching and mentoring

Ian Woodfield

Q9 Act upon advice and feedback and be open to coaching and mentoring.

Learning objectives

To promote an understanding of:

- the central importance of the 'professional conversation' based on a relationship of trust and mutual respect;
- the need to adopt an appropriate mentoring model;
- the need to develop a professional identity rooted in a culture of experience.

> **What experience and history teach is this – that people and governments never have learnt anything from history, or acted on principles deduced from it.**
>
> **G. W. Hegel (1822–1830 p. 21)**

Introduction

THE CHALLENGE FOR the new teacher is to overcome the understandable urge to reinvent everything about teaching – to avoid being seduced by a powerful *rhetoric* of change. The rhetoric of change can present 'streaming'[1] as if it were a new and fresh approach, it can use the language of 'appropriate pathways' to conceal mechanisms for selection and the labelling of a generation of children and young people as educational failures – it is only by drawing on the experiences of a past generation of teachers that these ideas can be fully exposed to critical review. It is essential that new teachers become engaged in an on-going professional conversation with experienced teaching colleagues about the nature of teaching and learning. It is only by engaging in such a professional conversation that the new teacher can give the lie to Hegel's often paraphrased sentiment that 'we never learn the lessons of history', this is not to say that talented young teachers will not innovate and change (see Chapter 8). Indeed, the nature of all professional life is to see a new generation take up the challenges presented by their time and to seek fresh solutions to those challenges – the problem lies in the adoption of strategies that are marketed as new but are in reality the failed attempts of previous generations repackaged for a new generation of teachers often kept ignorant of their own professional culture. A successful mentoring relationship will do much to 'bridge the cultural gap' between generations of teachers and should help to build a more secure sense of professional identity firmly founded on the somewhat unfashionable notion of *vocation*.

Approaches to mentoring

Brookes and Sikes (1997: 17–31) suggest a series of closely linked mentoring models for consideration:

- The apprenticeship model with the mentor as skilled craftsperson – this can be updated by reference to the theoretical model suggested by Anderson and Shannon (1988) (see below).
- The competence-based model with the mentor as trainer.
- Mentoring in the tradition of the reflective practitioner – the mentor as reflective coach, critical friend and co-enquirer – this can be compared with the empirical model suggested by Furlong and Maynard (1995) (see below).

Brookes and Sikes suggest that the apprenticeship model represents historically the 'first attempt to train teachers systematically' (ibid. p. 17). In its earliest form it is the 19th-century tradition of the pupil-teacher which, although clearly inappropriate as a model for 21st-century teacher education, as a system had at least the advantage of exposing its fledgling practitioners to the practical realities of teaching in the Victorian classroom. However, as Brookes and Sikes note, it was not in essence a system designed to promote insight or creative and critical engagement on the part of the new practitioner – although it should be said that to characterise all Victorian classrooms as the preserve of 'Mr. Gradgrind' (Dickens 1854)[2] would be to crudely stereotype a generation of teachers struggling to cope with the demands of that new creation – compulsory elementary state education. Some of these early teaching professionals struggled to break free from the constraints of 'payment by results' and a harsh regime of corporal punishment in order to inspire a new generation of educational reformers and teacher educators. Anderson and Shannon's theoretical model, as cited by Brookes and Sikes (ibid. pp. 28–9) can be seen as a 20th century updating of the apprenticeship ideal, embracing as it does the principles that mentoring is:

- fundamentally a nurturing process; and
- that the mentor must serve as a role model to the protégé; and
- that the mentor must exhibit certain dispositions that help define the process, e.g. the ability to relate and to inspire.

The apprenticeship model can be contrasted with the current dominance of the competence-based model; Brookes and Sikes (ibid. p. 20) characterise this model as one that is founded on 'pre-specified behavioural outcomes and skill-related competencies which the training and assessment procedures are tailored to meet'. I concur with their suggestion that this model is 'central to government thinking'; it is very much in tune with the demands of neo-liberal educational policies introduced over recent decades by both Conservative and New Labour governments (see the introductory chapter in this book). As such it encourages an approach to initial teacher education based on a series of competency checklists (DfES 2003). It is a model that fits comfortably with a view of teaching as an easily transferable body of 'skill sets' requiring of the mentor that they act as a trainer *and* assessor, with the power to 'weed out' unsuitable candidates who fail to meet a centrally determined set of criteria for the profession. Over the years I have worked with a number of student teachers and NQTs, it has been my responsibility as a head of department to wade through these lists and to check off the competencies displayed. I cannot in all conscience deny that the qualities listed are in any way inappropriate; for example, we should expect teaching professionals to be able to:

- liaise effectively with parents or carers on pupils' progress and achievements;
- seek and use opportunities to work collaboratively with colleagues in sharing practice.

To suggest otherwise would be patently absurd – but these are only two criteria amongst many against which the new teacher must be assessed – in practice, the list becomes the defining and all-consuming mechanical task at the centre of the relationship. I would suggest that if the mentoring process consists mainly of 'ticking off' a series of boxes on a vast checklist, it has become an impoverished and shallow experience both for the mentor and the student teacher or NQT involved. The professional conversation to which I alluded at the start of this chapter has to go beyond a centrally determined list of competencies and should seek to encourage a critical and reflective view of the nature of teaching and learning.

Schon's (1983) concept of the reflective practitioner is useful when considering how *more* rewarding and productive the relationship between mentor and student teacher or NQT can become. Brookes and Sikes (ibid. p. 23) suggest that such an approach allows the mentor to 'use their own professional experience as the basic material for learning about teaching'. This is *not* to suggest a passive and unfocused approach – but rather a more dynamic process of exploring shared experience based on mutual respect and a clear focus on an examination of models of best practice for the mentoring of student teachers:

> Coaching is an active process which depends on the mentor making planned and systematic interventions into the students' reflections in order to make them more meaningful and

analytical. Students, will of course, think about their teaching experiences with or without encouragement to do so, but without the support and guidance of more experienced teachers, too much of the learning that may be gleaned from the classroom experience is left to chance.

Brookes and Sikes (ibid.)

Such an approach can be found echoed in Cremin's (2006) work with a group of English primary teachers who were encouraged to reflect on their development as writers at their own level *and* their effectiveness as teachers of literacy. For some this process was not without a painful journey of self-realisation:

> Those first weeks were a nightmare, I thought it'd be easy to get started, I read loads and made plans, but none of them worked – it was awful, I felt at a complete loss. My husband told me to forget it, do something else, but I kept thinking about it, working at it and trying things out. Eventually one Sunday when I was gardening and not thinking about it, an idea just came out of the blue and intuitively I knew that was it – I'd found what I was after – I was going to write about a girl who couldn't write – it was such a relief.
>
> (Cremin 2006: 423)

Cremin (ibid. p. 427) notes that the teachers involved in the study experienced 'tension and affective discomfort', but that this experience 'appeared to mobilize a kind of creative energy, a response that often generated resolutions to their immediate dilemmas'. I would suggest that this process is analogous to the ideal of the professional conversation between mentor and student teacher or NQT; the process should be designed to *unlock* the creative potential of the new teacher and not simply to treat them as if they were the educational equivalent of a mechanic learning the order in which to replace certain engine parts. The concept of the professional conversation based on mutual respect is further enhanced by the ideal of the mentor as critical friend and co-enquirer, these models might appear at first to fit rather uncomfortably with the process of awarding QTS, or for more experienced professionals with that of threshold assessment. However, Brookes and Sikes (1997: 29–30) suggest that Furlong and Maynard's (1995) work with a group of student teachers gives rise to the idea of a staged mentoring relationship, one that changes to mirror the level of competency – closely matching the students developmental needs (see Table 9.1).

I would suggest that the current focus on performativity and the dominant culture of managerialism (see Chapter 8) stifles the effective development of this staged model; the lack of trust placed in teaching professionals effectively 'stalls' this staged approach at the level of *supervision*. It is my contention that without a more reflective approach to the mentoring relationship, we are in danger of encouraging the process to become merely the application of a crude series of measurable criteria, the antithesis of the ideal of the creatively engaged professional. This is not to say that teachers should be unaccountable for the performance of their professional

TABLE 9.1 A staged mentoring relationship

Beginning teaching	Focus of student learning: Rules, rituals and routines, establishing authority.	Mentoring role: Model. Key mentoring strategies: Student observation and collaborative teaching focused on rules and routines.
Supervised teaching	Focus of student learning: Teaching competences.	Mentoring role: Coach. Key mentoring strategies: Observation by the student; systematic observation and feedback on student's 'performance'.
From teaching to learning	Focus of student learning: Understanding pupil learning, developing effective teaching.	Mentoring role: Critical friend. Key mentoring strategies: Student observation; re-examining of lesson planning.
Autonomous teaching	Focus of student learning: Investigating the grounds for practice.	Mentoring role: Co-enquirer. Key mentoring strategies: Partnership teaching; partnership supervision.

Source: Adapted from Brookes and Sikes (ibid.) p. 30.

functions – it is to argue the case for a recapturing of a truly professional identity firmly founded on a relationship of mutual respect and trust between fellow professionals engaged in the business of teaching and learning. It must always be the case that those teachers who fail to achieve the requisite professional standards must either improve or ultimately be removed from their post, but the assumption that our schools are crowded with time-serving incompetents has no empirical basis. Rather, such assertions form part of the inheritance a discourse of derision (Ball 1990, Delamont 1999) formulated to suit the needs of a political rather than an educational agenda.

The purpose of coaching and mentoring

Parsloe and Wray (2000) draw upon the work of Senge (1992) and others to argue that coaching and mentoring are an essential element in the creation of a successful *learning organisation* – something that all schools should surely aspire to be (Hargreaves 2003; Wenger 1998, 2002):

> Most of us, at one time or another, have been part of a great 'team' or group of people who functioned together in an extraordinary way – who trusted each other, who complemented each other's strengths and weaknesses and compensated for each other's limitations, who had common goals that were larger than individual goals and who produced extraordinary

results ... Many say that they have spent much of their life looking for that experience again. What they experienced was a learning organization.

(Senge 1992, as quoted in Parsloe and Wray 2000: 18)

Parsloe and Wray (ibid.) use the work of Senge (1992) and Guest (1999) to present the ideal form of the learning organisation diagrammatically (see Figure 9.1).

It is their belief that the aim of the learning organisation must be to 'help and support people to manage their own learning in order that they may maximize their potential, develop their skills, improve their performance and enable them to become the person they want to be' (Parsloe and Wray 2000: 22).[3] For Parsloe and Wray, coaching and mentoring are 'preferred options' for a range of topics including, for example, the development of personal skills – an area of considerable relevance to the successful classroom practitioner. It is their contention that coaching and mentoring can often

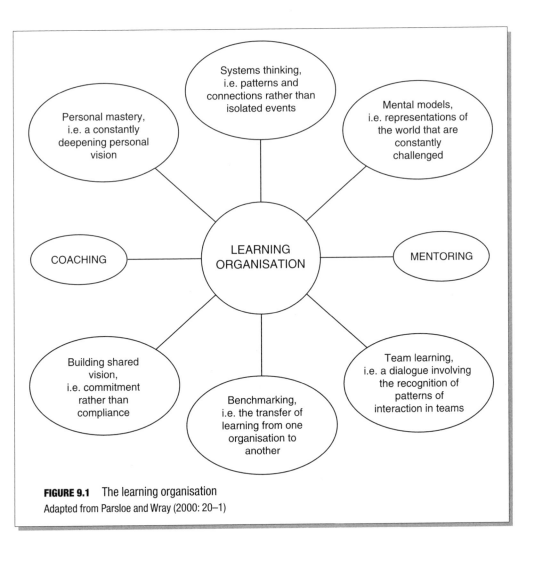

FIGURE 9.1 The learning organisation
Adapted from Parsloe and Wray (2000: 20–1)

overcome the 'learning inefficiencies' associated with the traditional training course. Whilst accepting that coaching and mentoring are frequently treated as synonymous, they go on to suggest that it can be useful to draw a distinction between them. They characterise 'coaching' as a process that *'enables* learning and development to occur' and that is best represented through a four-stage model (ibid. pp. 42–7):

1 *Analyse for awareness*, i.e. the learner develops a self-awareness of the need to improve their performance or change the way they have been doing things. Without ownership of this process Parsloe and Wray suggest that successful coaching *cannot* take place.

2 *Planning for responsibility*, i.e. the planning stage of the coaching process with the learner taking responsibility for outcomes. Parsloe and Wray suggest that managers frequently ignore this element. Unfortunately, to do so is to encourage an unstructured process that fails to focus on the real issues. Ideally this process should produce a formal personal development plan – a practice that is central to the process of performance management within teaching, certainly in its intended form.

3 *Implementing the plan, using appropriate coaching styles, techniques and skills*, i.e. the recognition that learners are located on a continuum from the inexperienced and incapable to the experienced and capable (this can be related to Furlong and Maynard's (1995) conception of a staged mentoring process). Coaching skills most frequently deployed include observation, feedback and questioning – again, this is directly applicable to the experience of the student teacher or NQT, or indeed of the 'performance review' of more experienced teachers.

4 *Evaluating for success*, i.e. a review of the successful outcomes associated with a personal development plan using a series of key questions, for example: Were the development goals achieved? Were there any unexpected benefits? Is there a need for a new personal development plan to improve performance still further? (Within the performance management process as applied to teachers there is an inbuilt assumption that such a plan will be generated annually.)

Parsloe and Wray (ibid. pp. 80–1) suggest that mentoring, on the other hand, is a process that *'supports and encourages* learning'. In their view, it may be distinguished from coaching through the application of three broad 'primary types' of mentor: the *corporate mentor*, a model that emphasises career guidance throughout the working life of the individual; the *qualification mentor*, a model that guides the individual through a particular form of study; the *community mentor*, the model of the professional friend or expert adviser who guides the individual through a potentially stressful situation. Parsloe and Wray accept that such ideal types are problematic in an environment where language is frequently used in a 'lazy' way that allows terms such as coaching and mentoring to mean 'different things to different people within the same organization' and indeed it is clear that the distinction they suggest between coach and mentor is not clearly defined in the world of education. As I have already indicated, current models as applied to the student teacher or NQT, or indeed the experienced teacher, involve centrally determined criteria for monitoring and assessment that actively *discourage* a productive learning process because they are often interpreted by performance-focused managers in such a way as to suggest teachers cannot be trusted and are not truly professional – the worst case scenario is that this will lead to the development of a culture of compliance rather than commitment.

Parsloe and Wray counsel that a clear understanding of the mutual expectations of any process of mentoring can best be founded on a clear code of practice, such as that suggested by the Working Party to establish National Standards for Mentoring (cited in Parsloe and Wray 2000: 178–9):

■ The mentor's role is to respond to the mentee's needs and agenda; it is not to impose their own agenda.

■ Mentors must work within the current agreement with the mentee about confidentiality that is appropriate within the context.

■ Mentors must be aware of any current law and must work within the law.

■ Mentor and mentee must be aware that computer-based records are subject to statutory regulations under the Data Protection Act.

■ The mentee should be aware of their rights and any complaints procedures.

■ Mentors and mentees should respect each other's time and other responsibilities, ensuring that they do not impose beyond what is reasonable.

■ The mentee must accept increasing responsibility for managing the relationship; the mentor should empower them to do so and must generally promote the learner's autonomy.

■ Either party may dissolve the relationship. However, both the mentor and the mentee have the responsibility to discuss the matter together, as part of mutual learning.

■ Mentors need to be aware of the limits of their own competence in the practice of mentoring.

■ The mentor will not intrude into areas the mentee wishes to keep private until invited to do so. However, they should help the mentee to recognise how other issues may relate to these areas.

■ Mentors and mentees should aim to be open and truthful with each other and themselves about the relationship itself.

■ Mentors and mentees should share the responsibility for the smooth winding down of the relationship when it has achieved its purpose – they must avoid creating dependency.

- The mentoring relationship must not be exploitative in any way; neither must it be open to misinterpretation.

These outline standards have been further developed by ENTO (Employment – National Training Organisation) – further information can be found on their website http://www.ento.co.uk – they can also be compared with the regulations regarding the performance management of teachers. Whilst the statutory regulations due to come into force in September 2007 (HMG 2006) appear to embrace some of the principles of successful mentoring and coaching and elements of the draft code (e.g. the clear establishment of the mentee's rights and of an appropriate complaints procedure), they also establish a statutory framework for an explicit and structured link between pay and performance. To those who have worked in a commercial or industrial environment such a connection would appear to be idiomatic, and in truth the successful teacher has always been rewarded for their performance. However, to those with experience of the world of education and in possession of an historical perspective such a direct link has other implications. The culture of performativity introduced by neo-liberal governments both Conservative and New Labour, has already produced negative outcomes associated with a focus on performance rather than learning, teaching to the test or seeking to cheat the test were the reasons for abandoning 'payment by results' in the 19th century. The danger for schools is that mentoring and coaching will become caught up in a 21st century version of 'payment by results'. It seems that in this sense we have failed to learn the lessons of history.

Problems faced by coaching and mentoring

The contextual issues and continuing practical problems associated with the mentoring process, have been highlighted by Colley (2003):

> . . . Mentoring is located within a far larger and more complex web of power relations that are specific to our historical era. The most fundamental structural forces in our society include capitalist economic and social relations. They also include gender and the patriarchal oppression of women, and other deep rooted inequalities . . . such macro-level power relations are bolstered further by the contemporary political climate.
>
> (Colley 2003: 29)

To these concerns I would add a consequential but nonetheless significant concern regarding the loss of professional experience caused by a generational drift of teaching professionals into early retirement. A very real danger for schools confronting the need to adapt to change is the potential loss of experienced, committed professionals available to advise and counsel newly qualified teachers. Goodson (2003) describes the consequences for schools of the loss of the 'old professionalism', by which he means 'a view of teaching where the professionalism is expressed and experienced as more than just a job, but as a caring vocationalism' (ibid. p. 78). He describes it as 'old' because it has ceased to be the commonly held perspective of new teachers entering the profession and he perceives three significant problem areas for schools in the future that result from this loss of vocation. The first is the loss of memory, a loss described in commercial terms as the absence of a 'corporate memory'. This amounts in Goodson's view to the loss of skills and experience that allow institutions and businesses to respond to the needs of their clients on the basis of many years of experience, utilising almost unconsciously skills that are embedded within their workforce. Second, the loss of mentoring skills, in his view 'if the elders . . . feel disenchanted and disvalued, this is a problem for the community of the school' (ibid. p. 81). In his research he discovered entire cohorts of teachers who have become disenchanted with the process of change and reform and, as a consequence, they opted either to retire early or remained 'in a disaffected, disengaged way' (ibid.). The 'elders' in the school community kept their skills and 'layers of unquantifiable knowledge, acquired through many years of experience' (ibid.) to themselves, breaking the chain of professional transmission and leaving a school bereft of 'passion and purpose' (ibid.). Finally, he cautions against any view of the evacuation of 'old professionals' as a sign of success, contrary to those who claim that schools will be 'rejuvenated and filled with eager advocates of the new reforms' (ibid. p.82). Indeed, Goodson finds clear evidence of widespread problems of retention and recruitment. Amongst others he cites the work of Ross (2001) and his three-year study of teacher retention and recruitment:

> What has happened to the profession that has caused these teachers, at least, to become so disillusioned that they seek alternative careers? This question to teachers is rhetorical. The ways in which teaching has become managed, has become 'accountable' and has been subjected to control and direction, have contributed to demotivation.
>
> (Ross 2001: 9)

Moore *et al.* (2002) use the term 'eclecticism' to describe the way in which teachers make choices from a wide variety of educational traditions, philosophies, theories and practices available to them. In their view, teachers have become 'far less openly and actively oppositional to unliked public educational policy', even that there may be a 'corresponding guilt and denial on many teachers' part as they are obliged to put such policies into practice at the local level'. They suggest that such factors as increased government control might even lead to a form of professional identity crisis for teaching professionals. Their fieldwork, notably interviews with young teachers, leads them to raise concerns regarding the sustainability of teaching as a career for young graduates. They suggest that many see teaching as an interim career choice with the option to review alternatives after four of five years experience. Woods and Jeffrey (2002) further develop the theme of professional identity in their study of the impact of radical change on the working lives of primary school teachers. They employ Giddens' (1991: 18) construct of the 'disembedding' of social relations from their local contexts, with the global growth of reliance upon economic rationalism and technicism, marketability, efficiency and performativity, the dominance of management systems and of audit accountability and an attack upon moral systems, such as child-centredness, that run counter to these developments. In Giddens' analysis (1991: 189–96) these developments present the 'self' with four major dilemmas:

- The degree to which the self is unified or becomes fragmented.
- Whether one appropriates the changes to one's own concerns, or feels powerless before the depth and scale of the changes.
- The question of authority versus uncertainty.
- Personalised versus commodified experience.

For Woods and Jeffrey, the reconstruction of teacher identity is a useful case study to explore Giddens' theory that these tensions can be positively resolved and productively managed. They conclude that the previously unified self of the primary teacher has become fragmented with the collapse of the child-centred approach and the new emphasis on managerialism. They believe that there has been an assault on teacher autonomy that has left the profession with a feeling of powerlessness: 'Little attention is paid to their views. They are no longer trusted. They are under almost constant surveillance' (p. 97). Woods and Jeffrey believe that teachers are exposed to constant pressure and criticism breeding uncertainty about their abilities, aims, relationships and commitment to teaching. A feeling that almost verges on anomie,[4] with all sense of identity being lost. They conclude that commodified experience has replaced personalised experience and that consumerism has replaced care with an emphasis on measurable quantities in assessment. In their words 'competencies have replaced personal qualities as criteria of the good teacher'. On the basis of their fieldwork, Woods and Jeffrey believe that resolution comes easiest to those teachers whose self-concept most accords with the new social identity. Teachers in their study tended to displace previously substantial aspects of their professional identity to their lives outside teaching. Their professional identity within teaching had become 'situational', constructed to meet different situations and purposes in an environment in which they felt they could not invest their full selves.

Conclusion

Ultimately, the loss of vocation and its replacement with 'playing the game', with teachers acting out the new assigned social identity in inspection situations is *not* a firm foundation upon which to build a committed and successful teaching force for the 21st century. What *is* needed, is the construction of a secure mechanism for the seamless transmission of professional values from one generation to the next – the adoption of successful models for mentoring and coaching that nurture a new generation of teachers seeking to avoid rather than repeat the errors of the past. Committed to the highest professional standards, founded on the best available classroom practice, but also secure in a sense of professional identity.

In his critique of Faith Schools, but prescient to current educational practice in general, Pring (2006) cites Sacks (1997):

> Civilization hangs suspended, from generation to generation, by the gossamer strand of memory. If only one cohort of mothers and fathers fails to convey to its children what *it* has learnt from its parents, then the great chain of learning and wisdom snaps. If the guardians of human knowledge stumble only one time, in their fall collapses the whole edifice of knowledge and understanding.
>
> (Cited in Pring 2006: 178–9)

Author's note

Parts of this chapter are drawn from an unpublished thesis submitted to the University of Brighton.

Notes

1   The term 'setting' is often used as more acceptable than 'streaming' – in reality the grouping of students based on *general ability* is a return to the principle of the grammar school stream – effectively selection on transition from primary school. Setting implies a more flexible approach based on the individual student's ability in certain curriculum areas as opposed to a cohort-based assessment of 'general ability'.

2   'Now what I want is, Facts. Teach these boys and girls nothing but Facts. Facts alone are wanted in life. Plant nothing else and root out everything else. You can only form the minds of reasoning animals upon Facts: nothing else will ever be of service to them.' (Dickens 1854, p.1.)

3   See the introductory chapter of this book for a discussion of the limitations of the idea of 'potential' as a fixed form of measurable ability.

4   Anomie can be defined as a sense of purposelessness caused by a steady erosion of standards and values previously regarded as secure and central to the individual's sense of identity.

References

Anderson, E.M. and Shannon, A.L. (1988) 'Towards a conceptualization of mentoring', *Journal of Teacher Education*, 39(1): 38–42.

Ball, D. (1972) 'Self and identity in the context of deviance: the case of criminal abortion' in R. A. Scott, and J. D. Douglas (eds) *Theoretical Perspectives on Deviance*. New York: Basic Books.

Ball, S. J. (1990) *Politics and Policy Making in Education: Explorations in Policy Sociology*. Cambridge: Cambridge University Press.

Brookes, V. and Sikes, P. (1997) *The Good Mentor Guide*. Buckingham: Open University Press.

Colley, H. (2003) *Mentoring for Social Inclusion*. London: Routledge/Falmer.

Convery, A. (1999) 'Listening to teachers' stories: are we sitting too comfortably?' *Qualitative Studies in Education*, 12: 131–46.

Coldron, J. and Smith, R. (1999) 'Active location in teachers' construction of their professional identities', *Journal of Curriculum Studies*, 31: 711–26.

Cremin, T. (2006) 'Creativity, uncertainty and discomfort: teachers as writers', *Cambridge Journal of Education*, 36(3): 415–33.

Delamont, S. (1999) 'Gender and the discourse of derision', *Research Papers in Education*, 14(1): 3–21.

DfES (2003) *The New Induction Standards*. http://www.teachernet.gov.uk.

Dickens, C. (1854) *Hard Times*. New York: Dover Publications (2001).

Furlong, J. and Maynard, T. (1995) *Mentoring Student Teachers: The Growth of Professional Knowledge*. London: Routledge.

Giddens, A. (1991) *Modernity and Self-Identity*. Cambridge: Polity.

Goodson, I. (2003) *Professional Knowledge, Professional Lives*. Maidenhead: Open University Press.

Guest, G. (1999) *Building Learning Organizations*. Paper delivered to the European Consortium of Learning Organizations Conference, Glasgow.

Hargreaves, A. (2003) *Teaching in the Knowledge Society: Education in the age of insecurity*. Maidenhead: Open University Press.

Hegel, G.W.F. (1822–1830) *Lectures on the Philosophy of World History: Introduction, Reason in History*, translated by H.B. Nisbet. Cambridge: Cambridge University Press (2002).

HMG (2006) *The Education (School Teachers Performance Management) (England) Regulations 2006*, Statutory Instruments 2006 No. 2661, http://www.teachernet.gov.uk.

Moore, A., Edwards, G., Halpin, D. and Rosalyn, G. (2002) 'Compliance, Resistance and Pragmatism: the (re)construction of schoolteacher identities in a period of intensive educational reform', *British Educational Research Journal*, 28(4).

Nias, J. (1989) *Primary Teachers Talking*. London: Routledge.

Parsloe, E. and Wray, M. (2000) *Coaching and Mentoring*. London: Kogan Page.

Pring, R. (2006) 'Faith Schools: Have they a place in the comprehensive system?' in M. Hewlett, R. Pring and M. Tulloch (eds) *Comprehensive Education: Evolution, achievement and new directions*. Northampton: University of Northampton.

Ross, A. (2001) 'Heads will roll', *Guardian Education*, 23 January, pp. 8–9.

Sacks, J. (1997) *The Politics of Hope*. London: Jonathan Cape.

Schon, D. A. (1983) *The Reflective Practitioner*. New York: Basic Books.

Senge, P. (1992) *The Fifth Discipline*. London: Century Business.

Snow, D. and Anderson, L. (1987) 'Identity work among the homeless: the verbal construction and avowal of personal identities', *American Journal of Sociology*, 92(6): 1336–71.

Wenger, E. (1998) *Communities of Practice: Learning, Meaning and Identity*. Cambridge: Cambridge University Press.

Wenger, E., McDermott, R. and Snyder, M. (2002) *A Guide to Managing Knowledge: Cultivating Communities of Practice*. Boston: Harvard Business School Press.

Woods, P. and Jeffrey, B. (2002) 'The Reconstruction of Primary Teachers' Identities', *British Journal of Sociology of Education*, 23(1).

10

Teaching, learning and behaviour strategies

Ian Woodfield

Q10 Have a knowledge and understanding of a range of teaching, learning and behaviour management strategies and know how to use and adapt them, including how to personalise learning and provide opportunities for all learners to achieve their potential.

Learning objectives

To promote an understanding of:

- the accelerating agenda for social inclusion;
- the tension between inclusion and a culture of performativity;
- the need to focus on the development of strategies for teaching, learning and behaviour management that are in the best interest of all learners.

Introduction

> When New Labour was elected to government in the UK in May 1997, it soon faced an urgent educational dilemma. While one of its central election slogans had been 'education, education, education', it had inherited a schooling context from the prior Conservative Government, in which, during the previous six years, recorded permanent exclusions from English schools for disciplinary reasons had risen from about 3,000 to over 13,000 per annum.
>
> (Vulliamy 2001: 177)

Some time during my third or fourth year at teacher training college, around 1977–1978, in the days when most if not all Cert. Ed. students took courses in sociology, psychology, history and philosophy of education, I had to write an assessed essay entitled: ' "Education cannot compensate for society": Discuss'. This title was taken from an article Basil

Bernstein wrote for a 1970 edition of *New Society*. In the following years, talking with friends and colleagues from similar educational backgrounds, I realise what a gift that title was to sociology of Ed. lecturers, since most of us were set something based on it!

(Sikes 2003: 243)

(Inclusion) is a synonym for exclusion. It has been approached differently in the two schools I have worked in since it was first brought in. It seems to me that it is an administrative response to the number of exclusions that were happening in the late 1990s when exclusions were running at an all time high. I have heard it referred to very cynically as a keep them off the streets measure.

(Head of department quoted in Woodfield 2007)

SOME YEARS AGO I was given the opportunity to join the University of Brighton's Professional Doctorate in Education programme, the basis of my thesis submitted in completion of this programme was a series of interviews with senior teachers working in a large comprehensive school on the south coast of England. This chapter draws heavily on part of that thesis and focuses on one of the dominant themes that emerged from the interview experience – the tension between elements of the Government's current agenda for schools, as expressed through policy initiatives such as *Every Child Matters* together with the emphasis placed on personalisation and inclusion, and the competitive culture of performativity inherent in the neo-liberal basis of the education policies of both New Labour and previous Conservative administrations (see the introductory chapter to this book).

The inclusion of pupils with special educational needs

Norwich and Kelly (2004) highlight the significance of two linked areas of policy and practice concerning the education of pupils with learning difficulties. One is the movement towards the greater inclusion of pupils with special educational needs into mainstream schools; the other is the recognition of the child's voice in education as part of a wider movement across various areas of social provision. For Norwich and Kelly these initiatives have their foundations in the Education Act of 1981 and the Children Act (1989), both introduced under a Conservative administration. In their view, the election of a Labour government in 1997 served to accelerate the process of inclusion partly in response to the unacceptable number of permanent exclusions, beginning with the SEN Green Paper (DfEE 1997) and subsequent Programme of Action (DfEE 1998). I would argue that there is a symbiotic relationship between the accelerating inclusion agenda and the need for teachers to adapt successful teaching, learning and behaviour management strategies to suit the needs of *all* learners within an educational environment in which *every* pupil can learn to the maximum. There is now a wealth of advice available to assist the pupil teacher or NQT with successful lesson planning, much of it freely available on-line from the

DCSF and the QCA.[1] But there is a note of caution here for the creative professional seeking to provide a worthwhile learning experience for all their pupils. As the ever readable Philip Beadle trenchantly comments:

> If nothing else the four-part lesson plan guarantees a modicum of pace. Only the most blindingly slack teacher will have the gall to write a four part lesson plan thus: 'Starter: word search. Guided: how to copy off the board. Independent: intense copying off the board. Plenary: how might we improve copying off the board?' It does, at least, build in some variety. But it's a dunce's dictat. The four-part lesson plan promotes and rewards teaching that is routine and formulaic; teaching in which there is no room to run with some brilliant idea that occurs to a pupil; because we, a set of fantastically creative professionals, are scared of being ticked off.
>
> (Beadle 2006)

However, as Tutt (2006: 215) suggests, there is also a need to recognise that 'it is *impossible* to implement ideas that are diametrically opposed to each other', indeed Tutt (ibid.) goes on to urge teachers to 'focus on what we feel is right for the children and young people we teach and to go all out to win the argument over the current pressures that stand in our way'.

Norwich and Kelly provide some startling statistics to support their view that inclusion of children with special educational needs has been accelerated under New Labour: in 2002 Norwich estimated that only about 1.3 per cent of school age children were in special schools in England (Norwich 2002). Over 60 per cent of all pupils with Statements of Special Educational Needs were receiving their schooling in mainstream settings, leaving only pupils with 'more and more severe difficulties' (Norwich and Kelly 2004: 44) in a declining number of Special Schools. For my generation of teachers, inclusion is undoubtedly one of the most significant 'sea changes' in the state education system. For many teachers this change was gradual and therefore less dramatic than the introduction of the National Curriculum but far-reaching and fundamental in its impact on working practices and on the ability of schools to manage and deliver an acceptable level of effective education. Inclusion has confronted schools with a high level of challenge, intertwined as it always has been with issues regarding the behaviour of pupils as distinct from their 'learning difficulties', a connection that is seldom apparent or simply passed over briefly in much of the literature. In the views of some of the senior teachers I interviewed, this demand presents an unacceptable level of challenge given current levels of resources:

> In the previous school that I was working in the Inclusion Suite was a highly decorated and pleasant environment with multiple workstations and dedicated staff trained to work with behaviourally challenged pupils, disaffected pupils, special needs. It was right opposite my classroom so I had a first-hand experience of what this kind of unit within a school actually meant, lots of pupils coming and going and disrupting other classrooms. It was a focus for

the most disruptive elements within the school, who perhaps might not have been on the premises in previous circumstances and who might have been better served elsewhere . . . there were some pupils being brought in who were quite clearly not being included in any meaningful way but were merely being contained on the premises.

(Head of department quoted in Woodfield 2007)

I think enabling pupils to access the curriculum, which they might not have been able to access five or ten years ago because they might have been in a different institution or they might have had a limited curriculum, needs a lot more staffing. I think that we haven't targeted staff at inclusion. I can't [but] think of the huge number of staff that we have got in this school, that not enough have been appointed to deal with issues related to inclusion.

(Assistant head teacher quoted in Woodfield 2007)

The consequences of inclusion

Sellman *et al.* (2002) in their critique of the literature on exclusion lay emphasis upon the 'commitment to the prevention of exclusion from society' demonstrated by the Labour administration (Sellman *et al.* p. 890). They refer to the creation of the Social Exclusion Unit in 1998, the development of targets to reduce permanent exclusions and truancy from schools (DfEE 1999a, 1999b) and the modest reductions in the number of recorded permanent exclusions in the years since 1996–1997. Sellman *et al.* conclude that the literature reveals exclusion from school to be 'associated with wider social exclusion from society' (Sellman *et al.* p. 890, Hayton 1999). They perceive exclusion as the product of a 'complex interplay between social institutions and individuals' (Sellman *et al.* p. 891) and they refer in detail to the work of Cole (1996) and his model of culture as the weaving together of layers of context, progressively wrapping the individual in a series of 'rings', a model which in turn draws upon the work of Bronfenbrenner (1979). The model emphasises the interconnections between layers of context and serves to focus attention on the dynamics between them; for example, the impact of national policy on school and classroom organisation. However, this analysis leads them to conclude that there are fundamental tensions between policies that are designed to raise standards and those intended to promote inclusion. Moreover, they believe that the 'quantitative focus' on reducing exclusions has detracted from the need to put greater resources into the socialising of primary classrooms – the implementation of programmes to provide training in anger management and conflict resolution, for example (Sellman *et al.* p. 897).

The tension between the drive to improve academic standards and policies to foster inclusion is apparent in the interviews I conducted with a group of senior teachers. In all of the transcripts there is a clearly apparent emphasis upon the need to satisfy a target driven culture of ever improving examination performance – a target culture that is seen by some as crude and insensitive to the needs of individual pupils:

> I think that although there is a nod in the direction of differentiation for a range of different learners contained within the framework [the National Literacy Strategy]; I think it is quite clearly the case that many pupils when they come into secondary are not yet ready for the objectives that are set out in Year 7, for example. I think there was an assumption that the catch up materials would work more effectively than they have done. I think there is an assumption on the part of a large number of people that the framework is going to sort out the problems of readers and writers in a large number of schools and I don't think that it automatically will. I think that the change of the tests make it impossible to make a comparison. The tests pre the strategy were very clear-cut in what they were analysing. The tests now are very much more focused in terms of the skills and they are much more tied to the framework, which I think is a good thing in terms that one can see the efficacy of what is being taught, it is analytical and diagnostic. But I don't think it is possible to make a valid statistical comparison in terms that it is the strategy that is working as opposed to what went before. There will be some attempt to correlate that but I treat that with some scepticism I am afraid.
>
> (Head of department quoted in Woodfield 2007)

> I was really concerned that at the (staff) meeting where we discussed this I came across as some sort of Luddite who wasn't accepting any changes. It is more to do with the fact that these (targets) are imposed from higher up in the school, by people who are not working in class or have limited experience now of working in class. I think that there is no substitute for a teacher who knows the kids they are teaching. I think that professional judgement – a phrase they bandy about so much – is not really taken into account. I think that I can set a much better target for a kid that I know, whose work I know, than some sort of CAT [Cognitive Abilities Test] average that might work or might not. It's good if it does and there are a lot of kids for whom it will work but what about those 'aberrations' [from the norm]?
>
> (Head of department quoted in Woodfield 2007)

Schools and social capital

The significance of inclusion as a policy rests with the interpretation that can be placed on the role that schools play in society; in my reading this is at the core of the issue. Are schools simply at the mercy of economic and social forces beyond their control or are they ultimately capable of acting as agents for social change (see Cole 2004)? Bourdieu and Passeron (1990) have suggested various forms of capital (social, cultural, symbolic and economic) to encompass the complex relationship between the individual and social institutions. In broad terms economic capital can be defined as command over economic resources; social capital as resources based on group membership; cultural capital as forms of knowledge, skill and education; symbolic capital as accumulated prestige and honour. Bourdieu and Passeron suggest a strong relationship between the possession of 'cultural capital' and success in the education system. In their view, there is a clear link between the possession of 'cultural capital' and success in the education system. They claim that societal relations are reproduced through education and the transmission of cultural capital. However, in the literature the terms social and cultural capital are used, if not interchangeably, certainly as inextricably linked concepts. The focus of many of those who have explored the area is principally on social capital, a term that is sometimes not clearly defined but generally taken to refer to social networks implicitly linked with levels of socio-economic power and status; cultural capital when it is referred to is generally seen as of secondary importance and as a by-product of social capital.[2]

Ecclestone and Field (2003) debate the value of social capital in 'academic milieus', they note the attractiveness of the concept to policy makers who perceive that it can 'empower people by engaging whole communities with education and learning' (Ecclestone and Field 2003: 267). However, they caution that the concept can also be connected with authoritarian as well as liberal-humanistic policy responses. Field (cited in Ecclestone and Field 2003: 269–70) emphasises that as well as contributing to inclusion and achievement in schools, social capital can also serve to reinforce exclusion, underachievement and poor cultural capital. He cautions that social capital is highly differentiated in nature and value, and that the resources that it provides are unequally distributed between individuals and groups. In his view, extremes of socio-economic inequality are harmful to social capital, they serve to reduce the possibility of cooperation and favour the use of social capital to gain status and power at the expense of others – witness the phenomenon of the 'middle-class flight' from 'failing schools' following an unfavourable Ofsted inspection and the imposition of Special Measures or the potentially terminal effect of including a school in the Fresh Start programme:

> Stacey James is living proof that the best laid policies don't necessarily work. The Brighton teenager was one of the pupils the government was trying to help when it promised to scrap failing schools and replace them with something better. Now she is one of the last pupils to complete exams at the East Brighton College of Media Arts (Comart). The school, which opened only six years ago as part of the flagship Fresh Start policy, officially closed last week . . . Fresh Start showed that middle-class flight, left unchecked, will trump flashy government policies every time. The echo of Fresh Start should be loud enough to cause tinnitus in the government's collective ear.
>
> (Mulholland 2005)

Ecclestone (cited in Ecclestone and Field 2003: 272) describes a worst case scenario where simply identifying someone as 'damaged' becomes an end in itself, replacing attempts to create social capital through meaningful educational experience. She identifies a 'thinly veiled line' between concerns about social exclusion and poor productivity, 'disaffected' young people can therefore be held accountable and strong moral judgements made regarding their lack of progress, such pupils she is suggesting can be 'blamed' for their failure in the same way that past generations of politicians have held the poor to be responsible for their poverty. Ecclestone suggests that some forms of social capital exclude those who do not conform. For Ecclestone this interpretation is rooted in the culture of 'performativity',[3] she suggests that definitions and indicators of social capital affect what we see as the 'right' sort of social capital or 'unhelpful' capital. For example, past attempts by some schools in the use of interviews to 'select' pupils reflects the idea that certain individuals are undesirable and unlikely to contribute to the school's 'league table' position, these pupils are deemed unlikely to meet the necessary standard in SAT tests or GCSE examinations on the basis of 'social' criteria that may well conceal unarticulated concerns relating to social class or ethnicity. In contrast, the desire to meet the needs of all pupils regardless of their ability to contribute to the measured performance of the school is made clear in the following remarks from one of the senior teachers I interviewed:

> . . . Lets chuck the National Curriculum out of the window. Lets introduce thinking skills, philosophy, listening skills for all pupils in Year 7 so that we maybe spark them into learning again. In the subject area that I am teaching in now, in English, they don't know how to write essays because they have got no imagination. We need to encourage them to play, to experiment, to get them away from the technology that we want so brilliantly to be able to use. DVD players, the internet at home are not used for educational purposes, not the educational purposes we would expect them to use. They don't play, they don't read and we have to rekindle and encourage that. I would kick the National Curriculum out of the window in Year 7 . . .
>
> (Assistant head teacher quoted in Woodfield 2007)

In response to this view, Field (cited in Ecclestone and Field 2003: 273–4) warns that 'we should not treat actors as passive victims' and that a discourse that ridicules 'blaming the victim' may ultimately serve as a 'poor substitute for rigorous analysis of social exclusion'. In turn, Ecclestone (cited in Ecclestone and Field 2003: 278) draws upon her experience of working with GNVQ pupils where 'safety and low expectations also encouraged pupils to resist work that was "too difficult", pressurising teachers to work within the boundaries of assessment criteria'. This experience would not be unfamiliar to some of the teachers I interviewed:

> . . . (The) entry data sounds as though it has a lot to say about the performance of a particular pupil but when you factor in the non-educational aspects of life and experience, the fact that a certain pupil comes in with a predicted grade at KS3 and KS4 does not necessarily mean that they have the skills or the motivation to achieve that grade. Motivating pupils to do it is a really big problem and yet the analysis of targets very rarely takes that into account.
>
> (Head of department quoted in Woodfield 2007)

Motivating all pupils

Case study: Working with pupil groups in the secondary classroom

Reflecting on behavioural problems and learning difficulties presented by some of his pupils, an experienced secondary school teacher decided to experiment with various forms of table groupings within the classroom setting. Following a period of trial and error, he settled on a regular pattern of randomised table groups, moving pupils to sit on tables that were broadly balanced in terms of gender and ability using an informal rotation on entry to the class. However, the allocation of certain pupils to certain tables was managed to avoid previously apparent behavioural problems. Friendship was not applied as a criteria but the rationale for the seating pattern was carefully explained to the pupils in terms of encouraging their focus on the content of the lesson rather than social interaction, creating opportunities to meet and work with pupils who they did not know socially, raising achievement through peer support and the free exchange of ideas with other members of their table group. Competition between table groups, for example, the award of points for answering questions correctly, and the sharing of knowledge and understanding was encouraged through mechanisms such as 'hot seating' (identifying a random member of the table group to answer questions rather than allowing the most able or vocal student to respond). The following positive outcomes were observed:

- Time on task increased significantly – pupils became generally more focused on the lesson. Inappropriate behaviour significantly declined and performance improved.

- Pupils became more involved with the lesson and more likely to share their understanding with others through discussion.

- Pupils increasingly identified 'success' with the performance of their table group and became more likely to share ideas with pupils who experienced difficulties. Some pupils became enthusiastic advocates of this approach – very few pupils were openly critical.

- As time passed the award of 'points' became less important – in many classes positive involvement with the lesson continued whether or not points were awarded.

- Pupils formed relationships with other pupils including some who had previously felt isolated within the class.

A note of caution – such an approach is not a 'magic formula' that can be applied in all circumstances. However, it does serve as an example of the powerful influence that group dynamics within the classroom can have on learning outcomes and pupil behaviour.

In seeking the means to motivate such pupils, teachers must also be cautious regarding the emergence of what Hargreaves has described as 'training sects' (Hargreaves 2003: 141), these can sometimes be seen as a 'what works', quick fix solution to complex problems that require a more considered approach. Take, for example, the rush to adapt Howard Gardner's (1983) conception of multiple intelligences to the classroom experience. When interviewed by the *TES* in 2006 (Passmore 2006), Gardner expressed some bemusement that his ideas have become interpreted as a recipe for classroom practice:

> . . . What about those children who wear badges saying, 'I'm a visual learner'? Or those who leap up and down in the back row, proudly announcing that they favour the 'kinaesthetic'? Isn't that Gardner's multiple intelligences in action? Well, no. He is sceptical about all of it. He doesn't like labelling children and he's puzzled when teachers proudly show him a 'bodily/spatial' corner in their classroom. 'Why?' is his reaction . . . when he first published his book introducing multiple intelligences 25 years ago (Gardner 1983) he was writing strictly as a psychologist. He did not have particular nostrums to disseminate . . . It is a mistake says Gardner to confuse the various intelligences with the sensory system. A visual learner, for instance, is not simply a child who likes to learn by looking. 'What matters is the operation they perform on the material they are absorbing, not how it got into the system,' he says.[4]
>
> (Passmore 2006: 20–1)

Moore (2004: 446) explores Bourdieu's concept of *habitus*, and takes from it the idea that consequent upon the quality and duration of formal education, the individual becomes equipped with 'social attributes' that can have either a positive or a negative effect on their educational achievement. This returns us to the implicit tension between inclusion and the desire to achieve high academic standards as highlighted by these remarks from one of the teachers interviewed:

> In principle obviously we would all agree [with inclusion], but I see other children suffering. Having certain children in my lessons is affecting the education of others. They might be included but others become excluded indirectly. There are certain sorts of children with special needs, I can think of some with physical disabilities who I think it is important that they are in school and not just for them. It is important for other children to understand that they have their own place and that they are individuals and important too. It is more to do with the disruptive element that I find quite hard. I think to some point that this school is working on that because for years we have been saying I can't teach this kid until someone has taught them how to behave and I think there is an element of that happening. But then again with kids who find it hard to behave in lessons I don't know how much I am helping them because I don't have Learning Support in my lessons. I don't really have a good picture of how it should be working to be honest.
>
> (Head of department quoted in Woodfield 2007)

Moore (2004: 447) refers to the power relationship that exists in the cultural field and to Bourdieu's characterisation of this relationship as a form of 'symbolic violence' (Bourdieu 1977); in simple terms, the education system can be seen as an agency of the state helping to preserve the established social order. This is *not* a characterisation with which many of the teachers I interviewed would concur, but undoubtedly there is an awareness that conventional provision is failing to reach some of their pupils and that the imposition of 'traditional' classroom values simply fails to work and that alternative provision has yet to fulfil its promise:

> I think we do inclusion. I think we are extremely slow to exclude pupils who might be excluded in other schools. I think we are quite quick to include pupils who have been excluded by a number of other schools. In some cases, we put together an alternative curriculum for them and where that has been along the lines of increased flexibility, step on projects etc, I think that has been quite positive for us. I must say that the [local FE] college in its increased flexibility programmes is not actually catering for those pupils, it is catering for pupils in the middle ground who should be getting level 2. As for pupils on the fringes – the NET [Not in Education or Training] pupils – they are struggling. I think we do inclusion – I am thinking of one or two pupils in particular who are occupied in the school partly on those programmes but partly on other things, which keep them in school, but I am not quite sure about the extent of the learning achieved.
>
> (Head of department quoted in Woodfield 2007)

> Extraction-group is not a phrase that I like. I am thinking of small areas where small groups of pupils could work with staff on the subject without having to cope with the large class situation or supporting what is being put into a large class situation. What we haven't got in this school is small areas for pupil use. I have been in some schools where next to each classroom there is a small study area. Where staff can work with a small a small group dealing with issues that inclusion throws up.
>
> (Assistant head teacher quoted in Woodfield 2007)

Maintaining order in the inclusive classroom

For the pupil teacher and the NQT, there remains the practical problem of maintaining a framework of order in the inclusive classroom. Here again there is a wealth of advice available – some of it sold at considerable expense by a variety of educational consultants. It is perhaps sometimes rather too easy for such undoubtedly skilled professionals to be parachuted into a difficult classroom situation and often convenient to overlook the impact of novelty value or the gravitas conferred by status. The report of the Practitioner Group on School Behaviour and Discipline (DFES 2005: 19–20) outlined a number of key principles that *should* feature in the learning environment of any successful school:

- There should be a clear policy for learning and teaching, including a behaviour code with agreed procedures.
- Lessons should be well planned and use *strategies that are appropriate to the ability of the pupils*.[5]
- There should be commonly agreed classroom management and behaviour strategies, e.g. a formal way to start lessons.

- Pupils should be offered the opportunity to take responsibility for aspects of their learning, working together in pairs, groups or as a whole class.

- The use of assessment for learning techniques, such as peer and self-assessment, to increase pupils' involvement in their lesson and promote good behaviour.

- Data on pupils' behaviour and learning should be collected *and used* to target support on areas where pupils have the greatest difficulty.

- All teachers should operate a classroom-seating plan as social interactions can inhibit teaching and create behaviour problems.

- Recognition that pupils are knowledgeable about their school experience, and have views about what helps them learn and how others' poor behaviour stops them from learning.

- Opportunities should be created for class, year and school councils to discuss and make recommendations about behaviour, including bullying, and the effectiveness of rewards and sanctions.

The existence of a differentiated curriculum

For some commentators the important distinction rests with our understanding of equality and inequality within the educational domain. Current concerns regarding the slowing of social mobility (Blanden *et al.* 2005) have led some commentators to call for a return of the 'grammar school' (Cohen 2005; Fernand and Gerard 2005), this despite the riposte that such conclusions 'misrepresent' the research and the Government's response to questions raised in the House of Lords (Blanden 2005; Adonis 2005):

> On grammar schools, the report of the London School of Economics . . . found that the countries with the highest rates of social mobility – namely Sweden, Norway and Finland – have non-selective school systems . . . also note that in this country there are only 160 grammar schools – the Government are leaving local communities to decide their future – and that of the pupils of those schools only 2.2 per cent are in receipt of free school meals and come from poorer backgrounds as against 14 per cent in secondary schools at large. Therefore, as agents of social mobility, this is not one of their strongest suits.
>
> (Adonis 2005; Column 1352)

However, this does not address the trend in some schools towards the creation of grammar school style 'express' streams. For example, the school where I conducted my fieldwork identified a group of pupils who will experience a collapsed Key Stage 3 core curriculum leading to SATs at the end of Year 8. This opens the door to a further differentiation of the curriculum for the highest achieving pupils – GCSE examinations in Year 10, AS levels in Year 11? Ultimately, we may still see in this trend the beginnings of a reassertion of the concept of the division of secondary education at 11 between the academic, for the 'most able,' and the vocational, for the rest. Inclusion in this context becomes simply the concept of pupils occupying a common geographical location; their experiences of school may become potentially so different that in virtually every other respect, they could be seen as belonging to different institutions, a very different outcome to that envisaged by the Warnock report in 1978, where 'locational integration' was merely the easiest and earliest step in a developmental programme leading to social and functional integration whereby at the final level 'pupils work together throughout the school day engaged in all social and academic activities' (Rose 2001). This is a far more egalitarian vision despite her more recent concerns that the intentions of her committee have become overtaken by a far wider definition of inclusion than she and they originally intended (Warnock 2005).

Sikes (2003: 245) notes the reluctance on the part of legislators, pupils and teachers to attribute inequality to social class. She regards the use of euphemisms such as 'disadvantage', 'ability' and 'socially excluded' to be simply ways of hiding the problematic definition of socio-economic class, she notes that in some ways it has become almost a 'taboo subject'. Hill and Cole (2001: 143–4) remind us of the link between pupils and their social class backgrounds; moreover, that consequent upon their respective socio-economic class pupils actually experience a differentiated curriculum that may either act to constrain or equip them with significant advantage in a competitive educational environment. In their view, it is primarily through the 'hidden curriculum'[6] that pupils attending schools such as the Ridings in Halifax 'tend to have different expectations, labelling and stereotyped work futures' than those attending 'prestigious' selective secondary schools such as the London Oratory. However, they also draw attention to the view that evidence exists of further differences in the teaching and learning methods used by teachers and pupils. They refer to the work of Brown, Riddell and Duffield (1997) who, amongst other differences, found that children in working-class schools spent between 3 and 6 per cent of their time in discussion in comparison with 17–25 per cent in the middle-class schools observed. Brown et al. establish a clear relationship between these constraints and the teachers' desire to maintain order in the classroom. Moreover, they suggest that whilst middle-class children were generally positive about their experience of school and the individual help they received, working-class children saw only the need to complete tasks. Hill and Cole observe a clear linkage between this observed behaviour and the conclusions drawn by Bowles and Gintis (1976) in their classic study 'Schooling in Capitalist America'.[7] At least one of the senior teachers I interviewed rejected an overt link between the immediate needs of capitalism and educational provision, although this denial cannot, in itself, serve to reject the existence of a 'correspondence' between such provision and the macro-economic system:

> . . . I certainly don't see us training for business. I think that is a very difficult and political argument that I can't accept entirely. I have seen the figures and I have seen the graphs they show of the gap between the skills. I think if schools started to go too much down that route I think that we would almost be trying to pick winners of a horse race when we don't know

where the race is going. You are trying to train for quite a considerable time in the future and what you are then in to saying is that somebody has to judge where our economy is going in the next 20 years and therefore you would have an education driven by a prediction of an economy not one that is driven by the economy. They are two different things and I think that in a world that is changing as quickly as our world is at the moment, the political and humanitarian changes that are taking place, I don't think that predicting a 20-year economy is a very easy thing to do.

(Assistant head teacher quoted in Woodfield 2007)

Conclusion

Ultimately, this returns us to the purpose of state education and to the informing philosophy behind our educational institutions. Is there any relevance to terms such as 'equality of opportunity' and 'parity of esteem' in relation to the business of education in the 21st century? Is inclusive education for pupils defined at an early age to be of 'below average ability' simply a return to the past prescriptions of the tripartite system,[8] where some prepare for university and others must 'learn to labour'? Recent research from the NfER suggests that new forms of vocational education for 14–16-year-olds may well produce a positive impact on pupils' attainment, self-confidence, attendance and involvement in further education and training (Golden *et al.* 2005). However, concerns remain amongst the senior teachers I interviewed regarding the validity of current policies:

> . . . What was it he said 'education, education, education', the same old rubbish that is churned out. We have been there and done that, there is very little new (in these) initiatives. They are just the old ones revamped.

(Assistant head teacher quoted in Woodfield 2007)

It is clear that if we are to remake an education system truly suited to the individual needs of pupils in the 21st century, then that system cannot simply be a crude reflection of the short-term needs of the global marketplace. It must be a system that is responsive to the differing needs of *all* pupils regardless of 'ability'. However, one thing above all else, the needs of our pupils can never be met with a return to the 'dead-end' of the tripartite system exemplified by a crude reliance on test measurements to decide future life chances.

Notes

1   http://www.standards.dfes.gov.uk/schemes3/?view=get

2   Fukuyama (1999: 1–2) has commented on the number of different definitions of social capital in use. He suggests the following definition: social capital is an informal norm that promotes cooperation between two or more individuals. For example, the norms that constitute social capital can range from a norm of reciprocity between two friends (the need to give a gift if one has been received), all the way up to complex and elaborate doctrines like Christianity or Confucianism. In this sense, in an educational setting social capital might well be represented as those you meet and come to know, these social contacts may well have an impact on your future life. For those who attend elite private schools, 'the old school tie' may also be seen as a mechanism for maintaining privilege.

3   Performativity refers to the undue emphasis that can be placed on test scores and examination performance – the competitive culture of league tables.

4   For the classroom teacher this clearly indicates the need to reflect on *how* individual pupils process the content of a lesson. It serves little or no purpose to simply identify a learner as 'visual'. However, allowing that pupil the *freedom* to use diagrams or pictures as memory aids may well achieve a positive outcome.

5   The danger here is that schools will simply close off large areas of knowledge to certain pupils, the National Curriculum establishes an entitlement curriculum but offers little or no guidance on how much time should be devoted to particular areas of knowledge. Some secondary schools may well seek the opportunity to adopt a rigid streaming system that offers pupils either an academic or a vocational route, e.g. geography for the academically able destined for university, leisure and tourism for those who must seek employment and should therefore not be encouraged to ask any searching or awkward questions of their prospective employers.

6   The 'hidden curriculum' refers to the various learning experiences that pupils encounter inside school beyond the confines of the formal taught curriculum, e.g. codes of conduct, uniforms, roles and responsibilities such as 'prefect' or school council representative.

7   Bowles and Gintis present a case for the existence of a 'correspondence principle' between the provision of state education and the needs of the capitalist economic system, e.g. for a subservient and cooperative workforce with basic skills of numeracy and literacy.

8   Following the 1944 Education Act the 'tripartite system' involved the selection of pupils based on examination at age 11 (the 11+) for different forms of secondary provision. For most pupils, this three-part system was effectively a choice of two paths, secondary moderns for those who were destined to leave at 15 or 16, the grammar school for the academic elite destined for university. The system was fundamentally unfair, it disadvantaged many pupils from working-class homes and female pupils – if a 'level playing field' had been allowed, far fewer boys would have achieved grammar school places at 11.

References

Adonis, M. (2005) Hansard 19 July, Column 1352.

Beadle, P. (2006) 'Four steps to being chucked on the scrapheap', the *Education Guardian* 24 October, p. 6.

Blanden, J., Gregg, P. and Machin, S. (2005) *Intergenerational Mobility in Europe and North America*. London School of Economics http://www.lse.ac.uk.

Blanden, J. (2005) 'Research Misrepresented', *Belfast Telegraph*, 20 May http://www.belfasttelegraph.co.uk.

Bourdieu, P. (1977) *Outline of a theory of practice*. Cambridge: Cambridge University Press.

Bourdieu, P. and Passeron, J. (1990) *Reproduction in Education, Society and Culture*. London: Sage.

Bronfenbrenner, U. (1979) *The Ecology of Human Development*. Cambridge, MA: Harvard University Press.

Bowles, S. and Gintis, H. (1976) *Schooling in Capitalist America*. London: Routledge & Kegan Paul.

Brown, S., Riddell, S. and Duffield, J. (1997) *Classroom approaches to learning and teaching: the social dimension*. Paper delivered to the ECER (European Educational Research Association Annual Conference), Seville.

Cole, M. (1996) *Cultural Psychology*. Cambridge, MA: Belknap Press.

Cole, M. (2004) 'Rethinking the future: the commodification of Knowledge and the Grammar of Resistance' in *A Tribute to Caroline Benn: Education and Democracy*, M. Benn and C. Chitty (eds) London: Continuum: 150–63.

DfEE (1997) *Excellence for all children: meeting special educational needs*. London: HMSO.

DfEE (1998) *Meeting special educational needs: a programme of action*. London: DfEE.

DfEE (1999a) *Social Inclusion: pupil support* Circular 10/99. London: DfEE.

DfEE (1999b) *Social Inclusion: the LEA role in pupil support* Circular 11/99. London: DfEE.

DfES (2005) *Report of the Practitioner Group on School Behaviour and Discipline.* http://www.dfes.gov.uk/.

Ecclestone, K. and Field, J. (2003) 'Promoting Social Capital in a "Risk Society": a new approach to emancipatory learning or a new moral authoritarianism?' *British Journal of Sociology of Education*, 24(3).

Furedi, F. (2002) *The Culture of Fear: risk taking and the morality of low expectations*, 3rd edn. London: Continuum.

Fukuyama, F. (1999) *Social Capital and Civil Society*. Paper prepared for the IMF Conference on Second Generation Reforms, http://www.imf.org/external/pubs/ft/seminar/1999/reforms/fukyama.htm.

Gardner, H. (1983; 1993) *Frames of Mind*, tenth anniversary edition. BasicBooks: New York.

Golden, S., O'Donnell, L., Benton, T. and Rudd, P. 2005 *Evaluation of Increased Flexibility for 14–16 year olds programme: Outcomes for the first cohort.* National Foundation for Educational Research, August 2005, www.nfer.ac.uk.

Hargreaves, A. (2003) *Teaching in the Knowledge Society: Education in the age of insecurity.* Maidenhead: Open University Press.

Hayton, A. (1999) *Tackling Disaffection and Social Exclusion.* London: Kogan Page.

Hill, D. and Cole, M. (2001) 'Social Class' in D. Hill and M. Cole (eds) *Schooling and Equality.* London: Kogan Page.

Moore, R. (2004) 'Cultural capital: objective probability and the cultural arbitrary', *British Journal of Sociology of Education*, 25(4).

Mulholland, H. (2005) 'The school that died of poverty', the *Guardian*, 9 August.

Norwich, B. (2002) *Special school placement and Statements for English LEAs 1997–2001.* Report for Centre for Study of Inclusive Education, University of Exeter.

Norwich, B. and Kelly, N. (2004) 'Pupils' views on inclusion: moderate learning difficulties and bullying in mainstream and special schools', *British Educational Research Journal*, 30(1).

Office of National Statistics (2005) http://www.statistics.gov.uk/socialcapital.

Passmore, B. (2006) 'MI: mission impossible?' *The TES Magazine*, 24 November.

Rose, R. (2001) 'Special Educational Needs' in D. Hill and M. Cole (eds) *Schooling and Equality.* London: Kogan Page.

Sellman, E., Bedward, J., Cole, T. and Daniels, H. (2002) 'A Sociocultural Approach to Exclusion', *British Educational Research Journal*, 28(6).

Sikes, P. (2003) 'Making the Familiar Strange: a new look at inequality in education', *British Journal of Sociology of Education*, 24(2).

Tutt, R. (2006) 'Reconciling the Irreconcilable: coping with contradictory agendas', *Forum*, 48(2): 209–16.

Vulliamy, G. (2001) 'A Sociology of School Exclusions', *British Journal of Sociology of Education*, 22(1).

Warnock, M. (1978) *Report of the Committee of Enquiry into the education of Handicapped Children and Young People.* London: HMSO.

Warnock, M. (2005) 'Special educational needs: a new look', *Impact 11*, Philosophy of Education Society of Great Britain.

Woodfield, I. (2007) *Leading specialist secondary school professionals on recent educational policies: a phenomenological analysis.* (Unpublished thesis submitted to the University of Brighton.)

Index